Complete Thai

Teach
Yourself®

Complete Thai

David Smyth

First published in Great Britain in 1996 as *Teach Yourself Thai* by Hodder Education, an Hachette UK company.

First published in US 1996 by The McGraw-Hill Companies, Inc.

This edition published in 2017 by John Murray Learning

British Library Cataloguing in Publication Data: a catalogue record for this title is available from the British Library.

Library of Congress Catalog Card Number: on file.

ISBN: 9781444101911

12

Cover image © Imagestate Media

Typeset by Cenveo® Publisher Services.

Printed and bound in Great Britain by CPI Group (UK) Ltd., Croydon, CR0 4YY.

John Murray Learning policy is to use papers that are natural, renewable and recyclable products and made from wood grown in sustainable forests. The logging and manufacturing processes are expected to conform to the environmental regulations of the country of origin.

Carmelite House
50 Victoria Embankment
London EC4Y 0DZ
www.hodder.co.uk

Contents

Meet the author

David Smyth has been successfully teaching Thai for more than 30 years to learners of all abilities. He is Senior Lecturer in Thai at the School of Oriental and African Studies (SOAS), University of London, and the author of the companion volume *Complete Thai Conversation* and the highly regarded *Thai: An Essential Grammar*.

In *Complete Thai* he provides a user-friendly introduction to speaking, reading and writing Thai for the complete beginner. Each unit is based around conversations between Thais and foreigners, which prepare you for the kind of questions you are certain to hear and show you how to respond correctly and appropriately. The conversations are accompanied by jargon-free explanations of the grammar, vocabulary and cultural points raised in the conversations.

Successful learners of Thai all acknowledge the huge importance and benefit of being able to read Thai from an early stage in the learning process. A considerable part of each unit of *Complete Thai* is therefore devoted to presenting the Thai script in a logical, step-by-step sequence, with numerous exercises for you to test yourself and listen to on the recording. The page layout of the book is conveniently organized so that once you have mastered the principles of the writing system you can cover up the romanized section of each conversation and work through them again entirely in Thai script.

Complete Thai has proved effective in equipping thousands of learners with a sound foundation in Thai. We hope that you, too – whether you are an ambitious learner, eager to become literate in Thai, or a more casual learner who wants rather more than a mere phrasebook – will enjoy and benefit from this revised edition of the course.

Meet the author

Only got a minute?

Thai is spoken exclusively in Thailand, by approximately 60 million people. It is closely related to Lao, the national language of neighbouring Laos, but quite different from Burmese, Cambodian and Malay, the languages spoken in its other neighbouring countries. Two features that strike the Western learner immediately are the unusual script, which is unique to Thailand, and the fact that Thai is a tonal language, which means that the meaning of a word is determined by the pitch at which it is pronounced. While script and tone represent a challenge, they are by no means the obstacle they might at first appear and, with regular practice, both can be readily mastered by the average learner.

The script in which Thai is written has developed over the years from a script that came originally from India. Like many of the scripts in use on the subcontinent of India, Thai is written across the page, from left to right, with some vowels appearing above the line of writing, and others below it. Another unusual feature of the script is that there is no space between words. Where you will find a space is when some form of punctuation is needed – the space acts as a comma or full stop, for instance.

The fact that Thai is a tonal language means that the pitch of a word is as much an integral part of that word as its consonant and vowel sounds. Most Westerners have some difficulty at first in both recognizing and producing tones and some give up learning Thai far too quickly because they expect instant success. The fact is that most successful learners have progressed gradually through practice and patience, gradually developing their pronunciation and hearing skills and constantly working on improving them. If you have Thai friends, try to listen for the tones when you hear them speak and encourage them to correct your pronunciation. Most importantly, don't get discouraged … and don't give up!

Only got a minute?

Only got five minutes?

Thai is a member of the Tai family of languages, which are spoken across an area that stretches from northern Vietnam in the east to northern India in the west. Within Thailand, distinct regional dialects are spoken in the north, northeast and south of the country; the dialect spoken in the Central Region is regarded as the standard, used both in schools and the media and for official purposes.

Thai is a *tonal* language, with the meaning of each syllable determined by the pitch at which it is pronounced. There are five tones in Thai – mid, low, high, rising and falling. Thus, **kao** means 'news' when pronounced with a *low* tone (**kào**), 'white' with a *rising* tone (**kǎo**), and 'rice' with a *falling* tone (**kâo**). While tones add a level of complexity to pronunciation, the western learner usually finds the grammar relatively easy to grasp at the initial stage. The order of words in a sentence is similar to English, while both nouns and verbs have a single fixed form, nouns showing no distinction between singular and plural and verbs no distinction between tenses. Although Thai has borrowed a lot of words from English, especially technical and scientific terms, most everyday words bear no resemblance to their English or European equivalents and so must be learned and memorized. Most learners find it is easier to remember new Thai words if they learn them in short phrases; this way you learn how to use the word at the same time and it's also easier to remember the tone of a word in a phrase rather than as an isolated item.

Thai is written across the page from left to right with no spaces between words. Spaces are used as punctuation markers, instead of commas or full stops. There is no universally agreed system for writing Thai in roman letters. If you look at menus in different restaurants, you may find the word 'stir fried' written as 'pad', 'phad', 'pat', 'phat', 'pud', 'put', or 'phud'. Many Thais have difficulty in making sense of Thai written in roman letters and very few would be able to romanize words in a systematic manner. For the learner, however, romanized Thai is an invaluable crutch to help you get started quickly; but the more quickly you can discard it, the better. While learning to read Thai does involve a certain investment of time and effort, it is not as difficult as many people imagine. There is a close match between spelling and pronunciation, so being able to read Thai will help to improve your pronunciation. It will also impress your friends, Thai and non-Thai alike, but more importantly, it will enable you to take responsibility for your own learning once you have completed this course.

Only got ten minutes?

Thai (formerly known as 'Siamese') is the most important member of the Tai family of languages. Tai languages are spoken by an estimated 70 million people across a vast area, stretching from northern Vietnam, through south-western China – where there are 15 million speakers – to northern India. It was once thought that Tai speakers originated from China and migrated southwards into present-day Thailand, but linguistic research now suggests that the border area between northern Vietnam and China's Guangxi province is a more likely origin, with Tai speakers migrating westwards and south-westwards into Thailand, from the 8th century AD.

Although Tai languages have developed from a single distant ancestor and retained some common grammatical features, the gradual development of phonological and lexical differences has made them mutually unintelligible. Lao, the national language of Laos, is the Tai language most closely related to Thai. Many Lao people are able to receive and enjoy Thai language television programmes, which are seen as culturally prestigious, but most Thais who live in Bangkok would struggle to understand a conversation between two Lao speakers.

Within Thailand, distinct regional dialects are spoken in the north, northeast and south of the country. The dialect spoken in the Central Region is regarded as the standard, used both in schools and the media and for official purposes. Many Thais in rural areas, apart from speaking the regional dialect and Central Thai, may also speak a minority language or dialect as well. The sizeable Cambodian-speaking population living in the provinces that border Cambodia, for example, will regard Cambodian as their first language, use north-eastern dialect outside Cambodian-speaking areas and Central Thai at school or perhaps in the workplace; but when they write, they write only in standard Central Thai.

Thai, like many major South East Asian languages (e.g. Burmese, Vietnamese and Lao) is a *tonal* language, with the meaning of each syllable determined by the pitch at which it is pronounced. There are five tones in Thai – mid, low, high, rising and falling. Thus, **kah** is a type of grass when pronounced with a *mid* tone, 'galingal' when pronounced with a *low* tone (**kàh**), 'leg' with a *rising* tone (**kǎh**), 'to trade' with a *high* tone (**káh**) and 'cost' with a *falling* tone (**kâh**).

Learning a tone language can be intimidating and 'What if I'm tone deaf?' is a commonly voiced fear. For some people, hearing unusual sounds and imitating them closely comes quickly and easily; others will find that this process takes longer. The important thing is not to give up if you can't hear tones immediately or produce new sounds; with patience and perseverance, most people will eventually overcome the obstacles.

For the English-speaking learner who has struggled with French, Spanish or German verb tenses at school, Thai grammar, in the initial stages, appears refreshingly uncomplicated. Word order is similar to English while nouns and verbs have a single fixed form, with neither singular/plural distinctions nor verb endings to memorize. But Thai also displays many features common in South East Asian languages but not found in European languages. These include a complex pronoun system (reflecting gender, age, social status, formality, intimacy), the use of *particles* (untranslatable words) to convey mood and noun *classifiers*, used in expressing quantity.

Thai has borrowed many words from the classical Indian languages, Sanskrit and Pali, Cambodian and, more recently, English. Most words of pure Thai origin are monosyllabic. As they bear no resemblance to their English or European equivalents, their meanings cannot readily be guessed. Learners often find it difficult to remember words in isolation; learning the word as part of a useful phrase, preferably with the Thai script spelling, is the most effective way of retaining vocabulary.

The Thai script has evolved from a script that originated in South India and was introduced into mainland South East Asia during the 4th or 5th century AD. An inscribed stone pillar, dated 1292 AD, is widely believed to be the first recorded example of Thai writing. In one section of the inscription, the author, King Ramkhamhaeng of Sukhothai, actually claims to have devised the script; in recent years, however, there has been heated academic debate about the authenticity of the inscription.

Thai is written across the page from left to right with no spaces between words. Spaces are used as punctuation markers, instead of commas or full stops. The Thai alphabet has 42 consonants. Many consonant symbols change their pronunciation at the end of a word because of the very limited number of final consonant sounds that exist in Thai.

There is no universally agreed system for romanizing Thai. Many Thais have difficulty in reading anything other than names of people or places written in roman letters and very few would be able to romanize words in any kind of systematic manner; indeed, two members of the same family may romanize their own family name differently. A brief glance through the menu in any Thai restaurant is likely to throw up numerous inconsistencies. For the learner, however, some kind of systematic romanization system provides a necessary crutch on the path to literacy. Every system has its shortcomings, whether through using esoteric symbols that only trained linguists can understand or through trying to represent strange sounds in letters that are inadequate for the purpose. The aim of every serious learner should be to discard romanization as quickly as possible and read Thai script. Once you are literate, you will be much more aware of what is going on around you and you are able to draw on authentic materials, such as posters, advertisements, magazines and so on to improve your Thai.

Introduction

About Thai

Thai is the national language of Thailand and is spoken by approximately 60 million people in that country. Lao, spoken in neighbouring Laos, is very closely related to Thai (although most Thais from Bangkok would have some difficulty understanding it), but the other neighbouring languages – Burmese, Cambodian and Malay – are completely different. Distinct dialects of Thai are spoken in the north, northeast and south of the country, but it is the language of the Central Region and Bangkok which is used throughout the country as the medium for education and mass media and which is taught in this course.

Thai is a *tonal* language. In tonal languages the meaning of a syllable is determined by the pitch at which it is pronounced. **kao,** for example, means 'news' when pronounced with a *low* tone, 'white' with a *rising* tone and 'rice' with a *falling* tone. If tones make pronunciation in Thai seem more complex than in more familiar European languages, the learner will probably find Thai grammar considerably easier to absorb, for there are no complex verb tenses and noun endings which seem to blight many people's experience of trying to learn a foreign language.

Thai is written in its own unique alphabetic script, which has developed from a script originally found in India. It is written across the page from left to right, with certain vowels appearing above the line of writing and others appearing below. There are no spaces between words; when spaces do occur, they act as a form of punctuation mark, similar to commas and full stops.

About the book

This book is intended for the complete beginner. It aims to equip the learner with the necessary vocabulary and grammar to cope with the day-to-day situations a foreigner is likely to encounter in Thailand. Another major aim of the course is to provide a solid introduction to the Thai writing system so that the learner will have the means to extend his or her knowledge of the language beyond this course.

Each unit is built around dialogues, followed by a brief cultural background note which draws out aspects of the linguistic or social context of the dialogues. Key phrases and expressions are highlighted, while the full vocabulary lists and explanatory language notes should enable you to understand conversations without too much difficulty. A variety of practice exercises help to reinforce the material covered in the dialogues and the key at the end of the book allows you to keep a close check that you are on the right track. A considerable part of each unit is devoted to reading and writing Thai. The script is presented in manageable chunks and tested in reading exercises.

Most of the material in each unit is reproduced in recorded form to accompany this book. You are strongly advised to purchase this to gain a clear idea of how Thai should sound.

How to use the book

Each individual will have their own preferred way of working through the course. If you have the recorded material, you might like to start each unit by listening to the dialogue a number of times with your book closed, simply to get your ear attuned to the language. Alternatively, you may prefer to work out what the dialogue means before you consider listening to it. It does not really matter what approach you adopt as long as you are happy with it and you are prepared to follow it regularly. Whatever approach you adopt, however, you are ultimately faced with the task of memorizing and accurately reproducing unfamiliar combinations of sounds. It is best to memorize words in meaningful phrases rather than in isolation and your pronunciation and intonation will obviously be greatly aided if you have the recording to use as a model. Frequent review of earlier lessons and exercises is essential if the language in them is to become almost second nature.

People learning a language written in an unfamiliar script may often say: 'Oh, I only want to learn to speak it, I'm not bothered about writing.' They usually imagine that learning a new script will be extremely difficult and time consuming and that they will be able to steam ahead much more quickly if they concentrate merely on the spoken language. You can, if you choose, work through this book in that fashion, simply ignoring the sections on script. But if you do, you won't be getting your money's worth from the course and you'll be adopting a short-sighted and self-limiting view. Just think how ridiculous you would think it was if a Thai told you he was studying English conversation from this dialogue because he couldn't be bothered to learn Western script:

A กุดมอร์นิง ไมเนมอิสจอห์น

B กุดมอร์นิง มิสเตอร์จอห์น เฮาอาร์ยูทูเด?

(When you have reached Unit 11 you will see just how silly it is!)

The familiar Thai script would encourage him to pronounce these English words with a Thai accent and he certainly wouldn't be able to get English speakers to write down new words for him if he were trying to expand his vocabulary; in short, he would never progress beyond the one or two books in which English is written phonetically in Thai letters.

You may not ever plan to write letters in Thai or read newspapers and novels, but if you want to build on what you can learn from a book such as this, becoming literate in Thai is an absolute must! It will also, as anyone who has mastered the script will tell you, improve your pronunciation immeasurably.

Now that you have decided that you do want to learn to read Thai, here is the good news. The Thai script is presented in this course in such a way as to persuade you that it is neither extremely difficult nor time consuming and that even if you are one of the least gifted language learners, you can, with regular practice, learn to read and write Thai. All it really requires is the patience to copy out letters, words and then phrases a sufficient number of times until it becomes almost second nature. Eventually copying out whole passages will improve not only your reading and writing skills but will also reinforce everything else you have learned about the language, including pronunciation and grammar. Keep going back over earlier lessons, because by reading material that is familiar, you will begin to read more quickly and develop the ability to recognize words instantly without having to labour over individual letters each time.

Remember that when learning a foreign language, 'little and often' is much more effective than long but infrequent sessions. Ten to 15 minutes every day is far more productive than one long session once a week.

Romanization of Thai

For westerners learning the language it is convenient to use romanized Thai at the beginning, but it must be stressed that this is no more than a learning aid. It is not an acceptable alternative to the Thai script and most Thais would not be able to read Thai written in romanized form. There are a number of different systems of romanizing Thai, each with its advantages and disadvantages. Like all systems, the one used in this book can offer only an approximate representation of the Thai sound. The most effective strategy is to learn pronunciation from the recording and to memorize Thai script spellings rather than romanized spellings. You should treat the romanization system as a crutch and you should aim to discard it as quickly as possible.

Pronunciation

There are a few sounds in Thai that do not exist in English and which can cause some problems. But the vast majority of Thai sounds have a reasonably close equivalent in English.

Consonants

🔊 **00.02**

At the beginning of a word, consonants are generally pronounced as in English. A few sounds, however, need further clarification:

g *as in* **g***et (not* **g***in)*

ng a single sound which we are familiar with in English at the end of words like 'wrong' and 'song', but which also occurs at the beginning of words in Thai:

ngahn   ngâi   ngahm   ngoo

bp a single sound which is somewhere between a **b** sound and a **p** sound in English. Many learners find it hard to both produce this sound accurately and to distinguish it from **b**. Don't be discouraged if you do have problems; you will probably find that over a period of time you will gradually master it:

bpai   bpen   bpoo   bplào

dt a single sound which is somewhere between a **d** sound and a **t** sound in English. Again, many learners find it difficult to distinguish from **t** at first, although usually such problems are short lived:

dtàir   dtìt   dtorn   dtrong

At the end of a word the sounds **k**, **p** and **t** are not 'released'. Examples of 'unreleased' final consonants in English include the **t** in 'rat' when 'rat trap' is said quickly and the **p** in the casual pronunciation of 'yep!' At first you may feel that words ending in **k**, **p** and **t** all sound the same, but within a very short time you will find that you can hear a distinct difference:

bpàhk   bàhp   bàht

yâhk   yâhp   yâht

Many Thais have difficulty pronouncing an **r** sound and will substitute a **l** sound instead. Thus, **a-rai?** (*what?*) becomes **a-lai?** In words that begin with two consonants, you might also hear some Thais omit the second consonant sound. **krai?** (*who?*) becomes **kai?** and **bplah** (*fish*) becomes **bpah**. An even more bewildering change, associated with Bangkok working-class speech, is when **kw** at the beginning of a word becomes **f**, so that **kwăh** (*right*) is pronounced **făh**!

Vowels

🔊 **00.03**

Most Thai vowels have near equivalents in English. In the romanization system used in this book, vowels are pronounced as follows:

a as in *ago*	**ay** as in *may*
e as in *pen*	**ee** as in *fee*
i as in *bit*	**er** as in *number*
o as in *cot*	**ew** as in *few*
u as in *fun*	**oh** as in *go*
ah as in *father*	**OO** as in *book*
ai as in *Thai*	**oo** as in *food*
air as in *fair*	**oy** as in *boy*
ao as in *Lao*	

Other sounds, however, have no near equivalent in English and you need to listen to the recording to have a proper idea of how they should be pronounced:

eu	**meu**	**séu**	**keu**
eu-a	**mêu-a**	**sêu-a**	**něu-a**
air-o	**láir-o**	**gâir-o**	**tǎir-o**
er-ee	**ler-ee**	**ker-ee**	**ner-ee**

Tones

🔊 **00.04**

There are five tones in Thai: mid tone, low tone, high tone, rising tone and falling tone. These are represented in the romanization system by the following accents: mid tone (*no mark*), low tone (ˋ), high tone (ˊ), rising tone (ˇ) and falling tone (ˆ). To help you attune your ears to the different tone sounds, listen to the recording of a Thai speaker saying the following words. Don't worry about the meanings at this stage – simply concentrate on listening:

mid tone	**kOOn**	**krai**	**mah**	**bpai**
	pairng	**mee**	**dairng**	**bpen**
low tone	**jàhk**	**bpàirt**	**sìp**	**bàht**
	yài	**jòrt**	**èek**	**nèung**
high tone	**mái**	**káo**	**lót**	**lék**
	róo	**rót**	**náhm**	**púk**

rising tone	sǒo-ay	pǒm	sǒrng	kǒr
	sěe-a	kǒrng	nǎi	děe-o
falling tone	mâi	châi	dâi	têe
	gâo	mâhk	chôrp	pôot

It is obviously important to be able both to hear and to reproduce tones correctly if you are going to make yourself understood. But don't let a fear of getting a tone wrong inhibit you from practising. Surprisingly, wrong tones are very seldom the cause of misunderstandings and communication breakdowns. Indeed, many non-Thais operate confidently and effectively in the language with far from perfect accuracy in their tones.

1 sa-wùt dee
Hello
สวัสดี

In this unit, you will learn:
▶ *how to say hello and goodbye*
▶ *how to use polite particles*
▶ *how to address people appropriately*
▶ *low class consonants (i)*
▶ *vowels (i)*
▶ *numbers 1–10*

Dialogues

sa-wùt dee krúp kOOn Mah-lee

Peter and Malee are saying hello to each other. Here are the words they use:

QUICK VOCAB

sa-wùt dee	*hello; good morning/afternoon/ evening; goodbye*	สวัสดี
krúp	male polite particle	ครับ
kOOn	polite title: *Mr/Mrs/Miss/Ms*	คุณ
kà/kâh	female polite particle	คะ

 01.01

Peter	สวัสดีครับคุณมาลี	sa-wùt dee krúp kOOn Mah-lee.
Malee	สวัสดีค่ะคุณปีเตอร์	sa-wùt dee kà kOOn Peter.

> **● INSIGHT**
> Sometimes you will hear female speakers say **kâh** – with a longer vowel and a falling tone – rather than **kà** at the end of a statement. Both are equally correct. You will also hear some male speakers say **kúp** instead of **krúp**.

sa-wùt dee kà ah-jahn wí-pah

When addressing teachers, college lecturers, sports coaches and others with specialist knowledge, **ah-jahn** (*teacher, lecturer*) is used before the personal name rather than **kOOn**. Here is a student greeting her college lecturer, whose name is Wipha:

🔊 **01.02**

| Student | สวัสดีค่ะอาจารย์วิภา | sa-wùt dee kà ah-jahn Wí-pah. |
| Wipha | สวัสดีค่ะ | sa-wùt dee kà. |

If you don't know the personal name, you can simply address a teacher as **ah-jahn**.

sa-wùt dee krúp, kOOn mǒr

Doctors are addressed as **kOOn mǒr** (*doctor*). Here is a male patient responding to his doctor's greeting:

🔊 **01.03**

| Doctor | สวัสดีครับ | sa-wùt dee krúp. |
| Patient | สวัสดีครับคุณหมอ | sa-wùt dee krúp, kOOn mǒr. |

'wùt dee krúp kOOn Mah-lee

In informal speech, **sa-wùt dee** is often abbreviated to **'wùt dee**.

🔊 **01.04**

| Damrong | หวัดดีครับคุณมาลี | 'wùt dee krúp kOOn Mah-lee. |
| Malee | หวัดดีค่ะ | 'wùt dee kà. |

bpai nǎi?

A more casual greeting is **bpai nǎi?** *Where are you going?* This does not necessarily require more than a vague reply, such as **bpai tÓO-rá** (*on business*) or **bpai têe-o** (*out*):

| Damrong | ไปไหนครับ | bpai nǎi krúp? |
| Malee | ไปเที่ยวค่ะ | bpai têe-o kà. |

When female speakers ask questions, the tone of the polite particle is high: **ká**.

Malee	ไปไหนคะ	bpai năi ká?
Damrong	ไปธุระครับ	bpai tÓO-rá krúp.

QUICK VOCAB

bpai năi?	*where are you going? (informal greeting)*	ไปไหน
bpai têe-o	*going out*	ไปเที่ยว
bpai tÓO-rá	*going on business*	ไปธุระ

bpai lá ná

When we want to say goodbye, we can also use **sa-wùt dee** or its shortened form, **'wùt dee**. A more casual way of saying goodbye is **bpai lá ná**, *I'm off now, right?* or *I'm going now, OK?* An appropriate response is to use the polite particle to acknowledge the farewell. Here we could translate it as *yes/right/OK*.

🔊 **01.05**

Damrong	ไปละนะครับ	bpai lá ná krúp.
Sue	คะ	kà.
Malee	ไปละนะคะ	bpai lá ná ká.
Peter	ครับ	krúp.

● INSIGHT

Thais use first names in both formal and informal situations in Thailand. Thais, both male and female, should normally be addressed by their first name preceded by the polite title **kOOn** (usually written *khun* in romanized Thai) in front of their name. This is especially important when addressing or referring to individuals of higher social status; to omit **kOOn** in such instances would appear either over-familiar or disrespectful. Thus, Mrs Patcharee Saibua, Mr Sompong Tongkum and Miss Araya Jaroenwong should be addressed as Khun Patcharee, Khun Sompong and Khun Araya respectively.

You can use *khun* in front of a Thai person's name when you are speaking English, too, as a sign of politeness. Thais dealing with Westerners in a formal professional context sometimes prefer to use *khun* followed by a surname, instead of a first name, Charles Phillips becoming Khun Phillips rather than Khun Charles. Surnames have only come into general usage in Thailand within the last 100 years and their usage is restricted largely to written documents.

The terms **ah-jahn** and **kOOn mŏr** are used instead of **kOOn**, when talking to college lecturers and medical doctors respectively.

Key phrases and expressions

🔊 **01.06**

How to

1 greet someone *or* say goodbye formally

   sa-wùt dee krúp (male speaking)   สวัสดีครับ

   sa-wùt dee kà (female speaking)   สวัสดีค่ะ

2 greet (a) Malee, (b) a teacher or college lecturer, (c) a doctor

   sa-wùt dee krúp/ kà kOOn mah-lee   สวัสดีครับ/ค่ะ คุณมาลี

   sa-wùt dee krúp/ kà ah-jahn   สวัสดีครับ/ค่ะ อาจารย์

   sa-wùt dee krúp/ kà kOOn mŏr   สวัสดีครับ/ค่ะ คุณหมอ

3 greet someone *or* say goodbye informally

   wùt dee krúp/ kà   หวัดดีครับ/ค่ะ

4 greet a friend in a casual manner and respond to such a greeting

   bpai năi krúp/ ká?   ไปไหนครับ/คะ

   bpai tÓO-rá krúp/ kà   ไปธุระครับ/ค่ะ

   or

   bpai têe-o krúp/ kà   ไปเที่ยวครับ/ค่ะ

5 say goodbye i n a casual manner

   bpai lá ná krúp/ ká   ไปละนะครับ/คะ

Language notes

1 POLITE PARTICLES

Particles are untranslatable words that occur at the end of utterances.

Polite particles are added at the end of a statement or question to make the speaker's words sound polite and respectful; they have no direct equivalent in English and therefore cannot be translated. The most common polite particles are **krúp, kà** (or **kâh**) and **ká**. Male speakers use **krúp** at the end of both statements and questions. Some speakers reduce the initial **kr-** sound to **k-** and say **kúp**. Female speakers use either low tone **kà** or falling tone **kâh** at the end of statements and high tone **ká** after questions.

It is not necessary to use these particles after every sentence in a conversation. You will gradually learn how frequently to use polite particles by listening to native speakers; in the meantime, it is best to use them frequently and risk sounding too polite.

2 GREETINGS

sa-wùt dee is used as a greeting regardless of the time of day. It is often accompanied by a *wai*, a gesture in which the head is bowed slightly and the hands held in a prayer-like position, somewhere between the neck and forehead. The higher the position of the hands, the greater the respect shown to the person being greeted.

3 COLLOQUIAL EXPRESSIONS

When we learn a foreign language, we frequently encounter colloquial expressions that we understand how and when to use, without understanding how the words *fit together*. In this unit, the informal **bpai lá ná** (*'I'm off now'*) consists of the verb **bpai** (*to go*) followed by the particles **lá** and **ná**. If you really want to know how these particles work, you can consult the reference grammar listed under the Taking it further section in the Appendices, but, at this stage, it is sufficient just to remember the expression.

Exercises

🔊 **01.07**

1 How would you say hello to:
   a *Malee?*
   b *a doctor?*
   c *a college lecturer?*

🔊 **01.08**

2 How would you respond to the following:
   a sa-wùt dee kà
   b wùt dee krúp
   c bpai năi ká?
   d bpai lá ná krúp

🔊 **01.09**

3 Listen to the recording and repeat after the speaker, paying special attention to the tones:

kà	dee kà	wùt dee kà	sa-wùt dee kà
krúp	dee krúp	wùt dee krúp	sa-wùt dee krúp
ká	năi ká	bpai năi ká	kOOn bpai năi ká
krúp	ná krúp	lá ná krúp	bpai lá ná krúp

Reading and writing

The Thai letters are not introduced in alphabetical order (which you will find in the Appendices), but rather by class and frequency of occurrence. Thai friends will find this approach strange because it differs radically from the way in which they learned to read at primary school. But it is a well-proven method, which can be traced back to B.O. Cartwright's *Elementary Handbook of the Siamese Language written* in 1906!

1 CONSONANTS

Thai consonants are divided into three classes – *low class*, *mid class* and *high class*. It is essential to remember which class a consonant belongs to as the class of the initial consonant in a word will play a part in determining the tone of that word.

The consonants in this lesson are all *low class* consonants.

Thai consonants are all pronounced with an inherent **'or'** sound; thus at the end of this lesson you can say that you know the letters **nor**, **ngor**, **mor**, **ror** and so on. Each Thai consonant also has a 'name' that links the letter to a common word that begins with that letter, rather like 'a for apple, b for bat', etc. The letter **nor** is known as **nor nǒo** (**nǒo** means 'rat'), **ngor** is **ngor ngoo** (**ngoo** means 'snake') and **mor** is **mor máh** (**máh** means 'horse'). When Thais learn their alphabet at school, they always learn the name of the letter. While a full list of the names of letters is provided in Unit 13, it is not necessary to know these names in order to be able to read.

Look carefully at the following letters. They are all written with a single stroke of the pen, starting from the inside of the loop and moving outwards. In letters in which there are two loops, the starting point is the top loop on the left-hand side.

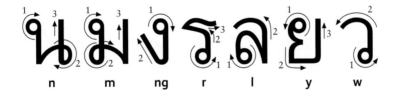

| n | m | ng | r | l | y | w |

Copy out each letter a number of times until you can reproduce it accurately and naturally; say the name of the letter (e.g. **nor**) each time you write it in order to help you memorize it.

2 VOWELS

Vowels are classified as either *long* or *short*. As each vowel symbol is introduced you will need to remember whether it is a long or short vowel, as vowel length plays a part in determining the tone of a word. A full list of long and short vowels appears in the Appendices.

The vowel symbols in this unit, with the exception of **-u-**, are written after a consonant symbol, the dash representing the position of the consonant. In subsequent units you will meet vowel symbols that are written above a consonant, below, in front and even surrounding the consonant on three sides.

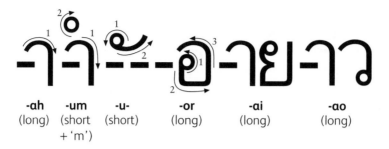

| -ah (long) | -um (short + 'm') | -u- (short) | -or (long) | -ai (long) | -ao (long) |

3 WORDS

Here are some common words that combine some of the consonants and vowels from this unit.

มา	งาน	นาน	นาย	ลาว
mah	**ngahn**	**nahn**	**nai**	**lao**
to come	*work*	*a long time*	*Mr*	*Lao(s)*

นำ	มัน	ยัง	รอ	ยอม
num	**mun**	**yung**	**ror**	**yorm**
to lead	*it*	*still*	*to wait*	*to agree*

4 NUMBERS

Although Arabic numerals are widely used in Thailand it is important to be familiar with the Thai system of writing numbers. These numbers are, incidentally, written the same way in Cambodian.

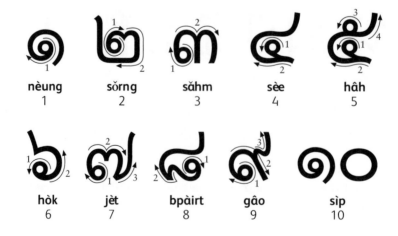

nèung 1	sŏrng 2	săhm 3	sèe 4	hâh 5

| hòk 6 | jèt 7 | bpàirt 8 | gâo 9 | sìp 10 |

Reading practice

1 Scan through this sample of Thai script for a couple of minutes and see how many letters you can identify. Put a faint pencil mark through each letter that you recognize.

ตลาดทางด้านยุโรปของเราในตอนนี้พูดได้ว่าไปได้สวย โดยเฉพาะที่อังกฤษ
ตอนนี้การไปเที่ยวเมืองไทยเป็นที่นิยมกันมากเหมือนกับเป็นแฟชั่นอีกอย่างหนึ่ง
เดิมเขาจะไปฮ่องกงกันมากกว่าเพราะฮ่องกงเป็นเมืองขึ้นของเขาและคนพูด
ภาษาอังกฤษกันได้เป็นส่วนมาก

🔊 **01.11**

2 In this and subsequent exercises, read the words and syllables aloud, first working across the page in rows and then down the page in columns. Practice until you can read quickly and fluently. Pick out words at random to test yourself. Copy out the table, saying aloud each word as you write it.

นา	มา	งา	รา	ลา	ยา	วา
นำ	มำ	งำ	รำ	ลำ	ยำ	วำ
นอ	มอ	งอ	รอ	ลอ	ยอ	วอ

🔊 **01.12**

3 Repeat the same procedure as in Exercise 2 in this exercise.

งาม	นาน	ยาม	นาง	งาน
นอน	รอง	ลอง	มอง	ยอม
มัน	ยัง	รัง	ลัง	วัน
ราย	ลาว	นาย	ราว	ยาง

🔊 **01.13**

4 In Thai writing, there are normally no spaces between words. Spaces are used for punctuation and tend to occur where there might be a comma, full stop or inverted commas in English. The western learner has to get used to recognizing where one word ends and another begins without the aid of spaces. Read each of the following lines, adding a word at a time, until you have a three-word sentence. Don't worry about the meaning at this stage – the purpose of the exercise is trying to accustom your eye to recognizing word boundaries.

นาย	นายมอง	นายมองนาง
ยาม	ยามมา	ยามมารอ
นาง	นางงาม	นางงามรำ

? Key points

1 **sa-wùt dee** means both *'hello'* and *'goodbye'*.

2 In informal situations, **sa-wùt dee** is often abbreviated to **wùt dee**.

3 Use **kOOn** in front of someone's personal name as a mark of politeness; if the person is a teacher, use **ah-jahn**.

4 Male speakers use the polite particle **krúp** at the end of statements and questions; some speakers omit the **r** and say **kúp**.

5 Female speakers use the polite particle **kà** or **kâh** at the end of statements and **ká** at the end of questions.

6 The polite particles **krúp** (male) and **kà** or **kâh** (female) are used in certain contexts to mean *'yes'*.

7 Low class consonants: น ม ง ร ล ย ว

8 Vowels: -า -ำ -ั -อ -าย -าว

9 Numbers: ๑ ๒ ๓ ๔ ๕ ๖ ๗ ๘ ๙ ๑๐

2 kOOn chêu a-rai?
What's your name?
คุณชื่ออะไร

In this unit, you will learn:
▶ *how to state your name, nationality and place of origin*
▶ *confirmation-seeking question: châi mái?*
▶ *what? questions*
▶ *mid class consonants*
▶ *vowels (ii)*
▶ *numbers 11–20*

Dialogues

pǒm chêu Peter krúp

Peter is about to introduce himself. Here are the new words he uses:

QUICK VOCAB

pǒm	*I (male)*	ผม
chêu	*first name; to have the first name ...*	ชื่อ
nahm sa-gOOn	*family name*	นามสกุล
bpen	*to be*	เป็น
kon	*person*	คน
ung-grìt	*English*	อังกฤษ
mah jàhk	*to come from*	มาจาก

◀)) 02.01

Peter	สวัสดีครับ	sa-wùt dee krúp.
	ผมชื่อ ปีเตอร์ครับ	pǒm chêu Peter krúp.
	นามสกุลกรีน	nahm sa-gOOn Green.
	เป็นคนอังกฤษ	bpen kon ung-grìt.
	มาจากแมนเช็สเตอร์	mah jàhk Manchester.

bpen kon tai

Now here's Malee introducing herself; here are the new words she uses:

QUICK VOCAB

di-chún	*I (female)*	ดิฉัน
kon tai	*Thai person*	คนไทย
grOOng-tâyp	*Bangkok*	กรุงเทพฯ

 02.02

Malee	สวัสดีค่ะ	sa-wùt dee kà.
	ดิฉันชื่อ มาลีค่ะ	di-chún chêu Malee kà.
	เป็นคนไทย	bpen kon tai.
	มาจากกรุงเทพฯ	mah jàhk grOOng-tâyp.

bpen kon pâhk něu-a

Next comes Damrong from the north of Thailand:

QUICK VOCAB

pâhk něu-a	*the north*	ภาคเหนือ
chee-ung mài	*Chiangmai*	เชียงใหม่

🔊 **02.03**

Damrong	สวัสดีครับ	sa-wùt dee krúp.
	ผมชื่อ ดำรงครับ	pǒm chêu Damrong krúp.
	เป็นคนภาคเหนือ	bpen kon pâhk něu-a.
	มาจากเชียงใหม่	mah jàhk chee-ung mài.

mah jàhk bpra-tâyt yêe-bpÒOn

And finally Mineko from Japan:

QUICK VOCAB

bpra-tâyt	*country*	ประเทศ
yêe-bpÒOn	*Japan*	ญี่ปุ่น

🔊 **02.04**

Mineko	สวัสดีค่ะ	sa-wùt dee kà.
	ดิฉันชื่อ มิเนโกะค่ะ	di-chún chêu Mineko kà.
	มาจากประเทศญี่ปุ่นค่ะ	mah jàhk bpra-tâyt yêe-bpÒOn kà.

mâi châi kon a-may-ri-gun

We have been using **bpen kon** ... to say things like *I'm Thai* (**bpen kon tai**) or *I'm a northerner* (**bpen kon pâhk něu-a**). If we want to say *I'm not Thai* or *I'm not a northerner*, then we use **mâi châi kon** ... :

QUICK VOCAB

mâi châi ...	*am/are/is not a ...*	ไม่ใช่ ...

🔊 **02.05**

Sue	ฉันไม่ใช่	chún mâi châi
	คนอเมริกันค่ะ	kon a-may-ri-gun kà.
	เป็นคนอังกฤษ	bpen kon ung-grìt.

Damrong	ผมไม่ใช่	pǒm mâi châi
	คนกรุงเทพฯครับ	kon grOOng-tâyp krúp.
	เป็นคนภาคเหนือ	bpen kon pâhk něu-a.

● INSIGHT

Do not use **mâi bpen** ... when you want to say '*I'm not* ...'! It's wrong!

Key phrases and expressions

How to

1 state your personal name

pǒm chêu ... (*male speaking*)	ผมชื่อ ...
di-chún (*formal*) **chêu** ... (female speaking)	ดิฉันชื่อ ...
chún (*informal*) **chêu** ... (female speaking)	ฉันชื่อ ...

2 state your family name

| **pǒm/chún nahm sa-gOOn ...** | ผม/ฉันนามสกุล ... |

3 state your nationality or regional identity

| **pǒm/chún bpen kon ...** | ผม/ฉันเป็นคน ... |

4 state where you come from

| **pǒm/chún mah jàhk ...** | ผม/ฉันมาจาก ... |

In the second part of this unit we are going to learn how to ask what someone's name and nationality is and how to confirm that we have heard, understood or inferred something correctly.

kOOn chêu a-rai ká?

Malee asks Mineko her name and checks that she has heard it correctly. Here are the new words:

QUICK VOCAB

a-rai	*what?*	อะไร
..., châi mái?	*..., is that right?*	...ใช่ไหม
châi	*yes to a ..., **châi mái?** question*	ใช่

02.06

Malee	คุณชื่ออะไรคะ	kOOn chêu a-rai ká?
Mineko	ชื่อ มิเนโกะค่ะ	chêu Mineko kà.
Malee	มิเนโกะใช่ไหมคะ	Mineko châi mái ká?
Mineko	ใช่ค่ะ	châi kà.

kOOn Mineko bpen kon châht a-rai krúp?

Damrong asks Mineko about her nationality:

QUICK VOCAB

châht	*nation*	ชาติ

 02.07

Damrong	คุณมิเนโกะเป็น คนชาติอะไรครับ	kOOn Mineko bpen kon châht a-rai krúp?
Mineko	เป็นคนญี่ปุ่นค่ะ	bpen kon yêe-bpÒOn kà.
Damrong	คนญี่ปุ่นใช่ไหมครับ	kon yêe-bpÒOn châi mái krúp?
Mineko	ใช่ค่ะ	châi kà.

> ● **INSIGHT**
>
> **kOOn** (*you*) is a pronoun that sounds rather impersonal; if you know a person's name you can use it with **kOOn** to sound more friendly.

kOOn Damrong bpen kon groong-tâyp châi mái krúp?

Peter assumes that Damrong is from Bangkok:

QUICK VOCAB

mâi châi	*no to a ..., **châi mái?** question*	ไม่ใช่

Peter	คุณดำรงเป็นคน	kOOn Damrong bpen kon
	กรุงเทพฯใช่ไหมครับ	grOOng-tâyp châi mái krúp?
Damrong	ไม่ใช่ครับ	mâi châi krúp.
	เป็นคนภาคเหนือ	bpen kon pâhk nĕu-a.
Peter	มาจากจังหวัดอะไรครับ	mah jàhk jung-wùt a-rai krúp?
Damrong	จังหวัดเชียงใหม่ครับ	jung-wùt chee-ung mài krúp.

● **INSIGHT**

Many Thais do not make any distinction between **r** and **l** sounds at the beginning of a word or syllable in informal speech. Thus they will pronounce **a-rai?** (*what?*) as **a-lai?** and **róo** (*to know*) as **lóo**.

Many speakers will also completely drop the **r** sound when it follows another consonant sound. So they may pronounce **ung-grìt** (*English*) as **ung-gìt**, **grOOng-tâyp** (*Bangkok*) as **gOOng-tâyp** and **bpra-tâyt** (*country*) as **bpa-tâyt**.

But many educated Thais regard the absence of **r** sounds as a sign of substandard speech and will look askance at the foreigner who has picked up the habit.

Key phrases and expressions

 02.09

How to

1 ask somebody their personal name

kOOn chêu a-rai?　　　　　　คุณชื่ออะไร

2 ask somebody their family name

kOOn nahm sa-gOOn a-rai?　　คุณนามสกุลอะไร

3 ask somebody their nationality

kOOn bpen kon châht a-rai?　　คุณเป็นคนชาติอะไร

4 ask somebody what region they are from

kOOn bpen kon pâhk a-rai?　　คุณเป็นคนภาคอะไร

5 ask somebody what province they are from

kOOn bpen kon jung-wùt a-rai?　คุณเป็นคนจังหวัดอะไร

6 confirm that you know someone's name

kOOn chêu ... châi mái?   คุณชื่อ ...ใช่ไหม

7 confirm that you know someone's nationality

kOOn bpen kon ... châi mái?   คุณเป็นคน ... ใช่ไหม

Language notes

1 PERSONAL PRONOUNS

There are many more personal pronouns in Thai than in English. The correct choice of pronoun depends on the relative status of the speakers and the degree of intimacy between them. The learner, however, can use Thai effectively with a limited number of pronouns. The most common of these are:

QUICK VOCAB

pǒm	*I* (male)	ผม
di-chún	*I* (female, formal)	ดิฉัน
chún	*I* (female, informal)	ฉัน
kOOn	*you* (singular and plural)	คุณ
káo	*he, she, they*	เขา
rao	*we*	เรา

Notice that the word for *I* is determined by the gender of the speaker, while a single word, **káo**, can mean *he, she or they*.

Thais frequently omit the personal pronoun when it is clear from the context who is speaking, being addressed or being referred to. In many of the examples in this course, you will find that the pronoun has been omitted in the Thai to make it sound more natural and that an arbitrary choice of pronoun has been included in the English translation. Thus, **bpen kon châht a-rai?** could mean *What's your nationality?* or *What's his/her/their nationality?*, while **bpen kon tai,** could mean *I'm Thai* or *He's/she's/they're Thai*.

The occupation terms **ah-jahn** (*teacher, college lecturer*) and **mǒr** (*doctor*) are also used as personal pronouns:

ah-jahn bpen kon tai

อาจารย์เป็นคนไทย

He's Thai (referring to a college lecturer)

You're Thai (addressing a college lecturer)

I'm Thai (college lecturer speaking)

18

2 NOUNS

Nouns in Thai have a single fixed form, with no distinction between singular and plural. Thus **kon** can mean either *person* or *people*, depending on the context.

An adjective follows the noun it modifies:

kon ung-grìt

คนอังกฤษ

English person/people

bpen kon tai

เป็นคนไทย

He is/they are Thai.

3 THE VERB 'TO BE': *bpen* + NOUN

bpen is one of several different Thai verbs that are used to translate *is/are, was/were*, etc. **bpen** does have other meanings, but when it means *to be*, it is always followed by a noun:

káo bpen kon pâhk něu-a

เขาเป็นคนภาคเหนือ

He's a northerner.

káo bpen kon yêe-bpÒOn

เขาเป็นคนญี่ปุ่น

She's Japanese.

In negative sentences such as *I'm not a …*, **bpen** is replaced by **mâi châi:**

chún mâi châi kon grOOng-tâyp

ฉันไม่ใช่คนกรุงเทพฯ

I'm not from Bangkok.

káo mâi châi kon a-may-ri-gun

เขาไม่ใช่คนอเมริกัน

He's not an American.

The negative word **mâi** may not be used before **bpen** to mean *is not*.

4 BANGKOK

The Thai name for Bangkok is **grOOng-tâyp** (often written as **Krungthep**) in guidebooks. This is a much abbreviated form of the enormously long official title. Western travel writers sometimes refer to Bangkok as the 'City of Angels' because **grOOng** means *city* and **tâyp** *angel*.

5 COUNTRIES AND NATIONALITIES

Names of countries are normally preceded by the word **bpra-tâyt** (*country*):

bpra-tâyt yêe-bpÒOn	*Japan*	ประเทศญี่ปุ่น
bpra-tâyt jeen	*China*	ประเทศจีน
bpra-tâyt tai	*Thailand*	ประเทศไทย
*meu-ung tai	*Thailand*	เมืองไทย

[NB ***meu-ung tai** is a more colloquial term for Thailand. **meu-ung** can mean *country or city*.]

Nationality, provincial identity and province of origin are expressed by the word **kon** (*person*) followed by the name of the country, region or province:

kon ung-grìt	*an English person*	คนอังกฤษ
kon pâhk něu-a	*a northerner*	คนภาคเหนือ
kon chee-ung mài	*a person from Chiangmai*	คนเชียงใหม่

6 REGIONS AND PROVINCES

Thailand has four regions (**pâhk**) each with its own distinct dialect and local customs and cuisine.

pâhk glahng	*the Central Region*	ภาคกลาง
pâhk dtâi	*the south*	ภาคใต้
pâhk něu-a	*the north*	ภาคเหนือ
pâhk ee-săhn	*the northeast*	ภาคอีสาน

For administrative purposes the country is divided into 76 provinces (**jung-wùt**).

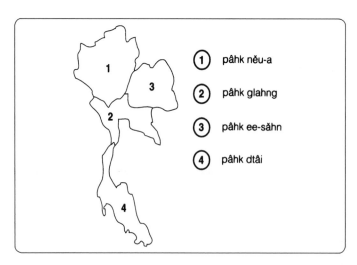

1. pâhk něu-a
2. pâhk glahng
3. pâhk ee-săhn
4. pâhk dtâi

7 'WHAT?' QUESTIONS

The Thai word for *what?* is **a-rai**. It normally occurs at the end of the sentence. Answers to these questions are formed by replacing **a-rai** with the appropriate piece of information:

kOOn chêu a-rai?

คุณชื่ออะไร

What's your name?

- chêu Mah-lee

- ชื่อมาลี

- My name is Malee.

káo nahm sa-gOOn a-rai?

เขานามสกุลอะไร

What's his surname?

- nahm sa-gOOn Green

- นามสกุลกรีน

- His surname is Green.

Note that the word **châht** (*nation*) is normally omitted in the answer to a question about nationality:

káo bpen kon châht a-rai?

เขาเป็นคนชาติอะไร

What nationality are they?

- bpen kon tai

- เป็นคนไทย

- They're Thai.

8 'YES/NO' QUESTIONS: ... châi mái?

Yes and *no* answers to questions in Thai are determined by the form of the question; there is no single word for either *yes* or *no*, so the learner has to listen carefully to the *question particle* in order to be able to answer correctly.

The question particle **châi mái?** is tagged onto the end of a statement to transform it into a confirmation-seeking question, like *...isn't it?, ... don't they?*, etc. in English. It is very useful for checking that you have heard or understood something correctly. The answer to a ... **châi mái?** question is either **châi** (*yes*) or **mâi châi** (*no*):

bpen kon tai châi mái?

เป็นคนไทยใช่ไหม

You're Thai, aren't you?

- châi

- ใช่

- Yes.

káo chêu Peter châi mái?

เขาชื่อปีเตอร์ใช่ไหม

His name is Peter, isn't it?

- mâi châi

- ไม่ใช่

- No.

9 NUMBERS 11–20

eleven	**sìp-èt**	*sixteen*	**sìp-hòk**
twelve	**sìp-sǒrng**	*seventeen*	**sìp-jèt**
thirteen	**sìp-sǎhm**	*eighteen*	**sìp-bpàirt**
fourteen	**sìp-sèe**	*nineteen*	**sìp-gâo**
fifteen	**sìp-hâh**	*twenty*	**yêe-sìp**

Exercises

🔊 **02.10**

1 How would you respond if a Thai asked you these questions?

  a kOOn chêu a-rai?

  b kOOn nahm sa-gOOn a-rai?

  c kOOn bpen kon châht a-rai?

  d kOOn bpen kon pâhk něu-a châi mái?

  e kOOn bpen kon jung-wùt a-rai?

🔊 **02.11**

2 How would you introduce the following people?

	1	2	3	4
Name	Somsak	John	Makoto	Paula
Surname	Torngkum	Stevens	Ito	Besson
Nationality	Thai	American	Japanese	French
Home town	Bangkok	New York	Tokyo	Paris

Example

káo chêu sŏm-sùk

nahm sa-gOOn torng-kum

bpen kon tai

mah jàhk grOOng-tâyp

 02.12

3 Using the information in the table, make sentences, using **bpen** and **mâi châi.**

	Peter	Nicole	Damrong	Soonyoung
mâi châi	a-may-ri-gun	sa-bpayn (Spanish)	jeen (Chinese)	yêe-bpÒOn
bpen	ung-grìt	fa-rung-sàyt (French)	tai	gâo-lĕe (Korean)

Example

Peter mâi châi kon a-may-ri-gun bpen kon ung-grìt

4 How would you ask the following questions?

   a *What's your name?*

   b *His name is Damrong, isn't it?*

   c *What is his surname?*

   d *What nationality is he?*

   e *She's from Bangkok, isn't she?*

   f *What province is he from?*

   g *He's a northerner, isn't he?*

 02.13

5 Listen to the recording and repeat after the speaker, paying special attention to the tones:

glahng	pâhk glahng	kon pâhk glahng	bpen kon pâhk glahng
dtâi	pâhk dtâi	kon pâhk dtâi	bpen kon pâhk dtâi
nĕu-a	pâhk nĕu-a	kon pâhk nĕu-a	bpen kon pâhk nĕu-a
ee-sǎhn	pâhk ee-sǎhn	kon pâhk ee-sǎhn	bpen kon pâhk ee-sǎhn

Reading and writing

1 CONSONANTS

 02.14

In the first unit, you learned the most common low class consonants. In this unit, you meet the main *mid* class consonants.

g   j   d   dt   b   bp   ('zero')

2 'ZERO' CONSONANT

Notice that the final symbol in this group is identical in appearance to the vowel **-or** that you learned in the last unit. When the symbol occurs at the beginning of a word, however, it is a consonant, which we can call 'zero' consonant because it has no inherent sound of its own. It is used when writing words that begin with a vowel sound:

อาง	อาว	อำ	อาย	อัน
ahng	**ao**	**um**	**ai**	**un**

3 VOWELS

The first three vowels are taller than other letters and are written in front of the consonant, even though the consonant is pronounced first. Although the first two vowels are pronounced exactly the same, they are not interchangeable in writing; the correct spelling of a word has to be memorized.

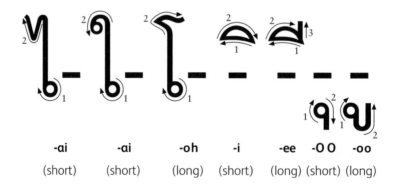

-ai	-ai	-oh	-i	-ee	-o o	-oo
(short)	(short)	(long)	(short)	(long)	(short)	(long)

Reading practice

1 LETTERS

Here is the same sample of Thai script that you met in Unit 1. Again, put a faint pencil stroke through all the letters you can recognize:

ตลาดทางด้านยุโรปของเราในตอนนี้พูดได้ว่าไปได้สวย โดยเฉพาะที่อังกฤษ ตอน
นี้การไปเที่ยวเมืองไทยเป็นที่นิยมกันมากเหมือนกับเป็นแฟชั่นอีกอย่างหนึ่ง เดิม

เขาจะไปฮ่องกงกันมากกว่าเพราะฮ่องกงเป็นเมืองขึ้นของเขาและคนพูดภาษา
อังกฤษกันได้เป็นส่วนมาก

2 WORDS

🔊 **02.15**

Try to read these words before listening to them on the recording. Don't worry if you find it difficult to hear the difference between ค and ต at this stage; it will come with practice.

กิน	กัน	กู	ใจ	จัง	จำ
ดู	ดี	ดัง	ตา	ตี	ตาย
บิน	ใบ	ไป	ปี	ปู	ยุง
อัน	ไอ	อาย	มี	โมง	โรง

3 SENTENCES

🔊 **02.16**

The sentences in the right-hand column all have five words. Read aloud across the page from left to right, gradually building up the sentence. Don't worry about meanings; the objective at this stage is simply to make the right noises. If you are having difficulty, it may help to draw a faint pencil line between each word, but beware of becoming dependent on this strategy. Note that all the words you are reading here have a mid tone.

บินมา	บินไปบินมา	ยุงบินไปบินมา
มาดู	ยินดีมาดู	ลุงยินดีมาดู
ปูดำ	มีปูดำ	ในนามีปูดำ
งูตาย	ตีงูตาย	ยามลาวตีงูตาย
นางงามดัง	ดูนางงามดัง	รอดูนางงามดัง

4 MATCH THE DATES

In Thailand the year is counted according to the Buddhist Era (BE). To convert a BE year to AD, subtract 543; thus BE 2500 is AD 1957, while AD 2000 is BE 2543.

i	๕/๑/๒๔๙๗	a	*19 June 1981*
ii	๒๕/๑๒/๒๕๓๖	b	*8 November 1948*
iii	๑๙/๖/๒๕๒๔	c	*5 January 1954*
iv	๘/๑๑/๒๔๙๑	d	*25 December 1996*

? Key points

1 **káo bpen** + NOUN *He is* ....

2 **káo mâi châi** + NOUN *He isn't* ....

3 The question word **a-rai?** (*what?*) occurs at the end of the sentence.

4 **... châi mái?** questions require a *yes* (**châi**) or *no* (**mâi châi**) answer.

5 NOUN + ADJECTIVE: an adjective *follows* the noun it modifies.

6 Bangkok: **grOOng-tâyp**; Thailand: **bpra-tâyt tai** or **meu-ung tai**; Thai: (*person/people*) **kon tai.**

7 Some speakers pronounce **'r'** sounds at the beginning of a word as **'l'**; some speakers omit an **'r'** sound when it is the second sound in a word.

8 Mid class consonants: ก จ ด ต บ ป อ

9 Vowels: ไ- ใ- โ- ◌ั ◌็ ◌ุ ◌ู

3 tum ngahn têe năi?
Where do you work?
ทำงานที่ไหน

In this unit, you will learn:
- ▶ *how to ask people about their job*
- ▶ *where? questions*
- ▶ *how to state the location of places*
- ▶ *how to express possession*
- ▶ *how to read 'live' and 'dead' syllables*
- ▶ *numbers 21–101*

Dialogues

In the following conversations, some Bangkok residents are being interviewed about their work. The two key questions are **tum ngahn a-rai?** (*What do you do?*) and **tum ngahn têe năi?** (*Where do you work?*). The question word **têe năi?** (*where?*), like **a-rai?**, occurs at the end of the sentence. Look at the following vocabulary and, if you have the recording, listen to it before reading the dialogues.

kOOn tum ngahn a-rai krúp?

QUICK VOCAB

tum ngahn	*to work*	ทำงาน
têe năi	*where?*	ที่ไหน
têe	*at*	ที่

 03.01

Interviewer	คุณทำงานอะไรครับ	kOOn tum ngahn a-rai krúp?
Dr Saowanee	ดิฉันเป็นหมอค่ะ	di-chún bpen mŏr kà.
Interviewer	ทำงานที่ไหนครับ	tum ngahn têe năi krúp?
Dr Saowanee	ทำงานที่กรุงเทพฯ ค่ะ	tum ngahn têe grOOng-tâyp kà.

tum ngahn têe năi ká?

In the next interview, the interviewee adds some information about the location of his place of work. Here are the new words you will need:

QUICK VOCAB

núk tÓO-rá-gìt	*businessman*	นักธุรกิจ
órp-fít	*office*	ออฟฟิศ
kŏrng	*of*	ของ
… kŏrng pŏm	*my (male speaker)*	… ของผม
yòo (têe)	*to be located (at/in/on)*	อยู่(ที่)
ta-nŏn sÒO-kŎOm-wít	*Sukhumwit Road*	ถนนสุขุมวิท

🔊 03.02

Interviewer	คุณทำงานอะไรคะ	kOOn tum ngahn a-rai ká?
Chartchai	ผมเป็นนักธุรกิจครับ	pŏm bpen núk tÓO-rá-gìt krúp.
Interviewer	ทำงานที่ไหนคะ	tum ngahn têe năi ká?
Chartchai	ทำงานที่	tum ngahn têe
	กรุงเทพฯ ครับ	grOOng-tâyp krúp.
	ออฟฟิศของผม	órp-fít kŏrng pŏm
	อยู่ที่ถนน	yòo têe ta-nŏn
	สุขุมวิท	sÒO-kŎOm-wít.

ah-jahn sŏrn têe năi krúp?

The third interview is with a university lecturer whose university is located in the Sukhumwit Road area (**tăir-o ta-nŏn sÒO-kŎOm-wít**). Here are the new words:

QUICK VOCAB

sŏrn	*to teach*	สอน
ma-hăh wít-ta-yah-lai	*university*	มหาวิทยาลัย
tăir-o	*locality, vicinity*	แถว

🔊 03.03

Interviewer	คุณทำงานอะไรครับ	kOOn tum ngahn a-rai krúp?
Prof. Araya	ดิฉันเป็นอาจารย์ค่ะ	di-chún bpen ah-jahn kà.
Interviewer	อาจารย์สอนที่ไหนครับ	ah-jahn sŏrn têe nǎi krúp?
Prof. Araya	สอนที่กรุงเทพฯ ค่ะ	sŏrn têe grOOng-tâyp kà.
	มหาวิทยาลัยดิฉัน	ma-hǎh wít-ta-yah-lai di-chún.
	อยู่แถวถนนสุขุมวิท	yòo tǎir-o ta-nŏn sÒO-kŏOm-wít.

● **INSIGHT**

kŏrng (*of*) is optional in expressing possession and here Prof. Araya omits it when she says *'my university …'* (**ma-hǎh wít-ta-yah-lai di-chún …**).

ree-un têe nǎi ká?

The final interviewee is a student:

QUICK VOCAB

núk sèuk-sǎh	*student*	นักศึกษา
ree-un	*to study*	เรียน
tum-ma-sàht	*Thammasat (University)*	ธรรมศาสตร์
tâh prá jun	*Ta Prachan (area of Bangkok; the original Thammasat campus)*	ท่าพระจันทร์

🔊 03.04

Interviewer	คุณทำงานอะไรคะ	kOOn tum ngahn a-rai ká?
Sunit	ผมเป็นนักศึกษาครับ	pŏm bpen núk sèuk-sǎh krúp.
Interviewer	เรียนที่ไหนคะ	ree-un têe nǎi ká?
Sunit	เรียนที่มหาวิทยาลัย	ree-un têe ma-hǎh wít-ta-yah-lai
	ธรรมศาสตร์ครับ	tum-ma-sàht krúp,
	ที่ท่าพระจันทร์	têe tâh prá jun.

Key phrases and expressions

◀)) 03.05

How to

1 ask somebody's occupation and state your own

kOOn tum ngahn a-rai?	คุณทำงานอะไร
pǒm/chún bpen …	ผม/ฉันเป็น …

2 ask where somebody works and say where you work

kOOn tum ngahn têe nǎi?	คุณทำงานที่ไหน
pǒm/chún tum ngahn têe …	ผม/ฉันทำงานที่ …

3 ask where somebody's place of work is and say where your place of work is

têe tum ngahn kǒrng kOOn yòo têe nǎi?	ที่ทำงานของคุณอยู่ที่ไหน
têe tum ngahn kǒrng pǒm/ chún yòo têe …	ที่ทำงานของผม/ฉันอยู่ที่ …

4 say something is located on Sukhumwit Road

yòo têe ta-nǒn sÒO-kǒOm-wít	อยู่ที่ถนนสุขุมวิท

5 say something is located in the Sukhumwit (Road) area

yòo tǎir-o (ta-nǒn) sÒO-kǒOm-wít	อยู่แถว(ถนน)สุขุมวิท

Language notes

1 núk …

núk (*one skilled in* …) occurs as the first element in numerous nouns; it can be followed by either a verb or a noun.

núk tÓO-rá-gìt (**tÓO-rá-gìt** *business*)	*businessman*	นักธุรกิจ
núk sèuk-săh (**sèuk-săh** *to study*)	*student*	นักศึกษา
núk kěe-un (**kěe-un** *to write*)	*writer*	นักเขียน
núk núng-sěu pim (**núng-sěu pim** *newspaper*)	*journalist*	นักหนังสือพิมพ์
núk gee-lah (**gee-lah** *sport*)	*sportsman*	นักกีฬา
núk moo-ay (**moo-ay** *boxing*)	*boxer*	นักมวย

2 'WHERE?' QUESTIONS

Where? questions follow the pattern VERB + **têe năi?** (*where?*). Note that **têe năi?** always occurs at the end of a sentence in Thai. Answers to *where?* questions often take the form, (VERB +) **têe** (*at*) + location:

kOOn tum ngahn têe năi?

คุณทำงานที่ไหน

Where do you work?

- (tum ngahn) têe grOOng-tâyp

- (ทำงาน)ที่กรุงเทพฯ

(I work) in Bangkok.

káo ree-un têe năi?

เขาเรียนที่ไหน

Where does he study?

- (ree-un) têe tum-ma-sàht

- (เรียน)ที่ธรรมศาสตร์

(He studies) at Thammasat.

órp-fit kǒrng kOOn yòo têe nǎi?

ออฟฟิศของคุณอยู่ที่ไหน

Where is your office?

- (órp-fit yòo) têe ta-nǒn sÒO-kǒOm-wít

- (ออฟฟิศอยู่)ที่ถนนสุขุมวิท

(My office is) on Sukhumwit Road.

3 LOCATION WORDS: têe AND *tǎir-o*

têe (*at*) is used to describe precise location, while **tǎir-o** (*in the vicinity of*) describes vaguer or more general location:

yòo têe ta-nǒn sÒO-kǒOm-wít

อยู่ที่ถนนสุขุมวิท

It's on Sukhumwit Road.

tum ngahn têe grOOng-tâyp

ทำงานที่กรุงเทพฯ

I work in Bangkok.

ree-un têe tum-ma-sàht

เรียนที่ธรรมศาสตร์

He studies at Thammasat.

tum ngahn tǎir-o sÒO-kǒOm-wít

ทำงานแถวสุขุมวิท

I work in the Sukhumwit area.

4 POSSESSION

Ownership or possession is expressed by the pattern NOUN + **kǒrng** (*of*) + OWNER. The word **kǒrng** is optional and frequently omitted:

órp-fit (kǒrng) chún

ออฟฟิศ(ของ)ฉัน

my office

têe tum ngahn (kǒrng) kOOn

ที่ทำงาน(ของ)คุณ

your place of work

ma-hǎh wít-ta-yah-lai (kǒrng) káo

มหาวิทยาลัย(ของ)เขา

his university

5 NUMBERS

Multiples of ten are formed in a regular way. Note, however that 20 is **yêe sìp**:

twenty	**yêe-sìp**	*seventy*	**jèt-sìp**
thirty	**sǎhm-sìp**	*eighty*	**bpàirt-sìp**
forty	**sèe-sìp**	*ninety*	**gâo-sìp**
fifty	**hâh-sìp**	*(one) hundred*	**(nèung) róy**
sixty	**hòk-sìp**		

Numbers between 21 and 100 are also formed in a regular way, but note the use of **èt** for one in 21, 31, 41, etc.:

21	**yêe-sìp èt**	*41*	**sèe-sìp èt**
22	**yêe-sìp sǒrng**	*91*	**gâo-sìp èt**
23	**yêe-sìp sǎhm**	*92*	**gâo-sìp sǒrng**
31	**sǎhm-sìp èt**	*101*	**(nèung) róy èt**
32	**sǎhm-sìp sǒrng**	*102*	**(nèung) róy sǒrng**

Exercises

1 Chantana, a Thai student is planning to take an intensive language course in London. Match the questions she was asked when she applied for a visa at the British Embassy with the answers she gave.

Questions
- **a** nahm sa-gOOn a-rai krúp?
- **b** ree-un têe nǎi krúp?
- **c** kOOn chêu a-rai krúp?
- **d** bpen núk sèuk-sǎh châi mái krúp?

Answers
- **i** châi kà
- **ii** di-chún chêu chǔn-ta-nah kà
- **iii** têe ma-hǎh wít-ta-yah-lai tum-ma-sàht kà
- **iv** nahm sa-gOOn bOOn-dee kà

2 How would you ask the following questions?
- **a** What (job) does he do?
- **b** Where do you work?
- **c** Where does Ajarn Araya teach?

d Where does Khun Sunit study?

e Where is Khun Chartchai's place of work?

🔊 03.06

3 Use the information in the table below to make statements about each person's occupation, place of work and the location of their place of work. Two new words occur in this exercise: **klí-nìk** (*clinic*) is not too hard to guess, while **bâhn** means *house* or *home*.

	Dr Saowanee	Khun Chartchai	Ajarn Araya	Khun Sunit
Occupation	doctor	businessman	lecturer	student
Home – **bâhn**	Bangkok	Sukhumwit area	Bangkok	Ta Prajan area
Place of work	clinic **klí-nìk**	office	university	Thammasat University
Location	Sukhumwit Road	Sukhumwit Road	Sukhumwit area	Ta Prajan

Examples

Dr Saowanee bpen mŏr
bâhn yòo têe grOOng-tâyp
tum ngahn têe klí-nìk
yòo têe ta-nŏn sÒO-kŎOm-wít

4 Using the information in the table in Exercise 3, answer the following questions:

a Khun Chartchai tum ngahn a-rai?

b bâhn Dr Saowanee yòo têe nǎi?

c Khun Sunit ree-un têe nǎi?

d ma-hǎh wít-ta-yah-lai ah-jahn Araya yòo tǎir-o nǎi?

🔊 03.07

5 Listen to the recording and repeat after the speaker, paying special attention to the tones. A new word you will hear is **bâhn** which means house or home.

nǎi?	têe nǎi?	yòo têe nǎi?	órp-fìt kOOn yòo têe nǎi?
nǎi?	têe nǎi?	yòo têe nǎi?	bâhn kOOn yòo têe nǎi?
nǎi?	têe nǎi?	yòo têe nǎi?	têe tum ngahn kOOn yòo têe nǎi?
nǎi?	tǎir-o nǎi?	yòo tǎir-o nǎi?	órp-fìt kOOn yòo tǎir-o nǎi?
nǎi?	tǎir-o nǎi?	yòo tǎir-o nǎi?	bâhn kOOn yòo tǎir-o nǎi?
nǎi?	tǎir-o nǎi?	yòo tǎir-o nǎi?	têe tum ngahn kOOn yòo tǎir-o nǎi?

Reading and writing

The words that you read in the first two units were all pronounced with a mid tone.

In this section, you will begin to read words with a high tone, a falling tone and a low tone. From now on, you will have to bear three things in mind when reading a Thai word:

(I) the *class* of the initial consonant – whether the initial consonant is *low class*, *mid class* or *high class*; (2) vowel length – whether the vowel is *long* or *short* and (3) syllable type – whether the syllable is 'live' or 'dead'.

1 LIVE SYLLABLES AND DEAD SYLLABLES

'Live' and 'dead' are translations of the Thai terms for two different types of syllable and refer to the way in which a syllable ends. A 'live' syllable can be prolonged in a droning voice; it is physically impossible to do this with a 'dead' syllable.

Live syllables end either with long vowels or a **m**, **n**, **ng** sound. Here are some examples:

-า	-อ	-าย	ไ-	-าว	◌ี	◌ู	-ม	-น	-ง
-ah	-or	-ai	-ai	-ao	-ee	-oo	-m	-n	-ng

e.g.

ยา	รอ	นาย	ไป	ลาว	มี	ดู	นาม	งาน	ยัง
yah	ror	nai	bpai	lao	mee	doo	nahm	ngahn	yung

Notice that all these examples are pronounced with a mid tone.

Dead syllables end with either a short vowel or a **k**, **p**, **t** sound. Here are some examples:

◌ิ	◌ุ	-บ	-ด	-ก
-i	-OO	-p	-t	-k

ติ	ดุ	รีบ	นิด	มาก
dtì	dÒO	rêep	nít	mâhk

Notice that these examples are pronounced with various tones. The next part of this section will explain how the *tone* of a dead syllable is determined by the class of the initial consonant and the *length* of the vowel.

Notice also that บ (**b**) and ด (**d**) have been transcribed as **p** and **t** respectively. This is because there are a limited number of sounds that can occur at the end of a word in Thai (or any language) and so the pronunciation of certain letters is modified when they occur at the end of a word.

Here are the consonants you learned in Unit 2 once more, showing how they are pronounced when they occur as an initial consonant and as a final consonant:

	ก	จ	ค	ต	บ	ป	อ
Initial	g	j	d	dt	b	bp	(Zero)
Final	k	t	t	t	p	p	-

A full list of initial and final consonant sounds appears in the Appendices.

2 DEAD SYLLABLES WITH LOW CLASS INITIAL CONSONANTS

🔊 **03.08**

If the initial consonant in a dead syllable is low class, the tone will be either *high* or *falling*. If the vowel is *short*, the tone is *high*:

รัก	ลุก	นิด	วัด	รับ	ยิบ
rúk	**lóOk**	**nít**	**wút**	**rúp**	**yíp**

If the vowel is *long*, the tone is *falling*:

มาก	นอก	ยอด	รีด	รีบ	ลูบ
mâhk	**nôrk**	**yôrt**	**rêet**	**rêep**	**lôop**

3 DEAD SYLLABLES WITH MID CLASS INITIAL CONSONANTS

🔊 **03.09**

If the initial consonant in a dead syllable is *mid* class, the tone will always be low, regardless of whether the vowel is long or short:

กับ	จาก	จุด	ดับ	ติด	บีบ	ปาก	อาบ
gùp	**jàhk**	**jÒOt**	**dùp**	**dtìt**	**bpèep**	**bpàhk**	**àhp**

4 SUMMARY OF TONE RULES

The tone rules you have just met are summarized in the following table. It is a good idea to make a copy of it and use it for reference and checking until you feel confident about the tone rules.

Initial consonant class	Live syllable	Dead syllable	
		Short vowel	Long vowel
Low class	Mid tone	High tone	Falling tone
Mid class	Mid tone	Low tone	Low tone

Reading practice

Use the summary table to help you work through these exercises. Don't worry if it takes you some time: if you understand the principles at this stage, you will find that your reading speed and accuracy will quickly improve. It is well worth taking the time to work through this unit two or three times, rather than to push on to the next with a rather shaky grasp of how tone rules work.

1 DEAD OR LIVE?

🔊 03.10

Which of these words are live syllables?

ไป   จอด   มาก   กัน   ดี   ติด

2 WHAT TONE?

🔊 03.11

The tone mark has been omitted in the transcription of these Thai words. What tone should they be pronounced with?

บีบ	นาง	กัด	จุด	นัด
beep	nahng	gut	jOOt	nut
ปี	ดาบ	จาน	จาก	ตาย
bpee	dahp	jahn	jahk	dtai
ลาบ	ราว	มีด	รอบ	ปาก
lahp	rao	meet	rorp	bpahk

3 WORDS

🔊 03.12

Practise reading the following words, taking your time to make sure you get the tone correct. Do the exercise several times until you can read through from right to left and top to bottom at a reasonable speed. If you really want to challenge yourself, use the recording of this exercise to give yourself dictation practice:

ยาก	มี	นัด	กับ	งาน
ยุง	กัด	มาก	จาก	รีบ
อาย	นอน	ยอม	ลูก	จอด

Key points

1 To ask *where X is*, use **X yòo têe nǎi?**

2 To say *X is located at/on,* use **X yòo têe ....**

3 To say *X is located in the vicinity of* ..., use **X yòo tǎir-o ....**

4 Possession or ownership is expressed by the pattern NOUN + **kǒrng** (*of*) + OWNER.

5 **kǒrng** (*of*) is frequently omitted in phrases expressing ownership: **órp-fìt pǒm** (*my office*).

6 When reading, the tone of a syllable is determined by (1) initial consonant class, (2) vowel length and (3) whether it is a 'dead' or 'live' syllable.

7 *Live* syllables end with long vowels or a **m**, **n**, **ng** sound.

8 *Dead* syllables end with either a short vowel or a **k**, **p**, **t** sound.

9 Understand and memorize the table summarizing the tone rules in Reading and writing, section 4.

tăir-o née mee bor-ri-gahn in-dter-net mái?
Is there an internet service around here?
แถวนี้มีบริการอินเตอร์เนตไหม

In this unit, you will learn:
▶ *polite expressions: excuse me, thank you, you're welcome*
▶ *yes/no questions: … mái?*
▶ *yes/no questions: … lĕr?*
▶ *more location expressions*
▶ *low class consonants (ii)*
▶ *vowels (iii)*
▶ *vowel shortener (i)*

Dialogues

tăir-o née mee bor-ri-gahn in-dter-net mái ká?

Sue stops a passer-by in a shopping mall to ask if there is an internet service nearby. Look at the new words before attempting to read or listen to the conversation:

QUICK VOCAB

kŏr-tôht	*excuse me*	ขอโทษ
tăir-o née	*this area, vicinity; around here*	แถวนี้
mee	*there is/are; to have*	มี
… mái?	*question particle used in yes/no questions*	ไหม
bor-ri-gahn	*service*	บริการ
chún	*floor, storey*	ชั้น
kòrp-kOOn	*thank you*	ขอบคุณ
mâi bpen rai	*you're welcome*	ไม่เป็นไร

Sue	ขอโทษค่ะ แถวนี้	kŏr-tôht kà, tăir-o née
	มีบริการ	mee bor-ri-gahn
	อินเตอร์เนตไหมคะ	in-dter-net mái ká?
Thai	มีครับ อยู่ชั้นสาม	mee krúp. yòo chún săhm.
Sue	ขอบคุณค่ะ	kòrp-kOOn kà.
Thai	ไม่เป็นไรครับ	mâi bpen rai krúp.

● INSIGHT

The verb in the **mái?** question is **mee**, so the 'yes' answer is **mee** (*not* **châi!**).

tăir-o née mee bprai-sa-nee mái?

Here's Peter asking if there is a post office in the area:

QUICK VOCAB

bprai-sa-nee	*post office*	ไปรษณีย์
... lĕr?	*confirmation-seeking question*	หรือ
	particle; eh?	
têe nôhn	*over there*	ที่โน่น
glâi	*near*	ใกล้
ta-na-kahn	*bank*	ธนาคาร

🔊 04.02

Peter	ขอโทษครับ แถวนี้	kŏr-tôht krúp, tăir-o née
	มีไปรษณีย์ไหม	mee bprai-sa-nee mái?
Thai	ไปรษณีย์หรือ มีครับ	bprai-sa-nee lĕr? mee krúp.
	อยู่ที่โน่น	yòo têe nôhn,
	ใกล้ๆ ธนาคาร	glâi glâi ta-na-kahn.
Peter	ขอบคุณครับ	kòrp-kOOn krúp.
Thai	ครับ	krúp.

glai mái ká?

And now Sue is asking if there is a bank nearby:

QUICK VOCAB

glai	far	ไกล
mâi … ròrk	not … at all	ไม่ …หรอก
dern	to walk	เดิน
bpai	to go	ไป
nah-tee	minute	นาที
tâo-nún	only	เท่านั้น
mâhk	much, many	มาก

🔊 04.03

Sue	ขอโทษค่ะ แถวนี้	kŏr-tôht kà, tăir-o née
	มีธนาคาร ไหม	mee ta-na-kahn mái?
Thai	ธนาคารหรือ มีค่ะ	ta-na-kahn lĕr? mee kà.
	อยู่ที่โน่น	yòo têe nôhn.
Sue	ไกลไหมคะ	glai mái ká?
Thai	ไม่ไกลหรอกค่ะ	mâi glai ròrk kà.
	เดินไปสองสาม	dern bpai sŏrng săhm
	นาทีเท่านั้น	nah-tee tâo-nún.
Sue	ขอบคุณมากค่ะ	kòrp-kOOn mâhk kà.
Thai	ไม่เป็นไรค่ะ	mâi bpen rai kà.

Key phrases and expressions

 04.04

How to

1 say 'Excuse me'

| **kŏr-tôht** | ขอโทษ |

2 ask if there is a … in the vicinity?

| **tăir-o née mee … mái?** | แถวนี้มี … ไหม |

3 say something is situated over there

| **yòo têe nôhn** | อยู่ที่โน่น |

4 express and acknowledge thanks

| **kòrp-kOOn (mâhk)** | ขอบคุณ(มาก) |
| **mâi bpen rai** | ไม่เป็นไร |

Language notes

1 kŏr-tôht

kŏr-tôht (*excuse me*) is used both as a polite opening when approaching a stranger and when asking someone to move aside. It also means *I'm sorry*, when apologizing; the appropriate response to an apology is **mâi bpen rai** (*never mind*).

2 THANK YOU/YOU'RE WELCOME

kòrp-kOOn (*thank you*) can be acknowledged by the expression **mâi bpen rai** (*you're welcome, don't mention it*). **mâi bpen rai** also means *never mind, it doesn't matter*. This is why you will sometimes find a Thai responds with a cheerful *never mind*, when you say *thank you* in English.

kòrp-kOOn kà

ขอบคุณค่ะ

Thank you.

- mâi bpen rai kà

- ไม่เป็นไรค่ะ

- You're welcome.

The polite particles **krúp** and **kà** can also be used to politely acknowledge someone's thanks.

kòrp-kOOn kà

ขอบคุณค่ะ

Thank you.

- krúp/kà

- ครับ/ค่ะ

- Right/OK.

3 'YES/NO' QUESTIONS: ... *mái?*

The question particle **mái?** occurs at the end of a sentence and is used in neutral questions requiring a *yes/no* answer. To answer *yes* to a **mái?** question, the verb in the question is repeated; to answer *no*, the pattern **mâi** + VERB is used. Be careful not to confuse the question word **mái?**, pronounced with a high tone, with the negative word, **mâi**, pronounced with a falling tone.

tăir-o née mee bprai-sa-nee mái?

แถวนี้มีไปรษณีย์ไหม

Is there a post office around here?

- mee/mâi mee

- มี/ไม่มี

- Yes/No.

glai mái?

ไกลไหม

Is it far?

- glai/mâi glai

- ไกล/ไม่ไกล

- Yes/No.

Notice the difference between the neutral **mái?** question and the confirmation-seeking **châi mái?** (see Unit 2) question:

tǎir-o née mee bprai-sa-nee mái?

แถวนี้มีไปรษณีย์ไหม

Is there a post office around here?

tǎir-o née mee bprai-sa-nee châi mái?

แถวนี้มีไปรษณีย์ใช่ไหม

There's a post office around here, isn't there?

glai mái?

ไกลไหม

Is it a long way?

glai châi mái?

ไกลใช่ไหม

It's a long way, isn't it?

4 'YES/NO' QUESTIONS: … *lěr?* (I)

The question particle **lěr?** occurs at the end of a sentence and, like **châi mái?**, it is used for seeking confirmation. In this lesson, the speaker simply repeats what he has just heard and adds **lěr?**, rather like ' …, *eh?*' in English, or a simple repetition with a question intonation; it is little more than a hesitation device, allowing the speaker time to prepare his answer.

tǎir-o née mee ta-na-kahn mái?

แถวนี้มีธนาคารไหม

Is there a bank around here?

- ta-na-kahn lěr? mee kà

- ธนาคารหรือ มีค่ะ

- A bank, eh? Yes.

5 REDUPLICATION

The repetition, or *reduplication*, of an adjective or adverb is a common feature of spoken Thai. One function of reduplication is to make the meaning of the reduplicated word less precise; it often corresponds to the English use of *-ish*. Thus, we could think of **glâi glâi** as meaning *nearish*. Often, however, Thais seem to reduplicate a word simply because it sounds nice to Thai ears, rather than to modify the meaning of the word.

6 'NEAR' AND 'FAR'

To every westerner learning Thai, it seems particularly perverse that two words with opposite meanings should sound almost identical – to the western ear. To a Thai, of course, there is a world of difference between **glâi** (*near*) and **glai** (*far*). If you have difficulty hearing the difference between the falling tone and the mid tone, don't despair: if you hear the word reduplicated, it is most likely to be the *near* word, **glâi glâi**. And if you hear the word in a question, it is very likely the *far* word, as in **glai mái?**

7 mâi … ròrk

The pattern **mâi** + VERB/ADJECTIVE + **ròrk** is used to contradict another person's stated opinion or assumption:

glai mái?

ไกลไหม

Is it far?

- mâi glai ròrk

-ไม่ไกลหรอก

- Not at all.

pairng

แพง

It's expensive.

- mâi pairng ròrk

-ไม่แพงหรอก

- No it isn't.

8 DIRECTION VERBS

The verbs **bpai** (*to go*) and **mah** (*to come*) occur after a number of verbs to show whether the action is directed away from the speaker (**bpai**) or towards the speaker (**mah**). They commonly occur after verbs of motion, such as *walk, run, fly, move house* and so on; they also occur after **toh** (*to telephone*).

dern bpai sŏrng săhm nah-tee tâo-nún

เดินไปสองสามนาทีเท่านั้น

It's just two or three minutes' walk. (lit., *walk-go-two-three-minutes-only*)

kOOn mah-lee toh mah

คุณมาลีโทรมา

Malee telephoned/called.

Exercises

 04.05

1 How would you ask if there was one of the following in the vicinity:
   a *post office?*
   b *bank?*
   c *internet service?*
   d *clinic?*

2 How would you say:
   a *Excuse me.*
   b *Thank you.*
   c *You're welcome.*
   d *It's on the third floor.*
   e *It's over there.*
   f *It's near the bank.*
   g *It's not far.*
   h *It's around here. It's in this area.*

3 Complete the dialogue with the words supplied:

glai	bpai	nah-tee	têe nôhn
mái?	kòrp-kOOn	kǒr-tôht	ta-na-kahn

Peter	... krúp tǎir-o née mee ta-na-kahn mái?
Thai	... lěr? mee krúp yòo ...
Peter	glai ... krúp
Thai	mâi ... ròrk krúp dern ... sǒrng sǎhm ... tâo-nún
Peter	... krúp
Thai	mâi bpen rai krúp

 04.06

4 Listen to the recording and repeat after the speaker, paying special attention to the tones:

têe nôhn	yòo têe nôhn	bprai-sa-nee yòo têe nôhn
ta-na-kahn	glâi glâi ta-na-kahn	yòo glâi glâi ta-na-kahn
nah-tee	sǒrng sǎhm nah-tee	dern bpai sǒrng sǎhm nah-tee

Reading and writing

1 CONSONANTS

🔊 **04.07**

The new consonants in this lesson are all low class consonants, like those in Unit 1. Be careful not to confuse ค (**k**) with ด (**d**); ช (**ch**) and ซ (**s**) are also easily confused.

k ch s t p f

2 VOWELS

🔊 **04.08**

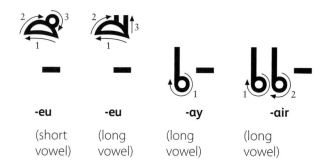

-eu	-eu	-ay	-air
(short vowel)	(long vowel)	(long vowel)	(long vowel)

The symbol ◌ื is unusual in that if there is no final consonant (i.e. the word ends with an **-eu** sound), the zero consonant symbol must be added:

with final consonant sound			no final consonant sound		
คืน	ลืม	มืด	คือ	ลือ	มือ
keun	leum	mêut	keu	leu	meu

The symbol เ- changes from an **-ay** sound to **er-ee** when it occurs with the consonant ย at the end of the word:

เ-			เ-ย		
เกม	เบน	เลน	เลย	เคย	เนย
gaym	bayn	layn	ler-ee	ker-ee	ner-ee

3 VOWEL SHORTENER SYMBOL ◌็

When the symbol ◌็ (which, incidentally, is identical to the number eight) appears above a consonant and in conjunction with the vowel symbols เ- and แ-, the vowels change from long to short vowels. The symbol ◌็ also occurs above the letter ก with no accompanying written vowel; this word is pronounced **gôr**:

เป็น	เล็ก	เก็บ	เจ็ด	แช็ก	ก็
bpen	lék	gèp	jèt	cháirk	gôr

4 WORDS WITH NO VOWEL SYMBOL (I)

When a word consists of two consonant symbols with no written vowel symbol, a short **-o** vowel must be supplied.

คน	นม	มด	ยก	จด	กบ
kon	nom	mót	yók	jòt	gòp

Remember that the tone rules from Unit 3 have to be applied. **kon** and **mót** both begin with a low class consonant, but **mót** has a high tone because it is a dead syllable and the vowel is short, while **kon** is a live syllable because it ends with an **-n** sound. **jòt** has a mid class initial consonant and because it is a dead syllable, it has a low tone.

Reading practice

1 WORDS

🔊 **04.09**

This exercise provides practice in reading words containing some of the new letters you have learned in this unit. Don't forget to distinguish between live and dead syllables. Refer back to the tone rules chart in Unit 3 or, better still, make a copy of it, so that you can keep referring to it when reading Thai words. This will ease the burden of memorization and help you to gradually absorb the rules through practice.

ชาย	ชาม	ซอย	บาท	คำ	ชอบ
ทาง	พา	พัก	ทำ	ทุก	คืน
ดึง	ตึก	คือ	เคย	เลย	แพง
แดง	แปด	เย็น	เล็ก	เป็น	เจ็ด
เก็บ	เปิด	ก็	คน	ลง	มด

2 SOME SHORT SENTENCES

🔊 04.10

แปด	แปดบาท	แปดบาทแพง	แปดบาทแพงไป
จีน	คนจีน	เป็นคนจีน	ลุงเป็นคนจีน
ไป	มากไป	เจ็ดจานมากไป	กินเจ็ดจานมากไป

How are you progressing?

One of the frustrating things about learning to read Thai is that you have to absorb so many rules initially before you can read even the simplest dialogue or passage. One good piece of news, however, is that once you have learned these rules, you will find a much closer match between the spelling of a Thai word and its pronunciation than you do in English. Another good piece of news is that you are nearly halfway there: by the end of Unit 8 you should be able to read most of the dialogues in this book. So keep working through the script sections, retracing your steps if necessary and reviewing earlier units regularly. Copying out exercises and later dialogues is enormously helpful for developing handwriting and actively reinforcing what has been learned.

? Key points

1 Polite expressions: **kǒr-tôht** (*excuse me*), **kòrp-kOOn** (*thank you*), **mâi bpen rai** (*you're welcome, don't mention it*).

2 Answers to VERB + **mái?** questions are either VERB (*yes*) or **mâi** + VERB (*no*).

3 **... lěr?** is often used as a hesitation device, like '..., *eh?*'.

4 Proximity: **glâi** (*near*), **glai** (*far*).

5 Low class consonants: ค ช ซ ท พ ฟ

6 Vowels: ◌ี ◌ ◌ือ เ- เ-ย แ-

7 Vowel shortener: ◌็ e.g. เป็น (**bpen**)

8 Words with no vowel symbol: e.g. คน (**kon**)

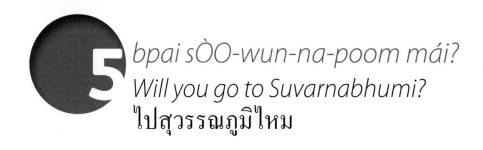

5 bpai sÒO-wun-na-poom mái?
Will you go to Suvarnabhumi?
ไปสุวรรณภูมิไหม

In this unit, you will learn:
- ▶ *taxi transactions*
- ▶ *how much? questions*
- ▶ *can: verb + dâi*
- ▶ *hesitation device: gôr*
- ▶ *high class consonants*
- ▶ *numbers 100–1,000,000*

Dialogues

bpai sÒO-wun-na-poom mái krúp?

Damrong wants to go to Bangkok's Suvarnabhumi Airport. Bangkok taxis have meters, so he needs to ask the driver whether he is willing to take him to his destination and, on arrival, how much the fare will be:

QUICK VOCAB

sÒO-wun-na-poom	*Suvarnabhumi* (Bangkok's main airport)	สุวรรณภูมิ
tâo-rài	*how much?*	เท่าไหร่

🔊 05.01

Damrong	ไปสุวรรณภูมิไหมครับ	bpai sÒO-wun-na-poom mái krúp?
Taxi	ไปครับ	bpai krúp.
......		
Damrong	เท่าไหร่ครับ	tâo-rài krúp?
Taxi	สามร้อยห้าสิบบาทครับ	sǎhm róy hâh-sìp bàht krúp.

bpai hǒo-a lum-pohng mái ká?

Sue wants to get to Hua Lampong, Bangkok's main railway station. How much does she have to pay?

hǒo-a lum-pohng   *Hua Lampong*   หัวลำโพง

🔊 **05.02**

Sue	ไปหัวลำโพงไหมคะ	bpai hǒo-a lum-pohng mái ká?
Taxi	หัวลำโพงหรือครับ	hǒo-a lum-pohng lěr krúp?
	ไปครับ	bpai krúp.
.....		
Sue	เท่าไหร่คะ	tâo-rài ká?
Taxi	สองร้อยยี่สิบบาทครับ	sǒrng róy yêe-sìp bàht krúp.

mâi bpai krúp. rót dtìt

Many taxi drivers rent their vehicles on a daily basis and have to return the vehicle at a certain time or face a stiff penalty; if a driver thinks he is short of time, he may refuse to take a passenger:

mâi	*no; not*	ไม่
rót	*car*	รถ
dtìt	*to stick/ be stuck*	ติด
rót dtìt	*traffic jam; the traffic is jammed*	รถติด

🔊 **05.03**

Peter	ไปธรรมศาสตร์ไหมครับ	bpai tum-ma-sàht mái krúp?
Taxi	ไม่ไปครับ รถติด	mâi bpai krúp. rót dtìt.

bpai sa-nǎhm bin tâo-rài ká?

Once you are outside Bangkok itself, you may have to negotiate the price. The simplest way is to respond to the quoted price with your alternative price + **dâi mái?** Do this before getting in the taxi; find out what a reasonable price would be before attempting to bargain.

Here's Sue about to take a taxi to the airport in Phuket:

sa-nǎhm bin	*airport*	สนามบิน
... dâi mái?	*can you ...?*	...ได้ไหม

| mâi dâi | *can't* | ไม่ได้ |
| pairng | *expensive* | แพง |

🔊 05.04

Sue	ไปสนามบินเท่าไหร่คะ	bpai sa-nǎhm bin tâo-rài ká?
Taxi	สามร้อยบาทครับ	sǎhm róy bàht krúp.
Sue	สามร้อยบาทหรือคะ	sǎhm róy bàht lěr ká?
	สองร้อยห้าสิบได้ไหม	sǒrng róy hâh-sìp dâi mái?
Taxi	ไม่ได้ครับ	mâi dâi krúp.
	สามร้อยไม่แพงครับ	sǎhm róy mâi pairng krúp.

1 What fare does the taxi driver quote?

2 How much does she try to knock off the fare?

3 Is she successful?

4 How does the taxi driver justify his decision?

bpai sa-tǎh-nee rót fai tâo-rài krúp?

Peter wants to get to the railway station to catch a train back to Bangkok:

QUICK VOCAB

sa-tǎh-nee rót fai	*railway station*	สถานีรถไฟ
kâh	*cost*	ค่า
núm mun	*petrol*	น้ำมัน

🔊 05.05

Peter	ไปสถานีรถไฟ	bpai sa-tǎh-nee rót fai
	เท่าไหร่ครับ	tâo-rài krúp?
Taxi	สองร้อยห้าสิบบาทครับ	sǒrng róy hâh sìp bàht krúp.
Peter	สองร้อยห้าสิบบา	sǒrng róy hâh sìp
	ทหรือครับ	bàht lěr krúp?
	สองร้อยได้ไหม	sǒrng róy dâi mái?
Taxi	ไม่ได้ครับ	mâi dâi krúp.
	ค่าน้ำมันแพง	kâh núm mun pairng.

1 How much will Peter have to pay?

2 Why won't the taxi driver lower the price?

róy bàht dâi mái krúp?

Damrong has more success in negotiating a discount for his journey, although the taxi driver's **gôr …** followed by a pause, shows that he has to think before conceding:

QUICK VOCAB

gôr …	er …	ก็ …

🔊 05.06

Damrong	ไปสถานีรถไฟ	bpai sa-tăh-nee rót fai
	เท่าไหร่ครับ	tâo-rài krúp?
Taxi	ร้อยห้าสิบบาทครับ	róy hâh sìp bàht krúp.
Damrong	ร้อยห้าสิบบาทหรือครับ	róy hâh sìp bàht lĕr krúp?
	ร้อยบาทได้ไหมครับ	róy bàht dâi mái krúp?
Taxi	ก็ … ได้ครับ	gôr … dâi krúp.

1 How much did the taxi ask for?

2 What fare did Damrong actually pay?

jòrt têe-nôhn kà ….

Sue has reached her destination and tells the driver where to stop:

QUICK VOCAB

jòrt	to park, pull up	จอด

🔊 05.07

Sue	จอดที่โน่นค่ะ	jòrt têe-nôhn kà ….
	ใกล้ๆไปรษณีย์	glâi glâi bprai-sa-nee.
Taxi	ที่นี่ใช่ไหมครับ	têe-nêe châi mái krúp?
Sue	ใช่ค่ะ เท่าไหร่คะ	châi kà. tâo-rài ká?
Taxi	สองร้อยยี่สิบบาทครับ	sŏrng róy yêe-sìp bàht krúp.

1 Where does Sue want the taxi to stop?

2 How much is the fare?

Key phrases and expressions

🔊 **05.08**

How to (ask or tell a taxi driver)

1 if he will take you to X

   bpai X mái?   ไป x ไหม

2 how much he will charge to go to X

   bpai X tâo-rài?   ไป x เท่าไหร่

3 suggest a price

   X bàht dâi mái?   x บาทได้ไหม

4 to pull up over there/here

   jòrt têe-nôhn/têe-nêe   จอดที่โน่น/ ที่นี่

Language notes

1 PLACE NAMES

The individual place name (e.g. Sukhumwit, Suvarnabhumi) follows the noun identifying the general category of place (e.g. road, airport):

sa-nǎhm bin sÒO-wun-na-poom

สนามบินสุวรรณภูมิ

Suvarnabhumi Airport

sa-tăh-nee rót fai hŏo-a lum-pohng

สถานีรถไฟหัวลำโพง

Hua Lampong Railway Station

ta-na-kahn grOOng-tâyp

ธนาคารกรุงเทพฯ

Bangkok Bank

ta-nŏn sÒO-kŎOm-wít

ถนนสุขุมวิท

Sukhumwit Road

ma-hăh wít-ta-yah-lai tum-ma-sàht

มหาวิทยาลัยธรรมศาสตร์

Thammasat University

2 HOW MUCH? QUESTIONS

tâo-rài? (*how much?*) can occur on its own (or, much better, followed by a polite particle). But in a sentence, it always occurs at the end:

tâo-rài krúp?

เท่าไหร่ครับ

How much is it?

bpai sa-năhm bin tâo-rài ká?

ไปสนามบินเท่าไหร่คะ

How much is it to the airport?

3 dâi

The meaning of the verb **dâi** depends on its position in a sentence. When it occurs after the main verb it means *can, be able to*. The question VERB + **dâi mái?** means *can you …?* A *yes* answer is **dâi**; a *no* answer **mâi dâi**:

sŏrng róy bàht dâi mái?

สองร้อยบาทได้ไหม

Will you go for 200 baht?

- dâi / mâi dâi

ได้/ไม่ได้

- Yes/No.

4 gôr

The word **gôr** serves a number of different functions. At the beginning of the sentence (as in this unit), it serves as a hesitation device, often showing some kind of reluctance, uncertainty or misgivings on the part of the speaker:

róy bàht dâi mái krúp?

ร้อยบาทได้ไหมครับ

How about a hundred baht?

- gôr … dâi krúp

- ก็ … ได้ครับ

- Well … alright.

glai mái?

ไกลไหม

Is it far?

- gôr … mâi glai

- ก็ … ไม่ไกล

- Well, er … no.

5 NUMBERS 100–1,000,000

Numbers from 100 upwards are formed in a regular way. Thai has specific words for 10,000 and 100,000:

100	**(nèung) róy**
101	**(nèung) róy èt**
102	**(nèung) róy sǒrng**
103	**(nèung) róy sǎhm**
200	**sǒrng róy**
300	**sǎhm róy**
1000	**(nèung) pun**
2000	**sǒrng pun**
10,000	**(nèung) mèun**
20,000	**sǒrng mèun**
100,000	**(nèung) sǎirn**
1,000,000	**(nèung) láhn**

Exercises

 05.09

1 How would you ask a taxi driver if he will take you to the following destinations:

   a *the railway station?*
   b *the airport?*
   c *Thammasat University?*
   d *Sukhumwit Road?*

2 How would you tell a taxi driver to pull up:

   a *here?*
   b *over there?*
   c *near the post office?*
   d *near the bank?*

05.10

3 Listen to the recording and repeat after the speaker, paying special attention to the tones.

krúp?	**mái krúp?**	**bpai sÒO-wun-na-poom mái krúp?**
ká?	**mái ká?**	**bpai hǒo-a lum-pohng mái ká?**
ká?	**tâo-rài ká?**	**bpai sa-nǎhm bin tâo-rài ká?**
krúp?	**tâo-rài krúp?**	**bpai sa-tǎh-nee rót fai tâo-rài krúp?**

Reading and writing

1 CONSONANTS

05.11

All the new consonants in this unit are high class consonants. High class consonants are pronounced with an inherent rising tone, so the letters below are read, **kǒr, chǒr, tǒr, pǒr,** etc. Notice that there are three different high class '**s**' symbols. Of these, the most common is the third, with the first two appearing mainly in words of foreign origin.

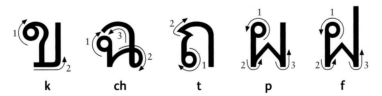

     k   ch   t   p   f

ศ	ษ	ส	ห
s	s	s	h

If you compare the consonants in this unit with the low class consonants we encountered in Unit 4, you will see that with the exception of **hǒr**, they can be paired together: a low class consonant shares the same sound as its high class partner, but the inherent tones differ.

Low class	ค	ช	ท	พ	ฟ	ซ
	kor	chor	tor	por	for	sor
High class	ข	ฉ	ถ	ผ	ฝ	ศ ษ ส
	kǒr	chǒr	tǒr	pǒr	fǒr	sǒr

High class consonants at the beginning of live syllables

 05.12

Live syllables with an initial high class consonant are pronounced with a rising tone:

ของ	ฉาย	ถุง	ผม	ฝา	สี	หู
kǒrng	chǎi	thǒOng	pǒm	fǎh	sěe	hǒo

Rare exceptions are **di-chún/chún** (I female speaker) and **káo** (he, she, they), where a high tone occurs in natural speech:

ดิฉัน	ฉัน	เขา
di-chún	chún	káo

High class consonants at the beginning of dead syllables

 05.13

Dead syllables that begin with a high class consonant are always pronounced with a *low* tone, regardless of whether the vowel is long or short:

ขับ	ผิด	สุด	ขาด	ฉีก	ถูก
kùp	pìt	sòOt	kàht	chèek	tòok

2 SILENT ห AT THE BEGINNING OF A WORD

There are a number of words in Thai that are spelt with an initial ห which is not pronounced. The function of this 'silent' ห is to convert the consonant that follows into a high class consonant. Such words then follow the tone rules of words that begin with a high class consonant:

ไหน	หมด	หงอก	หรู	หลัง	หยุด	หวาน
nǎi	mòt	ngòrk	rǎo	lǔng	yÒOt	wǎhn

Note that the question particle **mái?** looks as if it should be pronounced with a rising tone, but in normal speech is pronounced with a high tone:

ไหม

mái?

3 SUMMARY OF TONE RULES

The tone rules for syllables with initial high class consonants can be summarized as follows:

Initial consonant class	Live syllable	Dead syllable	
		Short vowel	Long vowel
High class	**Rising tone**	Low tone	Low tone

Reading practice

1 WORDS

 05.14

Here are some common words that begin with a high class consonant. The live syllables will have a rising tone and dead syllables a low tone. Read through the exercise several times until you can do it quickly and accurately.

ขาย	ขอ	ขับ	ฉีด	ถาม
ถูก	ผิด	ฝาก	สี	สุด
สอน	สาว	สัก	สิบ	หัก
หา	หลัง	หวัด	หนู	หลาย

2 MATCH THE NUMBERS

i	๒	a	แปด
ii	๓	b	หก
iii	๖	c	สิบ
iv	๗	d	สาม
v	๘	e	เจ็ด
vi	๑๐	f	สอง

3 SENTENCES

 05.15

Read across the page, building up to four-word sentences.

ไทย	คนไทย	เป็นคนไทย	ลุงเป็นคนไทย
ตาก	จังหวัดตาก	จากจังหวัดตาก	มาจากจังหวัดตาก

มาก	หลานมาก	มีหลานมาก	ยายมีหลานมาก
คน	สิบคน	ลูกสิบคน	มีลูกสิบคน
คน	สามคน	สาวสามคน	ลูกสาวสามคน

Key points

1 *How much?* questions: **... tâo-rài?**

2 *Can I/you/they ...?* questions: VERB + **dâi mái?**

3 Hesitation device: **gôr ...**

4 1000: **pun;** 10,000: **mèun;** 100,000: **săirn;** 1,000,000: **láhn**.

5 High class consonants: ข ฉ ถ ผ ฝ ส ศ ษ ห

6 Live syllables that begin with a high class consonant have a rising tone.

7 Dead syllables that begin with a high class consonant have a low tone.

8 Silent ห in front of low class consonants converts them to high class consonants.

6 loh la tâo-rài?
How much a kilo?
โลละเท่าไหร่

In this unit, you will learn:
- ▶ *how to buy various food items in the market*
- ▶ *how to ask what something is called*
- ▶ *how to ask someone to repeat something*
- ▶ *yes/no questions: ... lěr? and ... ná?*
- ▶ *script review*

Dialogues

sôm loh la tâo-rài ká?

Sue wants to buy some oranges. Pointing at the fruit and asking **nêe tâo-rài?** *How much are these?* would have been adequate, but Sue's question, **sôm loh la tâo-rài ká?** *How much a kilo are the oranges?*, shows off her grasp of more complex sentence patterns. Here are the new words that you'll meet:

QUICK VOCAB

sôm	*orange*	ส้ม
loh	*kilo*	โล
loh la ...	*... per kilo*	โลละ ...
lót	*to reduce, lower*	ลด
... nòy	*a little ...*	... หน่อย
... gôr láir-o gun	*let's settle for ...*	... ก็แล้วกัน

 06.01

Sue	ส้มโลละเท่าไหร่คะ	sôm loh la tâo-rài ká?
Vendor	โลละห้าสิบบาทค่ะ	loh la hâh sìp bàht kà.
Sue	โลละห้าสิบหรือคะ	loh la hâh sìp lěr ká?
	ลดหน่อยได้ไหม	lót nòy dâi mái?
Vendor	ก็ ... สองโลเก้าสิบ	gôr ... sǒrng loh gâo sìp
	บาทก็แล้วกัน	bàht gôr láir-o gun.

nêe rêe-uk wâh a-rai krúp?

Peter wants to know the name of an unfamiliar fruit. He could say **nêe a-rai?** *What's this?*, but **nêe rêe-uk wâh a-rai?** *What's this called?* sounds better. Here are the new words you will hear:

QUICK VOCAB

nêe	*this*	นี่
rêe-uk wâh ...	*to be called ...*	เรียกว่า
nóy-nàh	*custard apple*	นอยหน่า
a-rai ná	*pardon?*	อะไรนะ
lorng	*to try out*	ลอง
chim	*to taste*	ชิม
a-ròy	*to be tasty*	อร่อย

🔊 06.02

Peter	นี่เรียกว่าอะไรครับ	nêe rêe-uk wâh a-rai krúp?
Vendor	เรียกว่านอยหน่าค่ะ	rêe-uk wâh nóy-nàh kà.
Peter	อะไรนะครับ	a-rai ná krúp?
Vendor	นอยหน่าค่ะ	nóy-nàh kà.
Peter	นอยหน่าใช่ไหม	nóy-nàh châi mái?
Vendor	ใช่ค่ะ ลองชิมไหมคะ	châi kà. lorng chim mái ká?
	อร่อยนะ	a-ròy ná?
Peter	ขอบคุณครับ	kòrp-kOOn krúp.
Vendor	อร่อยไหมคะ	a-ròy mái ká?
Peter	อร่อยครับ โลละเท่าไหร	a-ròy krúp. loh la tâo-rài?
Vendor	โลละหกสิบบาทค่ะ	loh la hòk sìp bàht kà.

mǒo yâhng tâo-rài krúp?

Peter wants to buy some north-eastern food, including meat that has been *charcoal grilled* (**yâhng**), *sticky rice* (**kâo něe-o**) and **som tam** or *papaya salad* (**sôm dtum**).

QUICK VOCAB

mǒo	*pork, pig*	หมู
mǒo yâhng	*charcoal-grilled pork*	หมูย่าง

mái	*stick; wood; skewer*	ไม้
ao	*to want*	เอา
kâo	*rice*	ข้าว
kâo nĕe-o	*sticky rice*	ข้าวเหนียว
hòr	*packet*	ห่อ

🔊 **06.03**

Peter	หมูย่างไม้ละเท่าไหร่ครับ	mŏo yâhng mái la tâo-rài krúp?
Vendor	ไม้ละสิบบาทครับ	mái la sìp bàht krúp.
Peter	เอาสี่ไม้ครับ	ao sèe mái krúp.
Vendor	เอาข้าวเหนียวไหมครับ	ao kâo nĕe-o mái krúp?
Peter	เอาครับ เท่าไหร่ครับ	ao krúp. tâo-rài krúp?
Vendor	ห่อละสิบบาทครับ	hòr la sìp bàht krúp.
Peter	เอาสองห่อก็แล้วกัน	ao sŏrng hòr gôr láir-o gun.

ao sôm dtum krúp

Next, Peter stops at the *som tam* stall, where the vendor uses a pestle and mortar to pound the mixture of chillies, tomatoes, unripe papaya, lime juice, fish sauce and peanuts:

QUICK VOCAB

sôm dtum	*papaya salad;'som tam'*	ส้มตำ
pèt	*hot, spicy*	เผ็ด
tŏOng	*bag*	ถุง

🔊 **06.04**

Peter	เอาส้มตำครับ	ao sôm dtum krúp.
	ไม่เอาเผ็ดมากนะ	mâi ao pèt mâhk ná.
Vendor	ค่ะ ถุงละสามสิบบาทค่ะ	kà. tŏOng la săhm sìp bàht kà.
Peter	เท่าไหร่นะ	tâo-rài ná?
Vendor	สามสิบบาทค่ะ	săhm sìp bàht kà.
	เอาข้าวเหนียวไหม	ao kâo nĕe-o mái?
Peter	ไม่เอาครับ	mâi ao krúp.

Fresh food markets can be a good place for language practice and a place to watch Thais haggling over prices. Although prices are often clearly marked and increasingly less open to negotiation, markets are still an excellent venue to practise some useful language skills, such as asking the names of fruits and vegetables, confirming that you have heard the name correctly and asking the price. As your Thai gets better such conversations may naturally progress to talking about where you (and the vendor) come from, how long you have been learning Thai, whether you eat potatoes rather than rice and the prospects for this season's pineapple crop.

Key phrases and expressions

 06.05

How to

1 ask how much ... costs per kilo

... loh la tâo-rài? ... โลละเท่าไหร่

2 ask for a discount

lót nòy dâi mái? ลดหน่อยได้ไหม

3 ask what something is/is called

nêe a-rai? นี่อะไร

nêe rêe-uk wâh a-rai? นี่เรียกว่าอะไร

4 ask somebody to repeat something

a-rai ná? อะไรนะ

Language notes

1 PER KILO/BUNCH/FRUIT

The Thai word for *per* (as in *per kilo*) is **la**. Some fruits, such as oranges and custard apples, are bought by the kilo. Notice that the word order is: NOUN + *kilo* + **la** + *how much?/price*:

sôm loh la tâo-rài?

ส้มโลละเท่าไหร่

How much are the oranges per kilo?

nóy-nàh loh la hòk sìp bàht.

น้อยหน่าโลละหกสิบบาท

Custard apples are 60 baht a kilo.

Bananas are bought by the bunch (**wěe**), so **wěe** replaces **loh**:

glôo-ay wěe la tâo-rài?

กล้วยหวีละเท่าไหร่

How much are the bananas per bunch?

Other food items are bought by the container, such as a bag, packet, bottle and so on:

mǒo yâhng mái la tâo-rài?

หมูย่างไม้ละเท่าไหร่

How much is the barbecued pork per stick?

kâo něe-o hòr la sìp bàht

ข้าวเหนียวห่อละสิบบาท

Sticky rice is ten baht per packet.

sôm dtum tǒOng la sǎhm sìp bàht.

ส้มตำถุงละสามสิบบาท

Som tam is 30 baht a bag.

Large fruit, such as papayas and pineapples are bought individually; the word **lôok** occupies the same position in the sentence as **loh** or **wěe**:

sùp-bpa-rót lôok la tâo-rài?

สับปะรดลูกละเท่าไหร่

How much each are pineapples?

ma-la-gor lôok la hòk sìp bàht.

มะละกอลูกละหกสิบบาท

Papayas are 60 baht each.

The word **lôok** is called a *classifier*. Classifiers will be discussed more in Unit 7.

2 'YES/NO' QUESTIONS: ... *lĕr?* (II)

In the previous unit, we met **lĕr?** being used as a hesitation device. In this unit, it is used for seeking confirmation. While **châi mái?** questions tend to be neutral, **lĕr?** questions often convey a sense of surprise or disappointment about the information it seeks to confirm:

> **loh la hâh sìp lĕr?**
>
> โลละห้าสิบหรือ
>
> *(As much as) 50 baht a kilo?*

3 QUESTION WORD + *ná?*

The particle **ná?** is used after the question words *what?, how many?, who?, when?, why?, where?* and *how?* when asking someone to repeat a piece of information:

> **a-rai ná?**
>
> อะไรนะ
>
> *Pardon?*

> **tâo-rài ná?**
>
> เท่าไหร่นะ
>
> *How much was that again?*

4 'YES/NO' QUESTIONS: ... *ná?*

ná? also occurs as a question particle, inviting agreement with the preceding statement (e.g. *It's hot, isn't it?*):

> **pairng ná?**
>
> แพงนะ
>
> *It's expensive, isn't it?*

> **mâi ao pèt mâhk ná**
>
> ไม่เอาเผ็ดมากนะ
>
> *I don't want it very hot, right?*

The polite particle **krúp/ kà** is sufficient as a *yes* answer to a **... ná?** question, while a *no* response is **mâi** + VERB + **krúp/kà**:

> **a-ròy ná?**
>
> อร่อยนะ
>
> *It's tasty, isn't it?*

> **- krúp/kà; mâi a-ròy krúp/kà**
>
> - ครับ/ค่ะ ไม่อร่อยครับ/ค่ะ
>
> *- Yes/No.*

Exercises

1 How would you ask the price of the following food items:

   a *oranges (kilo)?*
   b *charcoal-grilled pork (skewer)?*
   c *sticky rice (packet)?*
   d *som tam (bag)?*

 06.07

2 Here are the replies you received. Confirm that you heard correctly and then say that you want two kilos/skewers/packets/bags. The first one is done for you.

   a **loh la hâh sìp bàht kà**

   – **loh la hâh sìp lěr krúp/ká?**

   ao sŏrng loh krúp/kà
   b **mái la sìp bàht krúp**
   c **hòr la sìp bàht krúp**
   d **tŏOng la săhm sìp bàht kà**

3 Peter is trying to find out the Thai word for *papaya*. This is what the fruit stall vendor said to him. What were his questions?

Peter	_____?
Vendor	rêe-uk wâh ma-la-gor kà.
Peter	_____?
Vendor	ma-la-gor kà.
Peter	_____?
Vendor	châi kà.
Peter	_____?
Vendor	lôok la yêe-sìp bàht kà.
Peter	_____?
Vendor	lót mâi dâi kà.

 06.08

4 Listen to the recording and repeat after the speakers:

krúp	tâo-rài krúp	loh la tâo-rài krúp	sôm loh la tâo-rài krúp?
ká?	tâo-rài ká?	wěe la tâo-rài ká?	glôo-ay wěe la tâo-rài ká?
krúp	tâo-rài krúp	hòr la tâo-rài krúp	kâo něe-o hòr la tâo-rài krúp
ká?	tâo-rài ká?	tŏOng la tâo-rài ká?	sôm dtùm tŏOng la tâo-rài ká?

Reading and writing

At this stage, it is worth pausing to review the key points that you have learned so far.

1 CONSONANTS

You have learned the following consonants. The consonant sound of each letter is given both when it occurs as an initial and as a final consonant.

Low class	น	ม	ง	ร	ล	ย	ว
Initial	n	m	ng	r	l	y	w
Final	n	m	ng	n	n		

	ค	ช	ซ	ท	พ	ฟ	
Initial	k	ch	s	t	p	f	
Final	k	t	t	t	p	p	

Mid class	ก	จ	ด	ต	บ	ป	อ
Initial	g	j	d	dt	b	bp	'zero'
Final	k	t	t	t	p	p	

High class	ข	ฉ	ถ	ผ	ฝ	ศ ษ ส	ห
Initial	k	ch	t	p	f	s	h
Final	k	t	t	p	p	t	

2 VOWELS

You have learned the following vowels:

Long	-า	-อ	โ-	◌ี	◌ู	◌ือ	เ-	แ-
vowels	-ah	-or	-oh	-ee	-oo	-eu	-ay	-air

Short	◌ั	ไ-	ใ-	◌ิ	◌ุ	◌ึ	เ◌ะ	แ◌ะ
vowels	-u	-ai	-ai	-i	-OO	-eu	-e	-air

3 LIVE SYLLABLES AND DEAD SYLLABLES

You have learned the difference between live syllables and dead syllables:

Live syllables   syllables that end with a long vowel or a **m, n, ng** sound or the vowels -**ai** and -**ao**

e.g.   มี   รอ   ดู   ไป   ดำ   จาน   ยัง

Dead syllables   syllables that end with a short vowel or a **p, t, k** sound

e.g.   ดุ   ติ   ดับ   สิบ   หมด   กด   จาก

4 SUMMARY OF TONE RULES

Initial consonant class	Live syllable	Dead syllable	
		Short vowel	Long vowel
Low class	Mid tone	High tone	Falling tone
Mid class	Mid tone	Low tone	Low tone
High class	Rising tone	Low tone	Low tone

5 READING WORDS

By now, whenever you read a Thai word or syllable, you will have learned to ask yourself three questions: (1) is it a live or dead syllable? (2) what class is the initial consonant? (3) is the vowel long or short? Once you have answered these questions, you should be able to identify the tone of the word correctly.

At this stage, don't worry if you are still finding it difficult to remember the tone rules. Copy the chart in the summary and keep it handy for subsequent lessons; the very act of copying itself will help you to memorize it. After a while you will find that you need to refer to it less and less and there will come a time when you feel ready to dispense with it altogether.

Reading practice

And now for your first reading passage. Read it through several times. Don't worry if it is slow going at first. When you have read and understood this passage, copy it out two or three times. This will improve your handwriting and help you to learn spellings, vocabulary and grammar. When you have completed the next unit, come back and re-read this passage. Keep doing this until you can read the passage confidently and accurately at normal speed.

QUICK VOCAB

ลำปาง	name of a province
แฟน	*girl/boyfriend; partner; spouse*
กับ	*and, with*

 06.09

วินัยเป็นคนไทย มาจากจังหวัดลำปาง

หลิงเป็นคนจีน เป็นแฟนของวินัย

วินัยกับหลิง ทำงานในออฟฟิศแถวสุขุมวิท

1 Where does Winai come from?

2 What is his girlfriend's name?

3 What is her nationality?

4 Where do they work?

? Key points

1 per kilo/bunch/fruit

2 *What's this called?* **nêe rêe-uk wâh a-rai?**

3 *Yes/No* questions: **... lĕr?**

4 *Yes/No* questions: **... ná?**

5 Asking someone to repeat something: QUESTION WORD **+ ná?**

7 bpai séu kŏrng
Going shopping
ไปซื้อของ

In this unit, you will learn:
- ▶ *how to carry out shopping transactions*
- ▶ *polite requests to do something*
- ▶ *too + adjective*
- ▶ *how? questions*
- ▶ *classifiers*
- ▶ *colours*
- ▶ *continuous actions*
- ▶ *tone mark: mái àyk*

Dialogues

dtôrng-gahn bàirp năi?

Sue wants to buy a mobile phone (**toh-ra-sùp meu tĕu** or **meu tĕu** for short). What is the main criterion she is looking for? Here are the new words you will hear:

QUICK VOCAB

dtôrng-gahn	*to need, want*	ต้องการ
séu	*to buy*	ซื้อ
meu tĕu	*mobile phone*	มือถือ
bàirp	*style, type, kind*	แบบ
bàirp năi?	*what kind?*	แบบไหน
bàirp năi gôr dâi	*any kind will do*	แบบไหนก็ได้
dtàir	*but*	แต่

Sue	สวัสดีค่ะ	sa-wùt dee kà.
	ฉันต้องการซื้อ	chún dtôrng-gahn séu
	มือถือค่ะ	meu těu kà.
Salesgirl	ต้องการแบบไหนคะ	dtôrng-gahn bàirp năi ká?
Sue	แบบไหนก็ได้	bàirp năi gôr dâi.
	แต่ไม่เอาแพงมากค่ะ	dtàir mâi ao pairng mâhk kà.

pairng bpai nòy

The salesgirl shows Sue a mobile phone. How much does it cost? What is Sue's reaction?

QUICK VOCAB

doo	to look at	ดู
lorng doo	to try out	ลองดู
rÔOn	model, version	รุ่น
rah-kah	price	ราคา
pun	thousand	พัน
tòok	cheap	ถูก

 07.02

Salesgirl	ลองดูรุ่นนี้ไหมคะ	lorng doo rÔOn née mái ká?
Sue	ราคาเท่าไหร่คะ	rah-kah tâo-rài ká?
Salesgirl	แปดพันบาทค่ะ	bpàirt pun bàht kà.
Sue	แพงไปหน่อย	pairng bpai nòy.
	เอาแบบถูกๆ ค่ะ	ao bàirp tòok tòok kà.

kŏr doo nòy dâi mái?

The next model that Sue looks at is considerably cheaper:

QUICK VOCAB

... yung-ngai?	how?	อย่างไร
jor	screen	จอ
sĕe	colour	สี

bâhng	(see Language notes)	บ้าง
sòng	*to send*	ส่ง
kôr kwahm	*message*	ขอความ
láir	*and*	และ
lên	*to play*	เล่น
gaym	*game*	เกม
dee	*good*	ดี
chôrp	*to like*	ชอบ

🔊 07.03

Salesgirl	รุ่นนี้เป็นอย่างไรคะ ราคาสามพันบาทค่ะ มีจอสี	rôOn née bpen yung-ngai ká? rah-kah săhm pun bàht kà mee jor sĕe.
Sue	ขอดูหน่อยได้ไหมคะ ทำอะไรได้บางคะ	kŏr doo nòy dâi mái ká? tum a-rai dâi bâhng ká?
Salesgirl	ส่งขอความ และเล่นเกมค่ะ	sòng kôr kwahm láir lên gaym kà.
Sue	ลดหน่อยได้ไหมคะ	lót nòy dâi mái ká?
Salesgirl	ได้ค่ะ คิดสองพันแปดร้อยค่ะ	dâi kà. kít sŏrng pun bpàirt róy kà.

1 How much does this phone cost?

2 What features does it have?

3 How much discount does the salesgirl offer?

mee sĕe a-rai bâhng krúp?

Peter is looking at t-shirts on a street stall:

QUICK VOCAB

sêu-a	*shirt, upper garment*	เสื้อ
dtoo-a	*classifier for shirts*	ตัว
nún	*that*	นั้น

sĕe dum	black	สีดำ
sĕe dairng	red	สีแดง
sĕe kaǒ	white	สีขาว
sĕe kĕe-o	green	สีเขียว
chôrp	to like	ชอบ
gum-lung ... yòo	to be ...ing	กำลัง ... อยู่
kít	to think; charge (money)	คิด

🔊 07.04

Peter	เสื้อตัวนั้นเท่าไหร่ครับ	sêu-a dtoo-a nún tâo-rài krúp?
Vendor	รอยห้าสิบบาทค่ะ	róy hâh sìp bàht kà.
Peter	มีสีอะไรบางครับ	mee sĕe a-rai bâhng krúp?
Vendor	สีดำ สีแดง สีขาว	sĕe dum sĕe dairng sĕe kǎo
	สีเขียว คุณชอบ	sĕe kĕe-o. kOOn chôrp
	สีอะไรคะ	sĕe a-rai ká?
Peter	กำลังคิดอยู่	gum-lung kít yòo.
Vendor	ลดราคาได้ค่ะ คิดสองตัว	lót rah-kah dâi kà. kít sŏrng dtoo-a
	สองรอยห้าสิบ	sŏrng róy hâh sìp.

1 How much do the t-shirts cost?

2 What deal does the vendor offer Peter?

kŏr lorng sài doo nòy dâi mái?

Now we find Peter in a shoe shop:

QUICK VOCAB

rorng táo	shoe(s)	รองเท้า
kôo	pair	คู่
sài	to wear, put on	ใส่
ber	number; size	เบอร์
kúp	tight	คับ
dtòk long	to agree	ตกลง

Salesgirl	ซื้ออะไรคะ	séu a-rai ká?
Peter	รองเท้าคู่นี้	rorng táo kôo née
	เท่าไหร่ครับ	tâo-rài krúp?
Salesgirl	เก้าร้อยห้าสิบบาทค่ะ	gâo róy hâh sìp bàht kà.
Peter	ขอลองใส่ดูหน่อย	kŏr lorng sài doo nòy
	ได้ไหม	dâi mái?
Salesgirl	ได้ค่ะ ใส่เบอร์อะไรคะ	dâi kà. sài ber a-rai ká?
Peter	เบอร์เก้าครับ	ber gâo krúp.
Salesgirl	เป็นอย่างไรคะ	bpen yung-ngai ká?
Peter	คับไปหน่อยครับ	kúp bpai nòy krúp.
	ขอลองเบอร์สิบได้ไหม	kŏr lorng ber sìp dâi mái?
Salesgirl	ได้ค่ะ ใส่ได้ไหม	dâi kà. sài dâi mái?
Peter	ได้ครับ	dâi krúp.
	ตกลงซื้อคู่นี้	dtòk long séu kôo née.

● INSIGHT

Notice the way the salesgirl asks *does it fit?* – **sài dâi mai?** –literally, *'Can you wear it?'*

1 What size shoe does Peter normally wear?

2 What size does he buy?

3 How much does he pay?

● INSIGHT

The Thai expression for *shopping* is **bpai séu kǒrng**, which literally means *go-buy-things*, although many Thais use the English word – but with an initial **ch** (**sh** sounds don't exist in Thai) and the stress on the second syllable. In some shops, small discounts are readily given to those who ask.

Key phrases and expressions

🔊 **07.06**

How to

1 say you want to buy ...

dtôrng-gahn séu ...   ต้องการซื้อ ...

2 ask the price of something

rah-kah tâo-rài?   ราคาเท่าไหร่

3 say something is a little too expensive

pairng bpai nòy   แพงไปหน่อย

4 say you want the cheap kind

ao bàirp tòok tòok   เอาแบบถูกๆ

5 ask to look at something

kŏr doo nòy dâi mái?   ขอดูหน่อยได้ไหม

6 ask what colours there are

mee sĕe a-rai bâhng?   มีสีอะไรบ้าง

7 ask to try something on

kŏr lorng sài doo nòy dâi mái?   ขอลองใส่ดูหน่อยได้ไหม

Language notes

1 ... gôr dâi

A number of question words also act as indefinite pronouns:

	Question word	Indefinite pronoun
a-rai	*what?*	*anything*
tâo-rài	*how much?*	*however much*
têe-năi	*where?*	*anywhere*
krai	*who?*	*anyone*
mêu-rài	*when?*	*whenever*
năi	*which?*	*any*

When a question word is followed by **... gôr dâi**, it indicates amenability or indifference on the part of the speaker, similar to the English *anything/anyone/whenever, etc., you like*:

bàirp năi gôr dâi

แบบไหนก็ได้

Any kind will do.

gin a-rai gôr dâi

กินอะไรก็ได้

I can eat anything you like.

kOOn bòrk krai gôr dâi

คุณบอกใครก็ได้

You can tell anyone you like.

jòrt têe-năi gôr dâi

จอดที่ไหนก็ได้

You can park anywhere you like.

2 A BIT TOO …

The idea of excess (*too …*) is expressed by the pattern ADJECTIVE + **(gern) bpai**. In spoken Thai, the word **gern** is very frequently omitted. The meaning can be toned down (*a bit too …*) by adding **nòy** (*a little*):

pairng (gern) bpai

แพง(เกิน)ไป

too expensive

pairng bpai nòy

แพงไปหน่อย

a bit too expensive

kúp bpai nòy

คับไปหน่อย

a bit too tight

3 POLITE REQUESTS: ASKING TO DO SOMETHING (YOURSELF)

When asking to do something yourself, the pattern **kŏr** + VERB + **nòy** is used: **dâi mái?** can be added at the end of the request for additional politeness:

kŏr doo nòy (dâi mái)?

ขอดูหน่อย(ได้ไหม)

Can I have a look, please?

kŏr lorng sài doo nòy (dâi mái)?

ขอลองใส่ดูหน่อย(ได้ไหม)

Can I try it on, please?

kǒr lorng ber jèt nòy (dâi mái)?

ขอลองเบอร์เจ็ดหน่อย(ได้ไหม)

Can I try size 7, please?

Remember that **kǒr** is only used when asking to do something yourself; you cannot use it when asking someone else to do something for you, such as give you a discount or bring you the bill.

4 'HOW?' QUESTIONS

How? questions which ask about the manner in which something is done follow the pattern VERB + **yung-ngai?**

bpen yung-ngai?

เป็นอย่างไร

How are things?

tum yung-ngai?

ทำอย่างไร

How do you do it?

bpai yung-ngai?

ไปอย่างไร

How are we going?

When you have completed all the script sections and can read Thai, you will notice that the normal pronunciation **yung-ngai** is not reflected in the spelling, which suggests it should be pronounced **yàhng-rai**. In normal speech, however, the first vowel is shortened, the low tone changes to a neutral mid tone and the final **ng** in the first syllable and the initial **r** in the second syllable are assimilated into an **ng** sound. In fact, Thais will often make a further reduction to **ngai** in informal greetings:

bpen ngai?

เป็นไง

How are things?

How? questions that ask how tall/heavy/long something is use **tâo-rài?** (*how much?*):

káo sǒong tâo-rài?

เขาสูงเท่าไหร่

How tall is she?

mun nùk tâo-rài?

มันหนักเท่าไหร่

How heavy is it?

ree-un pah-săh tai nahn tâo-rài?

เรียนภาษาไทยนานเท่าไหร่

How long have you studied Thai?

5 'WHAT?' QUESTIONS + *bâhng?*

bâhng (*some, somewhat*) occurs at the end of a *what?* question to show that the speaker expects a list of things in the answer:

tum a-rai dâi bâhng?

ทำอะไรได้บ้าง

What can it do?

mee sĕe a-rai bâhng?

มีสีอะไรบ้าง

What colours do you have?

bâhng also occurs at the end of *where?*, *how?* and *who?* questions:

bpai têe-o têe-năi bâhng?

ไปเที่ยวที่ไหนบ้าง

Where did you go/what places did you visit?

bpen yung-ngai bâhng?

เป็นอย่างไรบ้าง

How are things? (informal greeting)

jer krai bâhng?

เจอใครบ้าง

Who did you meet?

6 CLASSIFIERS

One striking difference between Thai and English is the way in which nouns and numbers are combined. In Unit 6, we met the following example and noted that the word **lôok** is called a *classifier*:

ma-la-gor lôok la hòk sìp bàht.

มะละกอลูกละหกสิบบาท

Papayas are 60 baht each.

In Thai, every noun has its classifier, which is used (1) in expressions involving numbers and (2) with **née** (*this*) and **nún/nóhn** (*that*).

Some common classifiers and the nouns they are used with are:

bai	*cups, bowls, plates, eggs, slips of paper*	ใบ
doo-ung	*stamps, lights, stars*	ดวง
dtoo-a	*items of clothing, animals, chairs, tables*	ตัว
hàirng	*places*	แห่ง
hôrng	*rooms*	ห้อง
kon	*people*	คน
kun	*vehicles*	คัน
lêm	*books*	เล่ม
lŭng	*houses*	หลัง
lôok	*fruit*	ลูก
pàirn	*flat objects*	แผ่น
un	*small objects*	อัน

All container words, such as *plate*, *bag*, *bottle*, and all words for measures, such as *kilometre*, *kilogram*, *day*, can be regarded as classifiers and will, therefore, be combined with numbers and *this/that* in the following patterns:

Numbers, nouns and classifiers are combined in the pattern, NOUN + NUMBER + CLASSIFIER:

kon tai săhm kon

คนไทยสามคน

three Thais

bâhn sŏrng lŭng

บ้านสองหลัง

two houses

ma-la-gor nèung look

มะละกอหนึ่งลูก

one papaya

nèung (*one*) can also occur after the classifier, in which case it can be translated as *a/an*:

mŏr nèung kon

หมอหนึ่งคน

one doctor

mŏr kon nèung

หมอคนหนึ่ง

a doctor

When **née** (*this*) and **nún/nóhn** (*that*) are used with a noun, the classifier is also used; the pattern is NOUN + CLASSIFIER + **née/nún/nóhn**:

sêu-a dtoo-a nún tâo-rài?

เสื้อตัวนั้นเท่าไหร่

How much is that shirt?

rorng táo kôo née gâo róy bàht.

รองเท้าคู่นี้เก้าร้อยบาท

This pair of shoes is 900 baht.

7 COLOURS

The word **sěe** is both the noun *colour* and the verb *to be the colour X*. **sěe** occurs before a specific colour word when describing the colour of something:

mee sěe èun mái?

มีสีอื่นไหม

Do you have other colours?

chôrp sěe a-rai?

ชอบสีอะไร

What colour do you like?

sěe dairng

สีแดง

Red/It is red.

mee sěe dairng mái?

มีสีแดงไหม

Do you have red?

The most common colour words are:

sěe dairng	*red*	สีแดง
sěe kěe-o	*green*	สีเขียว
sěe lěu-ung	*yellow*	สีเหลือง
sěe núm ngern	*blue*	สีน้ำเงิน
sěe núm dtahn	*brown*	สีน้ำตาล

| **sěe dum** | black | สีดำ |
| **sěe kǎo** | white | สีขาว |

8 *gum-lung* + VERB + *yòo*

The pattern **gum-lung** + VERB + **yòo** is used to indicate continuous actions, either in the present (*I am learning Thai*) or in the past (*I was learning Thai*):

gum-lung kít yòo

กำลังคิดอยู่

I'm thinking.

Either **gum-lung** or **yòo** may be dropped:

rao gum-lung doo tee-wee

เรากำลังดูทีวี

We're watching TV.

rao doo tee-wee yòo

เราดูทีวีอยู่

We're watching TV.

tum a-rai yòo?

ทำอะไรอยู่

What are you doing?

Exercises

1 How would you ask:

  a *what the price of something is?*
  b *to have a look at something?*
  c *to try something on?*
  d *for a discount?*

🔊 **07.07**

2 How would you say:

  a *It's too expensive. I don't want it.*
  b *It's too tight. I can't wear it.*
  c *It's too far. I can't walk.*
  d *It's too near. I don't like it.*

3 Supply the correct classifier from the selection in the box:

a ao kâo nĕe-o săhm …

b sêu-a … née róy hâh sìp bàht

c mŏo yâhng … la sìp bàht

d séu ma-la-gor nèung …

e mee kon tai hòk …

f ao sôm sŏrng …

g rorng táo … nún tâo-rài?

> loh mái kon hòr
> lôok kôo dtoo-a

🔊 **07.08**

4 Listen to the recording and repeat after the speaker, paying special attention to the tones:

ká?	mái ká?	dâi mái ká?	lót nòy dâi mái ká?
tĕu	meu tĕu	séu meu tĕu	dtôrng-gahn séu meu tĕu
bâhng	a-rai bâhng?	sĕe a-rai bâhng?	mee sĕe a-rai bâhng?

Reading and writing

The chart summarizing tone rules in Unit 6 will help you to read any dead syllable, but it covers only those live syllables that are pronounced with a mid or rising tone.

As you may have noticed, there are many live syllables that are pronounced with a falling, high or low tone – words such as **mâi**, **châi**, **chêu**, **láir-o**, **yòo**, **nòy** and so on.

In words like these, the tone is represented by a tone mark written above the initial consonant. If the initial consonant already has a vowel above it, then the tone is written above that vowel. The two most common tone marks are **mái àyk**, which you are about to meet, and **mái toh**, which will be introduced in the next unit.

1 *mái àyk* (◌่): TONE RULES

This tone mark looks like the number one. It is written above the initial consonant and in line with the right-hand perpendicular stroke. Unfortunately for the learner, due to changes in the language that have occurred over hundreds of years, this single tone mark no longer represents a single tone; words bearing this tone mark are pronounced with either a *falling* tone or a *low* tone. As with dead syllables, the determining factor is the class of the initial consonant. If **mái àyk** occurs above a low class initial consonant, the tone will be *falling*; if the initial consonant is either mid class or high class, then the tone is *low*.

Low class	ไม่	ใช่	ชื่อ	ที่	นี่
	mâi	**châi**	**chêu**	**têe**	**nêe**

If the initial consonant is either mid class or high class, then the tone is *low*:

Mid class	ไก่	ต่อ	จ่าย	บ่าย	ปู่
	gài	**dtòr**	**jài**	**bài**	**bpòo**
High class	แผ่น	ถ่าย	สี่	ห่อ	หน่อย
	pàirn	**tài**	**sèe**	**hòr**	**nòy**

2 SILENT อ AT THE BEGINNING OF A WORD

In Unit 5, you met words that began with a silent ห. There is also a very small number of words – only four, in fact – that begin with a silent อ. These are all pronounced with a low tone. All four words are very common and it is well worth copying them down and memorizing them at this stage. We have already come across two of them – **yòo** and **yàhng** – in the dialogues.

อยู่	อย่า	อย่าง	อยาก
yòo	**yàh**	**yàhng**	**yàhk**
to be situated at	*don't*	*like, kind*	*to like to*

Reading practice

1 WORDS

🔊 07.09

All these words are written with **mái àyk**, so they will be pronounced with either a falling tone or a low tone.

ไม่	นี่	พ่อ	แม่	หนึ่ง	คู่
อยู่	ไก่	แต่	สั่ง	หน่อย	ต่อ
ชื่อ	ใช่	พี่	ที่	อ่าน	ว่า

2 PHRASES

🔊 07.10

Next some short phrases with **mái àyk**:

ใช่ไหม	ไม่ใช่	นี่เท่าไหร่*	ยี่สิบบาท
แพงไปหน่อย	จอดที่นี่	ไม่แพงหรอก	อยู่ที่โน่น
ไม่เป็นไร	อยู่ที่ไหน	อ่านไม่ยาก	คิดว่าไม่มา

*The second syllable is **tâo**; see Unit 9.

3 Reading passage

QUICK VOCAB

สามี	*husband*	ลูก	*child*
เลย	*name of a province*	คน	*classifier for people*
ตาก	*name of a province*	ลูกชาย	*son*
กับ	*and, with*	ลูกสาว	*daughter*

🔊 07.11

ยุพาเป็นคนไทย มาจากจังหวัดเลย
สมโชคเป็นสามีของยุพา มาจากจังหวัดตาก
ยุพากับสมโชคมีลูก ๕ คน มีลูกชาย ๒ คน
มีลูกสาว ๓ คน

> ● INSIGHT
>
> ลูก has two meanings: (1) *child*; (2) classifier for fruit.

1 Where does Yupha come from?
2 What is her husband's name?
3 Where does he come from?
4 How many sons do they have?
5 How many daughters do they have?

Key points

1 QUESTION WORD + **gôr dâi** shows lack of preference.

2 *too* ...: ADJECTIVE + **(gern) bpai**.

3 Requests to do something oneself: **kŏr** + VERB + **nòy (dâi mái)?**

4 *How?* questions: VERB + **yung-ngai?**

5 Classifiers: NOUN + NUMBER + CLASSIFIER.

6 Classifiers: NOUN + CLASSIFIER + **née/nún/nóhn**.

7 Continuous actions: **gum-lung** + VERB + **yòo**.

8 Words with **mái àyk** tone mark have either a *falling tone* or a *low tone*.

9 Silent อ: อยู่ อย่า อย่าง อยาก

kǒr pùt tai jahn nèung
I'd like a plate of Thai-style fried noodles
ขอผัดไทยจานหนึ่ง

In this unit, you will learn:
- ▶ *how to order simple food dishes*
- ▶ *polite requests: kǒr + noun*
- ▶ *... réu yung? questions*
- ▶ *alternative questions: X réu Y*
- ▶ *location words: kûng and tahng*
- ▶ *two different uses of ... dôo-ay*
- ▶ *mái toh and other tone marks*

Dialogues

kǒr pùt tai jahn nèung

Peter and Sue have gone to eat at a small food shop. Here are the new words you'll hear:

QUICK VOCAB

pùt tai	*Thai-style fried noodles*	ผัดไทย
jahn	*plate*	จาน
kâo pùt	*fried rice*	ข้าวผัด
gài	*chicken*	ไก่
gÔOng	*shrimp*	กุ้ง
láir-o gôr	*and*	แล้วก็
náhm	*water; drink*	น้ำ
bpép-sêe	*Pepsi*	เป๊ปซี่
kòo-ut	*bottle*	ขวด

 08.01

Waitress	เอาอะไรคะ	ao a-rai ká?
Peter	ขอผัดไทยจานหนึ่ง	kǒr pùt tai jahn nèung.
Waitress	ผัดไทยไม่มีค่ะ	pùt tai mâi mee kà.

Peter	อ้อ ไม่มีหรือ	ôr mâi mee lěr?
	ข้าวผัดมีไหม	kâo pùt mee mái?
Waitress	มีค่ะ มีข้าวผัดไก่	mee kà. mee kâo pùt gài
	กุ้ง แล้วก็หมู	gÔOng láir-o gôr mǒo.
Peter	เอาข้าวผัดกุ้ง	ao kâo pùt gÔOng
	ก็แล้วกัน	gôr láir-o gun
Waitress	ค่ะ แล้วเอาน้ำอะไรคะ	kà láir-o ao náhm a-rai?
Peter	เอาเป๊ปซี่ขวดหนึ่ง	ao bpép-sêe kòo-ut nèung.

1 How does the waitress respond to Peter's initial order?

2 What does he order instead?

sùng réu yung?

Damrong is ordering **pùt see éw** – rice noodles fried in soy sauce:

QUICK VOCAB

sùng	*to order*	สั่ง
… réu yung?	*…yet?…*	หรือยัง
yung	*no* (in response to **réu yung?** question)	ยัง
pùt see éw	*rice noodles fried in soy sauce*	ผัดซีอิ๊ว
sên yài	*'broad strip' noodles*	เส้นใหญ่
sên lék	*'thin strip' noodles*	เส้นเล็ก
yài	*big*	ใหญ่
réu	*or*	หรือ
lék	*small*	เล็ก
sài	*to put in*	ใส่
kài	*egg*	ไข่
dôo-ay	*too, also*	ด้วย
núm sôm kún	*fresh orange juice*	น้ำส้มคั้น
gâir-o	*glass*	แก้ว

Waitress	สั่งหรือยังคะ	sùng réu yung ká?
Damrong	ยังครับ เอาผัดซีอิ๊ว	yung krúp. ao pùt see éw.
	จานหนึ่งครับ	jahn neùng krúp.
Waitress	เอาเส้นใหญ่หรือ	ao sên yài réu
	เส้นเล็กคะ	sên lék ká?
Damrong	เส้นใหญ่ครับ	sên yài krúp.
Waitress	ใส่ไก่หรือหมูคะ	sài gài réu mŏo ká?
Damrong	หมูครับ	mŏo krúp.
Waitress	ใส่ไข่ด้วยไหมคะ	sài kài dôo-ay mái ká?
Damrong	ใส่ครับ	sài krúp.
Waitress	เอาน้ำอะไร	ao náhm a-rai?
Damrong	เอาน้ำส้มคั้น	ao núm sôm kún
	แก้วหนึ่ง	gâir-o nèung.

● INSIGHT

In the last unit, you met **sài** meaning *to wear*. In this unit, it means *to put in*.

1 What kind of noodles does Damrong choose?

2 What kind of meat does he choose?

3 Does he want egg added, too?

gèp dtung dôo-ay krúp

At the end of the meal Peter calls the waitress over so that he can pay. How much does his meal cost?

QUICK VOCAB

nŏo	way of addressing young waitresses	หนู
gèp	*to collect, keep*	เก็บ
dtung	*money, satang*	สตางค์
... dôo-ay	particle used in commands	ด้วย
hôrng náhm	*toilet*	ห้องน้ำ

| kûng lǔng | behind; at the back | ข้างหลัง |
| tahng sái | on the left | ทางซ้าย |

 08.03

Peter	หนูเก็บสตางค์ด้วยครับ	nǒo gèp dtung dôo-ay krúp.
Waitress	เก้าสิบบาทค่ะ	gâo sìp bàht kà.
Peter	ขอโทษครับ	kǒr-tôht krúp.
	ห้องน้ำอยู่ที่ไหน	hôrng náhm yòo têe-nǎi?
Waitress	อยู่ข้างหลังค่ะ ทางซ้าย	yòo kûng lǔng kà, tahng sái.
Peter	ขอบคุณครับ	kòrp-kOOn krúp.
Waitress	ค่ะ	kà.

● **INSIGHT**

dtung is a shortened form of 'satang'. It has the more general meaning, 'money' in the expressions **gèp dtung** (lit., *collect the money*) and **mâi mee dtung** (*I haven't any money*). The satang is the smallest unit of Thai currency. There are 100 satang in one baht, although today it exists only in the 25-satang and 50-satang coins.

● **INSIGHT**

A striking feature of urban Thailand, especially Bangkok, is the number and variety of eating establishments, ranging from small, mobile pavement stalls, to exclusive, air-conditioned restaurants. Small stalls and food shops may specialize in certain kinds of food, such as curries and stir-fried dishes, regional favourites or roasted meats, such as duck, pork and chicken. Market stalls, student cafeterias and shopping mall 'food centres', provide an opportunity to sample a vast range of foods at very reasonable prices.

Key phrases and expressions

 08.04

How to

1 ask for a plate of …

| **kòr … jahn nèung** | ขอ … จานหนึ่ง |
| **ao … jahn nèung** | เอา … จานหนึ่ง |

2 ask for a glass/bottle of …

kòr … gâir-o/ kòo-ut nèung ขอ … แก้ว/ขวดหนึ่ง

3 ask for the bill

gèp dtung dôo-ay เก็บสตางค์ด้วย

4 ask where the toilet is

hôrng náhm yòo têe-năi? ห้องน้ำอยู่ที่ไหน

Language notes

1 POLITE REQUESTS: ASKING FOR SOMETHING

When politely asking for something, the pattern **kòr** + NOUN **+ nòy** (*a little*) is used. However, if the amount of the item requested is specified (e.g. *two* plates of fried rice, *one* bottle of beer), **nòy** is replaced by the number expression:

kòr náhm nòy (dâi mái)?
ขอน้ำหน่อย (ได้ไหม)
Can I have some water, please?

kòr náhm sŏrng gâir-o (dâi mái)?
ขอน้ำสองแก้ว (ได้ไหม)
Can I have two glasses of water, please?

In both cases, **dâi mái?** can be added at the end of the request for additional politeness.

Note that in restaurants it is perfectly acceptable to use **ao** (*I want*) instead of **kòr** when ordering food.

2 WATER

From the Thai script spelling, **náhm** (*water*) looks as if it should be pronounced with a short vowel.

The long vowel changes to a short vowel when it occurs as the first word in compound nouns (nouns made up of more than one word):

náhm	*water*	น้ำ
núm sôm kún	*fresh orange juice*	น้ำส้มคั้น
núm bplah	*fish sauce*	น้ำปลา

But when it is the second word in a compound, the vowel is pronounced long:

hôrng náhm	*toilet*	ห้องน้ำ
mâir náhm	*river*	แม่น้ำ

3 ALTERNATIVE QUESTIONS: . . . 'OR' . . . ?

The Thai word for *or* is **réu**. In Thai script, it is spelt exactly the same as the question particle **... lěr?** (Unit 4), but in normal speech it is pronounced with a short vowel and a high tone. Many speakers will pronounce the word with an initial **l** rather than **r**.

ao sên yài réu sên lék?

เอาเส้นใหญ่หรือเส้นเล็ก

Do you want broad strip or thin strip noodles?

sài gài réu mǒo?

ใส่ไก่หรือหมู

Do you want chicken or pork in it?

4 ... (láir-o) réu yung?

Questions that end in **... (láir-o) réu yung?** ask whether something has happened yet. The word **láir-o** (*already*) is often omitted and the question abbreviated to **... réu yung?**

sùng (láir-o) réu yung?

สั่ง(แล้ว)หรือยัง

Have you ordered yet?

séu (láir-o) réu yung?

ซื้อ(แล้ว)หรือยัง

Have you eaten yet?

A *yes* answer to a ... **(láir-o) réu yung?** question is verb + **láir-o**; a *no* answer is **yung:**

sùng (láir-o) réu yung?

สั่ง(แล้ว)หรือยัง

Have you ordered yet?

- sùng láir-o/yung

- สั่งแล้ว / ยัง

- *Yes/No.*

séu (láir-o) réu yung?

ซื้อ(แล้ว)หรือยัง

Have you eaten yet?

- séu láir-o/yung

- ซื้อแล้ว / ยัง

- *Yes/No.*

5 nǒo

nǒo (*rat*) is widely used as a first-person pronoun (*I*) by young children addressing parents and other adults and girls and women addressing superiors (such as teachers, bosses or older relatives). It is used as a second-person pronoun (*you*) by parents and adults addressing young children, and people of higher social status addressing servants, cleaners, waitresses and junior colleagues:

nǒo mâi bpai

หนูไม่ไป

I'm not going. (child speaking)

nǒo bpai mâi dâi

หนูไปไม่ได้

You can't go. (parent to child)

6 dôo-ay

In this unit, two distinct uses of **dôo-ay** are illustrated. One meaning of **dôo-ay** is *too, also*; but it is also used to indicate a polite command, as in the expression, **gèp dtung dôo-ay**, which literally means 'collect the money':

sài kài dôo-ay mái?

ใส่ไข่ด้วยไหม

Do you want egg in it, too?

gèp dtung dôo-ay

เก็บสตางค์ด้วย

The bill, please.

7 LOCATION WORDS: *kûng and tahng*

You have already met **têe** (*at*) and **tǎir-o** (*in the vicinity of*) as ways of describing the location of places; two further useful words are **kûng** (*side*) and **tahng** (*way*).

kûng commonly occurs before a number of prepositions; notice that it is pronounced with a short vowel in normal speech and not **kâhng**, as the spelling suggests.

kûng	bon	on; upstairs	ข้างบน
kûng	kâhng	beside	ข้างๆ
kûng	lâhng	under; downstairs	ข้างล่าง
kûng	lǔng	behind	ข้างหลัง
kûng	nâh	in front (of)	ข้างหน้า
kûng	nai	in; inside	ข้างใน
kûng	nôrk	outside	ข้างนอก

hôrng náhm yòo kûng lŭng

หองน้ำอยูขางหลัง

The toilet is at the back.

jòrt kûng nâh

จอดขางหนา

Park at the front.

If a noun follows the preposition, **kûng** is normally dropped:

hôrng náhm yòo lŭng bâhn

หองน้ำอยูหลังบาน

The toilet is behind the house.

jòrt nâh rót sĕe dairng

จอดหนารถสีแดง

Park in front of the red car.

tahng is used with **sái** (*left*) and **kwăh** (*right*):

hôrng náhm yòo tahng sái

หองน้ำอยูทางซาย

The toilet is on the left.

jòrt rót tahng kwăh

จอดรถทางขวา

Park your car on the right.

Exercises

1 How would you ask for:

  a *three plates of shrimp fried rice?*

  b *two bottles of water?*

  c *a glass of fresh orange juice?*

  d *the bill?*

 08.05

2 How would you ask someone if they have done the following?

  a *ordered yet?*

  b *bought a mobile phone yet?*

  c *tried something out yet?*

  d *been to Chiangmai yet?*

3 Listen to the recording and repeat after the speaker, paying special attention to the tones:

gâir-o	săhm gâir-o	núm sôm	ao núm sôm
		săhm gâir-o	săhm gâir-o
kòo-ut	hâh kòo-ut	bpép-sêe	ao bpép-sêe
		hâh kòo-ut	hâh kòo-ut
nèung	jahn nèung	pùt tai	kŏr pùt tai
		jahn nèung	jahn nèung

Reading and writing

In the last unit, you met the tone mark **mái àyk**. The other main tone mark is **mái toh**, which is introduced in this unit, together with the remaining two tone marks **mái dtree** and **mái jùt-dta-wah**. Once you have mastered these tone marks, you are well on the way to being able to read the dialogues in Thai script.

1 *mái toh* (◌̋): TONE RULES

This tone mark looks like the number two with an elongated tail and is written above the initial consonant. Words written with a **mái toh** tone mark have either a high tone or a *falling* tone.

When **mái toh** occurs on a word that begins with a low class consonant, it indicates that the word has a *high* tone:

Low class	น้อง	ม้า	รู้	แล้ว	ย้าย
	nórng	**máh**	**róo**	**láir-o**	**yái**

If the initial consonant is either mid class or high class, the tone is *falling*:

Mid class	แก้ว	ได้	ต้อง	บ้าน	ป้าย
	gâir-o	**dâi**	**dtôrng**	**bâhn**	**bpâi**
High class	ข้าง	ถ้า	ผู้	ห้อง	ให้
	kâhng	**tâh**	**pôo**	**hôrng**	**hâi**

2 *mái dtree* (◌́) AND *mái jùt-dta-wah* (◌̊): TONE RULES

The tone marks **mái dtree** (◌́) and **mái jùt-dta-wah** (◌̊) are much less common than **mái àyk** and **mái toh**. **mái dtree** is identical to the Thai number 7; it always produces a *high* tone. **mái jùt-dta-wah** is a cross; it always produces a *rising* tone.

เป๊ปซี่	ต๋อย
bpép-sêe	**dtŏy**

Tone marks are used to indicate tone in live syllables. The following chart summarizes the rules for their use.

Initial consonant class	mái àyk ่ -	mái toh ้ -	mái dtree ๊ -	mái jùt-dta-wah ±
Low class	**Falling tone**	**High tone**	**High tone**	**Rising tone**
Mid class	**Low tone**	**Falling tone**	**High tone**	**Rising tone**
High class	**Low tone**	**Falling tone**	**High tone**	**Rising tone**

Again, you might find it helpful to make your own copy of this chart and keep it handy for reference.

Reading practice

1 WORDS

 08.07

All these words are written with **mái toh** and are therefore pronounced with either a high tone or a falling tone:

ต้อง	ทิ้ง	บ้าน	ให้	รู้
ส้ม	นี้	ถ้า	ป้าย	น้ำ
แล้ว	กุ้ง	ร้อน	ห้อง	ซื้อ
ข้าว	โน้น	แก้ว	หน้า	ได้

2 PHRASES

 08.08

Now, some phrases from this and earlier units, using words with **mái toh:**

ได้ไหม	ไม่ได้	สามสิบห้า
รู้จักไหม	ก็แล้วกัน	ข้าวผัดกุ้ง
แก้วหนึ่ง	แถวนี้	สองร้อยบาท

3 DIALOGUE

🔊 08.09

Damrong and Sue are discussing her recent shopping trip:

Damrong	ซื้อมือถือหรือยัง
Sue	ซื้อแล้ว
Damrong	ขอดูหน่อยได้ไหม
Sue	ได้
Damrong	แพงไหม
Sue	ไม่แพง สี่พันบาท
Damrong	ซื้อที่ไหน
Sue	แถวสุขุมวิท

1 What purchase are Damrong and Sue discussing?

2 How much did it cost?

3 Where was it bought?

4 Dialogue

🔊 08.10

Somchai is ordering lunch for himself and a couple of friends:

QUICK VOCAB

duck rice	ข้าวหน้าเป็ด
red pork rice	ข้าวหมูแดง

Somchai	ขอข้าวหน้าเป็ดสองจาน
	ข้าวหมูแดงจานหนึ่ง
	แล้วก็น้ำส้มคั้นสามแก้ว
Waiter	น้ำส้มคั้นไม่มี เป๊ปซี่ได้ไหม

1 What food did Somchai order?

2 What problem did he have with his drinks order?

3 What solution did the waiter propose?

Key points

1 Asking for something: **kǒr** + NOUN.

2 **... réu yung?** questions.

3 Alternative questions: **X réu Y**.

4 **... dôo-ay:** (1) *too, also* (2) at the end of polite commands.

5 Location words **kûng** + PREPOSITION and **tahng** + *right/left*.

6 Words with **mái toh** tone mark have either a falling tone or high tone.

7 Words with **mái dtree** tone mark have a high tone.

8 Words with **mái jùt-dta-wah** tone mark have a rising tone.

9 tahn ah-hăhn pèt bpen mái?
Can you eat spicy food?
ทานอาหารเผ็ดเป็นไหม

In this unit, you will learn:
▶ *names of common food dishes*
▶ *would like to ...: yàhk (ja) + verb*
▶ *hâi: getting someone to do something*
▶ *can ...: verb + bpen*
▶ *if sentences*
▶ *verb + láir-o*
▶ *low class consonants (iii): ฒ ธ ภ ญ ณ*
▶ *vowels (iv): เ-า เ-ีย เ-ือ -ัว เ-ิ -ะ*

Dialogues

hâi kOOn Chanida sùng dee gwàh

At a restaurant, Chanida asks Peter what he would like to eat. How does he respond?

QUICK VOCAB

may-noo	menu	เมนู
yàhk ja	*like to*	อยากจะ
tahn	*to eat* (formal)	ทาน
hâi	*to get someone to do something*	ให้
dee gwàh	*better*	ดีกว่า
ah-hăhn	*food*	อาหาร
bpen	*to be able to*	เป็น

 09.01

Waiter	สั่งหรือยังครับ	sùng réu yung krúp?
Chanida	ยังค่ะ	yung kà.
	ขอดูเมนูหน่อย	kŏr doo may-noo nòy.
	คุณปีเตอร์อยากจะ	kOOn Peter yàhk ja

Peter	ทานอะไร	tahn a-rai?
	อะไรก็ได้ครับ	a-rai gôr dâi krúp.
	ให้คุณชนิดาสั่ง	hâi kOOn Chanida sùng
	ดีกว่า	dee gwàh.
	ผมสั่งอาหารไทย	pŏm sùng ah-hăhn tai
	ไม่เป็น	mâi bpen.

tahn ah-hăhn pèt bpen mái?

Chanida orders the food:

QUICK VOCAB

tâh	*if*	ถ้า
nórng	*way of addressing a younger waiter/waitress*	น้อง
gài pùt kĭng	*chicken fried with ginger*	ไก่ผัดขิง
pùt pùk roo-um mít	*mixed fried vegetables*	ผัดผักรวมมิตร
dtôm yum	*'tom yam'*	ตุ๋มยำ
dôo-ay	*too*	ด้วย
krúp pŏm	*yes*	ครับผม
náhm bplào	*plain water*	น้ำเปล่า
láir-o … lâ	*and how about …?*	แล้ว …ละ
rúp	*receive, take*	รับ

🔊 09.02

Chanida	คุณซูทานอาหาร	kOOn Sue tahn ah-hăhn
	เผ็ดเป็นไหม	pèt bpen mái?
Sue	เป็นค่ะ	bpen kà.
	ถ้าไม่เผ็ดเกินไป	tâh mâi pèt gern bpai.
Chanida	น้อง ขอไก่ผัดขิง	nórng! kŏr gài pùt kĭng
	ผัดผักรวมมิตร	pùt pùk roo-um mít
	แล้วก็ ตุ๋มยำกุ้ง	láir-o gôr dtôm yum gÔOng
	เอาข้าวด้วยค่ะ	ao kâo dôo-ay kà.

Waiter	ครับผม	krúp pǒm.
	แล้วรับน้ำอะไรครับ	láir-o rúp náhm a-rai krúp?
Chanida	น้ำเปล่าค่ะ	náhm bplào kà.
	แล้วคุณปีเตอร์ล่ะคะ	láir-o kOOn Peter lâ ká?

● INSIGHT

The waiter uses **krúp pǒm** instead of **krúp** as an alternative polite *yes* response. He also uses **rúp** as a polite alternative to **ao**. In smarter restaurants you are likely to hear the waiter or waitress ask **rúp a-rai?** *(What will you have?)*

1 Can Sue eat spicy food?

2 What kind of tom yam does Chanida order?

ìm láir-o kà

Chanida tries to persuade Sue and Peter to have dessert:

QUICK VOCAB

ka-nǒm	*dessert; cake*	ขนม
ìm	*to be full*	อิ่ม
láir-o	*already*	แล้ว
wǎhn	*to be sweet*	หวาน
mâi … ler-ee	*not … at all*	ไม่ …เลย
ngún	*in that case*	งั้น
gin	*to eat (informal)*	กิน
kon dee-o	*alone*	คนเดียว

🔊 09.03

Chanida	ขนมที่นี่อร่อยนะ	ka-nǒm têe-nêe a-ròy ná.
	คุณซูทานไหม	kOOn Sue tahn mái?
Sue	ไม่ค่ะ อิ่มแล้วค่ะ	mâi kà. ìm láir-o kà.
Chanida	แล้วคุณปีเตอร์ล่ะ	láir-o kOOn Peter lâ?
Peter	ไม่ครับ ไม่ชอบ	mâi krúp. mâi chôrp.

Chanida	ขนมไทยหวานไป	ka-nŏm tai wăhn bpai
	ไม่อร่อยเลย	mâi a-ròy ler-ee.
	งั้นฉันกินคนเดียวนะ	ngún chún gin kon dee-o ná.
	น้อง	nórng!

1 What reason does Sue give for declining dessert?

2 What is Peter's opinion of Thai desserts?

3 What does Chanida decide to do?

sòop bÒO-rèe mái krúp?

Somchai offers Peter a cigarette:

QUICK VOCAB

sòop	to smoke	สูบ
bÒO-rèe	cigarette	บุหรี่
lêrk	to give up	เลิก
gèng	to be good at	เก่ง
krêe-ut	to be stressed	เครียด
chék bin dôo-ay	Can I have the bill?	เช็คบิลด้วย

🔊 09.04

Somchai	สูบบุหรี่ไหมครับ	sòop bÒO-rèe mái krúp?
Peter	ไม่สูบครับ เลิกแล้ว	mâi sòop krúp. lêrk láir-o.
Somchai	เก่งนะ ผมเลิกไม่ได้	gèng ná. pŏm lêrk mâi dâi.
	ไม่สูบก็เครียด	mâi sòop gôr krêe-ut.
	น้อง ๆ ครับ	nórng, nórng krúp!
	เช็คบิลด้วยครับ	chék bin dôo-ay krúp.

1 What reason does Peter give for declining a cigarette?

2 Why can't Somchai give up smoking?

● INSIGHT

Food and eating is a major topic of conversation for Thais. As a foreigner, you may find a Thai friend drags you through endless traffic jams across town – or out of town – to visit a favourite restaurant where the food is allegedly unequalled. The appropriate reaction is to express appreciation for the food and admiration for your friend's discerning taste, not to complain that identical food – at least as far as you are concerned – could have been had without the journey.

A Thai meal typically consists of **kâo** (*rice*) and a number of **gùp kâo** (*with rice* or side dishes) and is eaten with a spoon and fork. Common side dishes include curries made with coconut milk, stir-fried meat dishes that blend vegetables, aromatic herbs and spices, and charcoal-grilled meat or fish accompanied by strongly flavoured sauces. Chillies feature prominently in most dishes and sauces.

Since the Thai tourism boom began in the 1980s, Thai cuisine has become enormously popular throughout the world with overseas Thais opening up restaurants not only in the big cities but also in provincial towns. Exotic foodstuffs, once only imported by, and available in specialist oriental stores, are now sold in main supermarket chains, many of which now produce their own brands of 'authentic' bottled, tinned or packaged curry sauces.

Key phrases and expressions

🔊 **09.05**

How to

1 ask a friend to order for you

hâi kOOn X sùng dee gwàh ให้คุณ X สั่ง ดีกว่า

2 say you are full

ìm láir-o อิ่มแล้ว

3 say you can't eat something

tahn/gin … mâi bpen ทาน/กิน … ไม่เป็น

4 say something is too sweet/spicy

wăhn/pèt bpai หวาน/เผ็ดไป

5 say you don't smoke

mâi sòop ไม่สูบ

Language notes

1 *yàhk ja* … WANT TO …/WOULD LIKE TO …

yàhk ja (*want to, would like to*) is an auxiliary verb that occurs in the pattern **yàhk (ja)** + verb; **ja** is optional and often omitted.

kOOn yàhk (ja) tahn a-rai?

คุณอยาก(จะ)ทานอะไร

What would you like to eat?

yàhk (ja) … mái? (*Would you like to…?*) questions are answered **yàhk** (*yes*) or **mâi yàhk** (*no*):

yàhk (ja) lorng chim mái?

อยาก(จะ)ลองชิมไหม

Would you like to taste it?

- yàhk/ mâi yàhk

อยาก/ไม่อยาก

Yes / No.

Be careful not to confuse **yàhk (ja)** with **chôrp** (*to like*). **chôrp** can be followed by either a verb or a noun; **yàhk (ja)** is always followed by a verb:

chôrp ah-hăhn tai

ชอบอาหารไทย

I like Thai food.

chôrp gin ah-hăhn tai

ชอบกินอาหารไทย

I like eating Thai food.

yàhk (ja) gin ah-hăhn tai

อยาก(จะ)กินอาหารไทย

I'd like to eat Thai food.

2 *hâi*

hâi is an important word with a number of distinct meanings. One usage is as a causative verb, which ranges in meaning from the possibly coercive *to get someone to do something/ have someone do something* to the more benevolent *to let someone do something*. The listener has to decide from the context which meaning is implied.

(pŏm) hâi kOOn Chanida sùng

(ผม)ให้คุณชนิดาสั่ง

I'll let Khun Chanida order.

káo hâi kOOn tum a-rai?

เขาให้คุณทำอะไร

What did he have/get you to do?

chún hâi káo jòrt têe nôhn

ฉันให้เขาจอดที่โน่น

I got him to park over there.

3 POLITE VOCABULARY

One way of indicating politeness is to use polite particles, such as **krúp** and **kà/ká?** Another way is to select the more formal of two words with the same meaning. In this unit, the waiter uses **rúp** instead of **ao** when asking the diners what they want to eat, and Chanida uses the formal word for *to eat*, **tahn** instead of the informal **gin** when she asks if Sue can eat spicy food.

4 VERB + *bpen*

In Unit 2, you met the pattern **bpen** + NOUN (e.g. **bpen kon tai**) where **bpen** meant *is/are*.

When **bpen** occurs in the pattern VERB + **bpen**, the meaning of **bpen** is *to know how to do something* or *can*. When it has this meaning, it occurs in the same position as **dâi** (*to be able to do something, can*); **bpen** and **dâi** are sometimes used interchangeably.

gin bpen

กินเป็น

I can eat it.

sùng ah-hăhn tai mâi bpen

สั่งอาหารไทยไม่เป็น

I can't order Thai food.

Questions that take the form VERB + **bpen mái?** are answered either **bpen** (*yes*) or **mâi bpen** (*no*):

kOOn tahn ah-hăhn pèt bpen mái?

คุณทานอาหารเผ็ดเป็นไหม

Can you eat spicy food?

- bpen / mâi bpen

-เป็น/ ไม่เป็น

- Yes/No.

5 IF

Sentences including an 'if' clause, typically follow the pattern, **tâh** (*if*) **... gôr** (*then*) + VERB:

tâh mâi pèt gern bpai rao gôr gin dâi

ถ้าไม่เผ็ดเกินไปเราก็กินได้

If it's not too hot, we can eat it.

tâh mâi sòop pŏm gôr krêe-ut

ถ้าไม่สูบผมก็เครียด

If I don't smoke I feel stressed.

tâh rót dtìt káo gôr mâi mah

ถ้ารถติดเขาก็ไม่มา

If the traffic is bad, he's not coming.

Either **tâh** or **gôr** can be omitted:

mâi pèt gern bpai rao gôr gin dâi

ไม่เผ็ดเกินไปเราก็กินได้

If it's not too hot, we can eat it.

tâh mâi sòop pŏm krêe-ut

ถ้าไม่สูบผมเครียด

If I don't smoke I feel stressed.

And in contracted speech, you may find that both **tâh** and **gôr** have disappeared:

rót dtìt mâi mah

รถติดไม่มา

If the traffic is bad, he's not coming.

6 VERB + *láir-o*

The word **láir-o** – which can often be translated as *already* – occurs in the pattern VERB/ADJECTIVE + **láir-o** to show that the action of the verb has been completed or the state of the adjective achieved:

káo bpai láir-o

เขาไปแล้ว

He's gone.

ìm láir-o

อิ่มแล้ว

I'm full.

7 láir-o … lâ?

The expression **láir-o … lâ?** means *And how/what about …?* The speaker assumes that the listener understands the context of the question:

láir-o kOOn lâ?

แล้วคุณล่ะ

And how about you?

láir-o ah-haˇhn lâ?

แล้วอาหารล่ะ

And how about the food?

láir-o rót lâ?

แล้วรถล่ะ

And what about the car?

8 mâi … ler-ee

mâi + VERB/ADJECTIVE + **ler-ee** is a stronger negative statement than **mâi** + VERB/ADJECTIVE; it can be translated as *not … at all*:

mâi a-ròy ler-ee

ไม่อร่อยเลย

It's not tasty at all.

mâi pairng ler-ee

ไม่แพงเลย

It's not expensive at all.

mâi chôrp ler-ee

ไม่ชอบเลย

I don't like it at all.

In Unit 4, you met the pattern **mâi** + VERB/ADJECTIVE + **ròrk**, which often translates as *not … at all*. Note, however, that **mâi … ròrk** and **mâi … ler-ee** are not interchangeable; the first is used for contradicting someone, while the second is used for intensifying the negative expression.

Exercises

1 How would you answer if a Thai asked you:

   a tahn ah-hǎhn tai bpen mái?

   b ah-hǎhn tai pèt mái?

   c tahn pèt bpen mái?

   d ka-nǒm tai a-ròy mái?

   e sòop bÒO-rèe mái?

2 Translate the following sentences, using the pattern ADJECTIVE + **(gern)** **bpai** to justify the initial negative comment:

   a *I can't eat Thai food. It's too spicy.*

   b *Thai desserts aren't tasty. They're too sweet*

   c *We can't walk. It's too far.*

   d *She's not buying it. It's too expensive.*

   e *I can't wear them. They're too tight.*

 09.06

3 Use the pattern **(tâh)** ... **gôr** ... to join the two sentences and then translate into English:

   a mâi sòop bÒO-rèe   krêe-ut

   b pèt gern bpai   mâi a-ròy

   c mâi pèt mâhk   gin dâi

   d mâi glai bpai   dern dâi

   e pairng bpai   mâi séu

Reading and writing

1 CONSONANTS

🔊 **09.07**

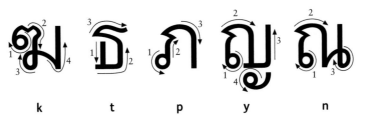

| k | t | p | y | n |

This third group of low class consonants have the same sounds as other low class consonants that you have already learned in Units 1 and 4. The new consonants do not occur as frequently as those you met earlier, but they cannot be ignored as they appear in a number of common words. These include:

ฆ่า	ภาษา	หญิง	ใหญ่	ญี่ปุ่น	คุณ
kâh	**pah-sǎh**	**yǐng**	**yài**	**yêe-bpÒOn**	**kOOn**
to kill	*language*	*female*	*big*	*Japan*	*you*

🔊 **09.08**

เา	เีย	เือ	◌ัว	เิ◌	-ะ
-ao	**-ee-a**	**-eu-a**	**-oo-a**	**-er**	**-a**
(short)	(long)	(long)	(long)	(long)	(short)

Several new vowels are now being added, most of which are combinations of symbols you have already met. From now on, whenever you meet the symbol เ-, you will need to scan the next couple of letters to see whether it is the **-ay** vowel (Unit 4) or part of one of the 'wrap-around' vowels above.

* When ◌ัว is followed by another consonant the top part of the vowel symbol (◌ั) is omitted:

หัว	ตัว	วัว
hǒo-a	**dtoo-a**	**woo-a**

but

ด้วย	สวน	ขวด
dôo-ay	**sǒo-un**	**kòo-ut**

** When เิ◌ is *not* followed by a consonant, the top part of the vowel symbol (◌ิ) is *omitted* and the zero consonant symbol (อ) *added*:

เดิน	เปิด	เกิด
dern	**bpèrt**	**gèrt**

but

เธอ	เจอ
ter	**jer**

Reading practice

1 WORDS

🔊 **09.09**

ภาค	ภาษา	ใหญ่	หญิง	คุณ	ฆ่า
เรา	เขา	เอา	เข้า	เท่าไหร่	เท่านั้น
เรียน	เขียน	เลี้ยว	เมื่อ	เหมือน	เพื่อน

ตัว	หัว	วัว	สวย	ช่วย	ด้วย
เกิน	เกิด	เชิญ	เดิน	เจอ	เธอ
จะ	คะ	ค่ะ	นะ	อะไร	บะหมี่

2 MENUS

Thai food has become extremely popular in the west following the tourism boom of the 1980s. Menus in Thai restaurants often list dishes both in Thai script and romanized Thai. Each restaurant may have its own way of romanizing Thai words. The term for 'stir fried', for example, might appear as 'pat', 'pad', 'pud', 'put', 'phat', 'phad', 'phud' or 'phut', depending on the whim of the restaurant owner or author. Of course, if you can read Thai script you can bypass all this confusion.

Cover up the romanized Thai words in the following and see how many of these basic menu items you can read. (Note that there are one or two items that involve spelling rules that you have not yet met.)

Curries and soups

แกง	**gairng**	'wet' curry (i.e. with a lot of liquid)
แพนง	**pa-nairng**	'dry' curry
แกงไก่	**gairng gài**	chicken curry
แกงเนื้อ	**gairng néu-a**	beef curry
แกงจืด	**gairng jèut**	bland, clear soup
ต้มยำ	**dtôm yum**	'tom yam' (spicy soup)
ต้มยำกุ้ง	**dtôm yum gÔOng**	shrimp 'tom yam'
ต้มยำปลา	**dtôm yum bplah**	fish 'tom yam'

Meat and fish

ไก่	**gài**	chicken
เป็ด	**bpèt**	duck
เนื้อ	**néu-a**	beef
หมู	**mŏo**	pork
ปลา	**bplah**	fish
ปลาหมึก	**bplah mèuk**	squid
กุ้ง	**gÔOng**	shrimp
ปู	**bpoo**	crab

Egg

ไข่	**kài**	*egg*
ไข่ดาว	**kài dao**	*fried egg*
ไข่เจียว	**kài jee-o**	*omelette*
ไข่ยัดไส้	**kài yút sâi**	*stuffed omelette*

Stir fried dishes

ไก่ผัดพริก	**gài pùt prík**	*chicken fried with chillies*
เนื้อผัดขิง	**néu-a pùt kǐng**	*beef fried with ginger*
เนื้อผัดน้ำ	**néu-a pùt núm**	*beef fried in*
มันหอย	**mun hǒy**	*oyster sauce*
หมูผัดหน่อไม้	**mǒo pùt nòr mái**	*pork fried with bamboo shoots*
กุ้งผัดใบกระเพรา	**gÔOng pùt bai gra-prao**	*shrimp fried with basil leaves*

3 DIALOGUE

 09.10

Chanida and Mineko have finished their meal. How does Mineko respond to Chanida's suggestion of coffee?

Chanida	อิ่มหรือยังคะ
Mineko	อิ่มแล้วค่ะ
Chanida	อาหารที่นี่อร่อยไหม
Mineko	อร่อยมากค่ะ
Chanida	รับกาแฟไหมคะ
Mineko	ไม่ค่ะ อิ่มมาก

Key points

1 *Would like to ...*: **yàhk (ja)** + VERB.

2 **hâi**: getting someone to do something.

3 *Can ...*: VERB + **bpen**.

4 If sentences: **tâh** (*if*) ... **gôr** (*then*) + VERB.

5 Verb + **láir-o** indicates that the action of the verb has been completed.

6 *Not ... at all*: **mâi** + VERB/ADJECTIVE + **ler-ee**.

7 Consonants: ฆ ธ ภ ญ ฌ

8 Vowels: เ-า เ-ีย เ-ือ -ัว เ-ิ -ะ

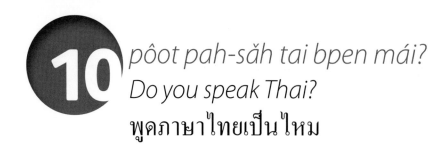

10 pôot pah-săh tai bpen mái?
Do you speak Thai?
พูดภาษาไทยเป็นไหม

In this unit, you will learn:
▶ *how to talk about your knowledge of Thai*
▶ *verb* + bpen + *adverb*
▶ *Why? questions*
▶ *how to compare things*
▶ mâi kôy ... tâo-rài *(not very...)*
▶ *how to read words beginning with consonant clusters*

Dialogues

kOOn pôot pah-săh tai bpen mái?

Damrong asks Katie if she can speak Thai:

QUICK VOCAB

pôot	to speak	พูด
pah-săh	language	ภาษา
nít-nòy	a little bit	นิดหน่อย
bâhn	house, home	บ้าน
mâir	mother	แม่
pôr	father	พ่อ

 10.01

Damrong	คุณพูดภาษาไทย	kOOn pôot pah-săh tai
	เป็นไหมครับ	bpen mái krúp?
Katie	เป็นนิดหน่อยค่ะ	bpen nít-nòy kà.
Damrong	เรียนที่ไหน	ree-un têe năi?
Katie	ที่บ้านค่ะ	têe bâhn kà.
	คุณแม่เป็นคนไทย	kOOn mâir bpen kon tai.
Damrong	ออหรือครับ	ôr lěr krúp?

Katie	แล้วคุณพ่อล่ะ	láir-o kOOn pôr lâ?
	คุณพ่อเป็นคนอังกฤษค่ะ	kOOn pôr bpen kon ung-grìt kà.
	พูดไทยไม่เป็นเลย	pôot tai mâi bpen ler-ee.

1 How well does Katie speak Thai?

2 Where did she learn Thai?

3 What nationality are her parents?

tum-mai kOOn pôot tai gèng

A taxi driver admires Peter's command of Thai:

QUICK VOCAB

tum-mai	why?	ทำไม
see	particle used in contradicting a negative statement	ซี
mâi kôy ... tâo-rài	not very; hardly, scarcely	ไม่ค่อย ... เท่าไหร่
nahn	a long time	นาน
deu-un	month	เดือน
fairn	boy/girlfriend; spouse	แฟน

🔊 **10.02**

Taxi	ทำไมคุณพูดไทยเก่ง	tum-mai kOOn pôot tai gèng?
Peter	ไม่เก่งหรอกครับ	mâi gèng ròrk krúp.
	พูดได้นิดหน่อยเท่านั้น	pôot dâi nít-nòy tâo-nún.
Taxi	เก่งซีครับ	gèng see krúp.
	อยู่เมืองไทยนานไหม	yòo meu-ung tai nahn mái?
Peter	ไม่ค่อยนานเท่าไหร่ครับ	mâi kôy nahn tâo-rài krúp
	สองสามเดือนเท่านั้น	sŏrng săhm deu-un tâo-nún.
Taxi	สองสามเดือนเท่านั้นหรือ	sŏrng săhm deu-un tâo-nún lĕr?
	เก่ง มีแฟนคนไทย	gèng. mee fairn kon tai
	ไหมครับ	mái krúp?
Peter	ไม่มีครับ	mâi mee krúp.

1 How long has Peter been in Thailand?

2 What does the taxi driver suspect lies behind Peter's linguistic proficiency?

pah-săh tai yâhk mái?

Chanida asks Sue how she finds learning Thai:

QUICK VOCAB

yâhk	*difficult*	ยาก
mĕu-un gun	*fairly*	เหมือนกัน
prór	*because*	เพราะ
sĕe-ung sŏong	*tones*	เสียงสูงเสียงต่ำ
sĕe-ung dtùm		
kít wâh ...	*to think that ...*	คิดว่า ...
àhn	*to read*	อ่าน
kĕe-un	*to write*	เขียน
ngâi	*easy*	ง่าย
gwàh	*more than*	กว่า

🔊 10.03

Chanida	ภาษาไทยยากไหมคะ	pah-săh tai yâhk mái ká?
Sue	ก็ ... ยากเหมือนกันค่ะ	gôr ... yâhk mĕu-un gun kà.
	คิดว่าพูดยากเพราะมี	kít wâh pôot yâhk prór mee
	เสียงสูงเสียงต่ำ	sĕe-ung sŏong sĕe-ung dtùm.
Chanida	แลว อานเขียนเป็นไหม	láir-o àhn kĕe-un bpen mái?
Sue	เป็นนิดหน่อยค่ะ	bpen nít-nòy kà.
	กำลังเรียนอยู่	gum-lung ree-un yòo.
Chanida	เป็นอย่างไร ยากไหม	bpen yung-ngai? yâhk mái?
Sue	คิดว่า อ่านง่ายกว่าพูด	kít wâh àhn ngâi gwàh pôot
	แต่เขียนไม่ค่อยได	dtàir kĕe-un mâi kôy dâi.

● INSIGHT

The colloquial word for tones – **sĕe-ung sŏong sĕe-ung dtùm** – literally means *'sounds-high-sounds-low'*.

1 Why does Sue think Thai is difficult?

2 Can Sue write Thai?

3 How does Sue rate speaking reading and writing Thai in order of difficulty?

> ● **INSIGHT**
>
> One of the enjoyable things about speaking Thai in Thailand is that there always seem to be lots of Thais eager to tell you how well you speak their language. Even the most inept attempts can prompt a complimentary **pôot tai gèng** (*you speak Thai well*). Such encouragement is a wonderful incentive to practise more, but don't take it too literally: mutual compliments are an important part of Thai social interaction and Thais are simply being friendly rather than objectively evaluating the foreigner's linguistic competence. A polite denial, such as **mâi gèng ròrk**, or **pôot dâi nít-nòy tâo-nún**, is an appropriately modest response.

Key phrases and expressions

 10.04

How to say

1 I only speak a little Thai.

pôot tai dâi nít-nòy tâo-nún พูดไทยได้นิดหน่อยเท่านั้น

2 I'm studying Thai.

gum-lung ree-un pah-săh tai yòo กำลังเรียนภาษาไทยอยู่

3 It's difficult to speak because it has tones.

pôot yâhk prór mee พูดยากเพราะมี

sěe-ung sŏong sěe-ung dtùm เสียงสูงเสียงต่ำ

4 I can hardly write Thai.

kěe-un pah-săh tai mâi kôy dâi เขียนภาษาไทยไม่ค่อยได้

Language notes

1 VERB + *bpen/dâi* + ADVERB

Adverbs and adjectives are identical in form in Thai. Thus **dee** is both the adjective *good* and the adverb *well*. To describe how competently someone can do something, the pattern VERB + **bpen/dâi** + ADVERB can be used:

pŏm pôot pah-săh dâi nít-nòy

ผมพูดภาษาไทยได้นิดหน่อย

I can speak Thai a little.

kOOn kĕe-un pah-săh tai dâi dee

คุณเขียนภาษาไทยได้ดี

You can write Thai well.

káo àhn pah-săh tai bpen nít-nòy

เขาอ่านภาษาไทยเป็นนิดหน่อย

She can read Thai a little.

When the adverb is **gèng** (*expertly*) or **klôrng** (*fluently*) it is normal to drop **bpen/dâi**:

káo pôot tai gèng/ klôrng

เขาพูดไทยเก่ง/คลอง

He speaks Thai very well/fluently.

2 'WHY?' QUESTIONS

The question word **tum-mai?** (*why?*) normally occurs at the beginning of the question, although in informal speech it can occur at the end:

tum-mai kOOn pôot tai gèng?

ทำไมคุณพูดไทยเก่ง

Why do you speak Thai so well?

tum-mai pah-săh tai pôot yâhk?

ทำไมภาษาไทยพูดยาก

Why is Thai difficult to speak?

kOOn bpai tum-mai?

คุณไปทำไม

Why are you going?

You can answer *why?* questions using **prór** (**wâh**) (*because*):

prór (wâh) kOOn mâir bpen kon tai

เพราะ(ว่า)คุณแม่เป็นคนไทย

Because my mother is Thai.

prór (wâh) mee sĕe-ung sŏong sĕe-ung dtùm

เพราะ(ว่า)มีเสียงสูงเสียงต่ำ

Because it has tones.

prór (wâh) yàhk bpai

เพราะ(ว่า)อยากไป

Because I want to go.

3 mâi kôy … tâo-rài

mâi kôy … tâo-rài (*not very…*) 'softens' negative statements or responses; **tâo-rài** at the end of the phrase is optional and often omitted:

mâi kôy nahn (tâo-rài)

ไม่ค่อยนาน(เท่าไหร่)

Not very long.

mâi kôy pairng (tâo-rài)

ไม่ค่อยแพง(เท่าไหร่)

Not very expensive.

káo pôot mâi kôy gèng (tâo-rài)

เขาพูดไม่ค่อยเก่ง(เท่าไหร่)

He doesn't speak very well.

When **mâi kôy … (tâo-rài)** is used with **dâi**, it can be translated as *hardly* or *scarcely*:

kěe-un pah-sǎh tai mâi kôy dâi (tâo-rài)

เขียนภาษาไทยไม่ค่อยได้(เท่าไหร่)

I can scarcely write Thai.

4 MOOD PARTICLE: see (I)

The particle **see** is used in a number of different ways. In this unit, it is used when contradicting a negative statement:

mâi gèng

ไม่เก่ง

I'm not good at it.

- gèng see

- เก่งซี

- Yes you are.

mâi pairng

ไม่แพง

It's not expensive.

- pairng see

- แพงซี

- Yes it is.

dern bpai mâi glai

เดินไปไม่ไกล

It's not far to walk.

- glai see

- ไกลซี

- Yes it is.

5 . . . měu-un gun

měu-un gun literally means *likewise, similarly*:

měu-un gun mâhk

เมมือนกันมาก

They are very similar.

mâi měu-un gun

ไม่เหมือนกัน

They are not the same.

měu-un gun is also used in qualified or lukewarm *'yes'* responses:

pah-săh tai yâhk mái?

ภาษาไทยยากไหม

Is Thai difficult?

- gôr ... yâhk měu-un gun

- ก็ ... ยากเหมือนกัน

- Well, yes, fairly difficult.

6 COMPARISONS

When comparing two things, the pattern X + ADJECTIVE + **gwàh** (+ Y) is used:

àhn ngâi gwàh pôot

อ่านง่ายกว่าพูด

Reading is easier than speaking.

kOOn sùng dee gwàh

คุณสั่งดีกว่า

It's better if you order.

yòo glai gwàh

อยู่ไกลกว่า

It's further away.

pah-săh jeen yâhk gwàh

ภาษาจีนยากกว่า

Chinese is more difficult.

Comparisons can be modified by adding **mâhk** (*much*) or **nít-nòy** (*a little*) at the end of the sentence:

káo pôot gèng gwàh chún mâhk

เขาพูดเก่งกว่าฉันมาก

She speaks much better than me.

nêe pairng gwàh nít-nòy

นี่แพงกว่านิดหน่อย

This is a little bit more expensive.

Exercises

1 How would you respond to the following questions?

  a kOOn pôot pah-săh tai bpen mái?

  b ree-un pah-săh tai nahn mái?

  c àhn pah-săh tai bpen mái?

  d kĕe-un pah-săh tai bpen mái?

  e pah-săh tai yâhk mái?

 10.05

2 How would you say that something is:

  a *not very expensive?*

  b *not very far?*

  c *not very tasty?*

  d *not very good?*

  e *not very difficult?*

 10.06

3 And how would you say something is:

  a *more expensive?*

  b *further?*

  c *tastier?*

  d *better?*

  e *more difficult?*

4 This is how a number of languages have been ranked in terms of relative difficulty for the English-speaking learner:

		Speaking	Reading
Difficult	****	Japanese	Chinese
	***	Chinese	Japanese
	**	Thai	Thai
Easy	*	French	French

Complete the following sentences using either **yâhk gwàh** or **ngâi gwàh**:

    a pah-săh tai pôot ... pah-săh fa-rùng-sàyt
    b pah-săh jeen pôot ... pah-săh yêe-bpÒOn
    c pah-săh fa-rùng-sàyt àhn ... pah-săh jeen
    d pah-săh yêe-bpÒOn àhn ... pah-săh tai

Reading and writing

1 WORDS BEGINNING WITH CONSONANT CLUSTERS

All the words that you have read up to now have begun with either a single consonant or a vowel sound. In this unit, you will learn how to read words that begin with a consonant cluster (two consonant sounds) – words like **krúp, glùp, gwàh**, and so on. Consonant clusters are listed below; knowing which clusters can exist at the beginning of a word will help you to avoid misreading certain two-syllable words.

กร- **gr-**	คร- **kr-**	ขร- **kr-**	ตร- **dtr-**	ปร- **bpr-**	พร- **pr-**
กล- **gl-**	คล- **kl-**	ขล- **kl-**		ปล- **bpl-**	พล- **pl-**
กว- **gw-**	คว- **kw-**	ขว- **kw-**			

When it comes to reading a word like **krúp**, the tone should clearly be high, since (1) it is a dead syllable, (2) both consonants in the cluster are low class and (3) the vowel is short. In many words, however, the two consonants at the beginning of the word belong to different classes. In such cases, it is the class of the first consonant that determines the tone:

ครับ	กว่า	ใกล้	ปลูก
krúp	**gwàh**	**glâi**	**bplòok**

2 WORDS WITH NO VOWEL SYMBOLS (II)

In Unit 4, you met words like **kon** and **gòt** which consisted of two consonants but no written vowel symbol. Two-syllable words, consisting of three consonant symbols and no vowel symbols, are much less common. In such cases the first vowel is **-a** and the second **-o**:

ถนน	สงบ	ขนม	ตลก
ta-nǒn	**sa-ngòp**	**ka-nǒm**	**dta-lòk**

More common are words in which there is a vowel symbol in the second syllable, but where a short **-a** vowel has to be supplied in the first:

ตลาด	สนาม	สบาย	ชนิดา
dta-làht	**sa-nǎhm**	**sa-bai**	**cha-n í-dah**

Since these words begin with two consonants, they look very similar to those that begin with a consonant cluster. But if you check the consonant cluster chart, you will see that the sounds, **dtl-**, **sn-**, **sb-** and **chn-** do not exist at the beginning of Thai words. A short **-a** vowel therefore has to be inserted after the first consonant to make the first syllable. This first syllable is unstressed and pronounced with a mid tone.

The tone of the second syllable is then determined by the second consonant in the word (i.e. the first consonant of the second syllable) unless it is one of those consonants you learned in Unit 1 (น ม ง ร ล ย ว); if the second consonant is a Unit 1 consonant, then it is the class of the first consonant that determines the tone:

สบาย	สภาพ	สง่า	สนาม
sa-bai	**sa-pâhp**	**sa-ngàh**	**sa-nǎhm**

Words beginning with บร are pronounced with an initial **-or** vowel between the first and second consonants, not an **-a** vowel:

บริการ	บริเวณ	บริษัท
bor-ri-gahn	**bor-ri-wayn**	**bor-ri-sùt**

Reading practice

1 WORDS

 10.07

The first two letters in these words form a consonant cluster:

กว่า	ขวา	กรุง	ประตู	ปลา
เปล่า	ตรง	ไกล	ใกล	กลับ
ใคร	คล้าย	ครับ	ความ	ประเทศ

2 MORE WORDS

 10.08

The first two letters in the following words do not form a cluster and therefore require a short
-a vowel to be supplied for the first syllable:

ถนน	ตลก	ขยัน	สยาม	สภาพ
ขนาด	สนุก	สถาน	สบาย	บริษัท
ฉลอง	ฉลาด	ฝรั่ง	ขยะ	บริการ

3 DIALOGUE

🔊 **10.09**

Interviewer	คุณพูดไทยเก่งครับ
	อยู่เมืองไทยนานไหม
Sarah	ไมค่อยนานเท่าไหร่ค่ะ
Interviewer	คุณพูดภาษาจีนเป็นใช่ไหมครับ
Sarah	ใช่ค่ะ ฉันอยู่เมืองจีนห้าปี
Interviewer	ทำอะไรที่โน่นครับ
Sarah	สอนภาษาอังกฤษค่ะ
Interviewer	อ่านเขียนภาษาจีนเป็นไหมครับ
Sarah	เป็นนิดหน่อยค่ะ

1 Has Sarah been in Thailand long?

2 How long was she in China?

3 What was she doing there?

4 Can she speak Chinese?

5 Does she read and write Chinese?

Key points

1 To talk about how well someone can do something, use the pattern VERB + **bpen** + ADVERB.

2 **tum-mai?** (*why?*) normally occurs at the beginning of a question.

3 Use **mâi kôy ... tâo-rài** (*not very...*) to soften negative statements.

4 The colloquial word for tones is **sěe-ung sǒong sěe-ung dtùm**.

5 **měu-un gun** means (1) *likewise, similarly* or (2) *fairly* in lukewarm *'yes'* responses.

6 To compare two things, use the pattern X + ADJECTIVE + **gwàh** (+ Y).

7 The following consonant clusters can occur at the beginning of a word: **gr- gl- gw- kr- kl- kw- dtr- bpr- bpl- pr- pl-**.

8 When two consonants at the beginning of a word do not form a permissible cluster, a short **-a** vowel is normally inserted after the first consonant to make an unstressed syllable.

9 If a Thai tells you, **kOOn pôot tai gèng**, don't nod in agreement and say, 'Yes I do, don't I?'

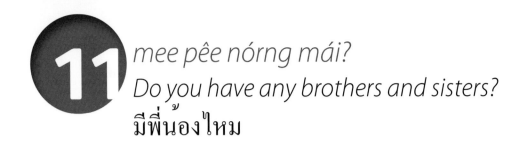

11 mee pêe nórng mái?
Do you have any brothers and sisters?
มีพี่น้องไหม

In this unit, you will learn:

▶ *kin terms: brothers and sisters, sons and daughters*
▶ *how many? questions*
▶ *who? questions*
▶ nâh + *verb*
▶ *consonants:* ฌ ฎ ฏ ฐ ฑ ฒ ฬ ฮ
▶ *vowel shortener (ii):* -ะ

Dialogues

mee pêe nórng mái?

Chanida is asking Peter if he has any brothers and sisters:

QUICK VOCAB

pêe nórng	*brothers and sisters*	พี่น้อง
nórng sǎo	*younger sister*	น้องสาว
dtàirng ngahn	*to get married*	แต่งงาน
èek	*another*	อีก
yung	*still*	ยัง

 11.01

Chanida	คุณปีเตอร์มี	kOOn Peter mee
	พี่น้อง ไหมคะ	pêe nórng mái ká?
Peter	ผมมีน้องสาว	pǒm mee nórng sǎo
	สองคนครับ	sǒrng kon krúp.
Chanida	แต่งงานแล้ว	dtàirng ngahn láir-o
	หรือยังคะ	réu yung ká?
Peter	คนหนึ่งแต่งงาน	kon nèung dtàirng ngahn

แล้ว อีกคนหนึ่ง	láir-o. èek kon nèung
ยัง ไม่แต่งงาน	yung mâi dtàirng ngahn.
ยังเรียนอยู่ครับ	yung ree-un yòo krúp.

● **INSIGHT**

Note two different uses of **yung**: (1) **yung mâi …** (*not yet …*) and (2) **yung … yòo** (*still …*).

1 How many brothers and sisters does Peter have?

2 Are they older or younger than him?

3 Are they married?

mee pêe nórng gèe kon?

Sue is asking Malee about her family:

QUICK VOCAB

gèe	*how many?*	กี่
pêe chai	*older brother*	พี่ชาย
pêe săo	*older sister*	พี่สาว
pôo-jùt-gahn	*manager*	ผู้จัดการ
bor-ri-sùt	*company*	บริษัท

🔊 11.02

Sue	ขอโทษค่ะ คุณมาลี	kŏr-tôht kà. kOOn Mah-lee
	มีพี่น้องกี่คนคะ	mee pêe nórng gèe kon ká?
Malee	สองคนค่ะ	sŏrng kon kà.
	พี่ชายคนหนึ่ง	pêe chai kon nèung
	พี่สาวคนหนึ่ง	pêe săo kon nèung.
Sue	พี่ชายทำงานอะไรคะ	pêe chai tum ngahn a-rai ká?
Malee	เป็นผู้จัดการ	bpen pôo-jùt-gahn
	บริษัทเล็ก	bor-ri-sùt lék.
Sue	แลวพี่สาวล่ะคะ	láir-o pêe săo lâ ká?
Malee	เป็นครูค่ะ	bpen kroo kà.

● **INSIGHT**

Personal questions are often prefaced by **kŏr-tôht** (*excuse me*) as a sign of politeness.

1 What does Malee's brother do?

2 And her sister?

mee lôok réu yung?

Chanida is asking Somchai about his younger brother:

QUICK VOCAB

nórng chai	*younger brother*	น้องชาย
jing	*to be true*	จริง
jing lĕr?	*really?*	จริงหรือ
lôok	*child*	ลูก
lôok chai	*son*	ลูกชาย
ah-yÓO	*age*	อายุ
kòo-up	*years old*	ขวบ

🔊 **11.03**

Chanida	น้องชายแต่งงาน หรือยังคะ	nórng chai dtàirng ngahn réu yung ká?
Somchai	แต่งแล้วครับ	dtàirng láir-o krúp.
Chanida	จริงหรือคะ มีลูกหรือยัง	jing lĕr ká? mee lôok réu yung?
Somchai	มีแล้วครับ มีลูกชายคนหนึ่ง	mee láir-o krúp. mee lôok chai kon nèung.
Chanida	อายุเท่าไหร่คะ	ah-yÓO tâo-rài ká?
Somchai	สองขวบครับ	sŏrng kòo-up krúp.

● **INSIGHT**

Notice that Somchai has dropped the word **ngahn** from his answer to Chanida's first question when he replies, **dtàirng láir-o.**

1 Does Somchai's younger brother have a son or a daughter?

2 How old is the child?

nêe krai?

Sue shows Malee some family snapshots:

QUICK VOCAB

krai?	who?	ใคร
rôop lòr	handsome	รูปหล่อ
nâh sĕe-a dai	what a shame!	น่าเสียดาย
nâh rúk	lovely, cute	น่ารัก
jing jing	really, truly	จริงๆ
pôo-chai	boy, male	ผู้ชาย
pôo-yĭng	girl, female	ผู้หญิง

🔊 11.04

Malee	นี่ใครคะ	nêe krai ká?
Sue	พี่ชายค่ะ	pêe chai kà.
Malee	รูปหล่อนะ	rôop lòr ná?
	มีแฟนหรือยังคะ	mee fairn réu yung ká?
Sue	มีแล้ว	mee láir-o!
Malee	น่าเสียดาย	nâh sĕe-a dai.
	แล้วเด็กคนนี้เป็นใคร	láir-o dèk kon née bpen krai?
Sue	เป็นลูกของพี่ชาย	bpen lôok kŏrng pêe chai.
Malee	น่ารักจริงๆ	nâh rúk jing jing.
	เป็นผู้หญิงหรือผู้ชายคะ	bpen pôo-yĭng réu pôo-chai ká?
Sue	ผู้หญิงค่ะ	pôo-yĭng kà.

1 Who is the man in the photo?

2 Why is Malee disappointed?

3 Who is the child?

Father's side

pôr	father	พ่อ
bpòo	paternal grandfather	ปู่
yâh	paternal grandmother	ย่า
lOOng	uncle (father's older brother)	ลุง
ah	uncle (father's younger brother)	อา
bpâh	aunt (father's older sister)	ป้า
ah	aunt (father's younger sister)	อา

Mother's side

mâir	mother	แม่
dtah	maternal grandfather	ตา
yai	maternal grandmother	ยาย
lOOng	uncle (mother's older brother)	ลุง
náh	uncle (mother's younger brother)	น้า
bpâh	aunt (mother's older sister)	ป้า
náh	aunt (mother's younger sister)	น้า

Key phrases and expressions

 11.05

How to ask

1 whether someone has any brothers and sisters

mee pêe nórng mái? มีพี่น้องไหม

2 how many brothers and sisters someone has

mee pêe nórng gèe kon? มีพี่น้องกี่คน

3 whether someone is married

dtàirng ngahn (láir-o) réu yung? แต่งงาน(แล้ว)หรือยัง

4 whether someone has any children

mee lôok (láir-o) réu yung? มีลูก(แล้ว)หรือยัง

5 how old someone is

ah-yÓO tâo-rài? อายุเท่าไหร่

Language notes

1 pêe nórng

pêe nórng (*brothers and sisters*) literally means *older siblings-younger siblings* and does not indicate gender at all. You may hear someone refer to a member of their family as **pêe** and you will not know whether it is an older brother or older sister. When it is necessary to be specific, the word **chai** (male) or **săo** (female) is added after **pêe** or **nórng**:

pêe nórng	*brothers and sisters*	พี่น้อง
pêe chai	*older brother*	พี่ชาย
pêe săo	*older sister*	พี่สาว
nórng chai	*younger brother*	น้องชาย
nórng săo	*younger sister*	น้องสาว

Both **pêe** and **nórng** are also used as pronouns. They create a sense of both intimacy and hierarchy between speakers. **pêe** has an especially wide range of usage, which includes, for example, younger work colleagues addressing older colleagues, shop assistants addressing older customers, wives addressing husbands and complete strangers striking up a conversation with someone older. In Unit 9, you met **nórng** used in restaurants to summon a waiter or waitress:

pêe bpai mái?

พี่ไปไหม

Are you going? (to an older friend)

pêe mâi bpai

พี่ไม่ไป

I'm not going. (to younger friend)

My older brother/sister isn't going.

2 'HOW MANY?' QUESTIONS

How many? questions are formed by the pattern, VERB + (NOUN) + **gèe** + CLASSIFIER; the answer normally takes the form (NOUN) + **number** + CLASSIFIER:

mee pêe nórng gèe kon?

มีพี่น้องกี่คน

How many brothers and sisters do you have?

- sŏrng kon

- สองคน

- Two.

3 pôo

pôo (*one who …*) occurs as the first element in a number of common nouns:

pôo-jùt-gahn	*manager*	ผู้จัดการ
pôo-chai	*male*	ผู้ชาย
pôo-yǐng	*female*	ผู้หญิง
pôo-yài	*adult*	ผู้ใหญ่

4 CHILDREN

The word **lôok** (*child, children*) means children in the sense of 'offspring'. Thais use **lôok** in sentences such as *How many children do you have?*, *Her children are lovely!*, *Whose child is that?* and so on. When talking about children as an age category, in statements such as *Thai children are very polite*, *Children under 12 not admitted* and so on, the word **dèk** is used:

mee lôok réu yung?

มีลูกหรือยัง

Do you have any children?

dèk tai dtôrng ree-un pah-săh ung-grìt

เด็กไทยต้องเรียนภาษาอังกฤษ

Thai children have to learn English.

The gender of one's children are specified in the same way as brothers and sisters, using **chai** for males and **săo** for females:

lôok chai	*son*	ลูกชาย
lôok săo	*daughter*	ลูกสาว

5 AGE

For children up to the age of 12 or 13, age is expressed using the patterns **ah-yÓO** (*age*) + NUMBER + **kòo-up** (*years old*). For people older than that, the pattern is **ah-yÓO** (*age*) + NUMBER + **bpee** (*year*), although **bpee** is often omitted. When asking someone's age, the question word **tâo-rài?** (*how much?*) is used:

lôok săo ah-yÓO sìp kòo-up

ลูกสาวอายุสิบขวบ

My daughter is 10 years old.

lôok chai ah-yÓO sìp hâh (bpee)

ลูกชายอายุสิบห้า(ปี)

My son is 15.

ah-yÓO tâo-rài?

อายุเท่าไหร่

How old is she?

6 *nâh* + VERB

nâh occurs before a verb to form an adjective that conveys the sense *worthy of …*:

rúk	*to love*	**nâh rúk**	*loveable, cute*	น่ารัก
yòo	*to live*	**nâh yòo**	*nice to live in*	น่าอยู่
gin	*to eat*	**nâh gin**	*tasty*	น่ากิน

nâh sĕe-a dai!

น่าเสียดาย

What a shame!

nâh rúk jing jing

น่ารักจริงๆ

It's really cute.

Chee-ung-mài nâh yòo

เชียงใหม่น่าอยู่

Chiangmai is a nice place to live.

7 'WHO?' QUESTIONS

The question word **krai** (*who?*) occurs either at the beginning of the question or at the end, depending on its function:

dèk kon née bpen krai?

เด็กคนนี้เป็นใคร

Who is this child?

krai pôot?

ใครพูด

Who is speaking?

kOOn yàhk ja pôot gùp krai?

คุณอยากจะพูดกับใคร

Who do you want to speak to?

Exercises

 11.06

1 How would you ask someone:
- **a** *how many brothers and sisters they have?*
- **b** *how many older sisters they have?*
- **c** *how many younger brothers they have?*
- **d** *how many children they have?*
- **e** *how many sons they have?*
- **f** *how many daughters they have?*

 11.07

2 How would you ask someone:
- **a** *how many pairs of shoes they bought?*
- **b** *how many shirts they bought?*
- **c** *how many bottles of Pepsi they drank?*
- **d** *how many glasses of orange juice they drank?*
- **e** *how many kilos of oranges they want?*
- **f** *how many mangoes they want?*

 11.08

3 Listen to the recording and repeat after the speaker, paying special attention to the tones:

réu yung?	**láir-o réu yung?**	**dtàirng ngahn láir-o réu yung?**
réu yung?	**láir-o réu yung?**	**mee lôok láir-o réu yung?**
réu yung?	**láir-o réu yung?**	**sùng a-hǎhn láir-o réu yung?**

Reading and writing

1 CONSONANTS

🔊 **11.09**

The consonants in this unit are not very common and you need not worry too much about memorizing them at this stage. The class of each consonant is indicated beneath the letter:

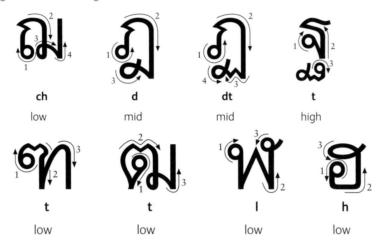

ch	d	dt	t
low	mid	mid	high

t	t	l	h
low	low	low	low

2 VOWEL SHORTENER: -ะ

You have already met the vowel symbol –ะ as a short **-a** vowel (Unit 9).

The same symbol also has a completely different function in shortening the long vowels เ-, แ-, โ-, เ-อ and radically changing the pronunciation of เ-า:

เะ	แะ	โะ	เอะ	เาะ
-e	-air	-o	-er	-or

Reading practice

1 WORDS

🔊 **11.10**

เยะ	เละเทะ	เตะ	เกะกะ
และ	แกะ	แพะ	แตะ
โต๊ะ	เลอะเทอะ	เยอะ	เยอะแยะ
เพราะ	เกาะ	เหมาะ	หัวเราะ

2 DIALOGUE

 11.11

Malee	พี่ชายมีลูกกี่คนคะ
Somchai	มีสองคนครับ
	ผู้ชายคนหนึ่ง ผู้หญิงคนหนึ่ง
Malee	อายุเท่าไหร่คะ
Somchai	ลูกชายอายุสิบห้าปีครับ ลูกสาวอายุสิบขวบ

1 What are Malee and Somchai talking about?

2 How old is the son?

3 And the daughter?

3 DIALOGUE

Sue has gone to register at a local clinic. A receptionist is taking down details from the answers Sue gives. Write down the questions the receptionist asked:

Receptionist	_____?
Sue	ชื่อ Susan ค่ะ
Receptionist	_____?
Sue	นามสกุล Ford ค่ะ
Receptionist	_____?
Sue	อายุ ๓๕ ค่ะ
Receptionist	_____?
Sue	แต่งงานแล้วค่ะ
Receptionist	_____?
Sue	มีแล้วค่ะ มีลูกชายคนหนึ่ง ลูกสาวคนหนึ่ง

Key points

1 **pêe nórng** (*brothers and sisters*) tells us about relative age, but not gender.

2 Female gender-specific words are: **pôo-yǐng** (*girl, female*); **pêe sǎo** (*older sister*); **nórng sǎo** (*younger sister*); **lôok sǎo** (*daughter*).

3 Male gender-specific words are: **pôo-chai** (*boy, male*); **pêe chai** (*older brother*); **nórng chai** (*younger brother*); **lôok chai** (*son*).

4 *How many?* questions: VERB + (NOUN) + **gèe** + CLASSIFIER.

5 **krai?** (*who?*) can occur at the beginning or end of a question depending on the meaning.

6 **nâh** + verb means *'worth ...ing'*.

7 Consonants: ฌ ฎ ฏ ฐ ฑ ฒ ฬ ฮ

8 Vowel shortener: -ะ

12 kǒr pôot gùp kOOn Sǒmchai nòy dâi mái?
Can I speak to Khun Somchai, please?
ขอพูดกับคุณสมชายหน่อยได้ไหม

In this unit, you will learn:

▶ *the language of telephone transactions*
▶ *how to talk about the future:* ja + *verb*
▶ *when? questions*
▶ *polite requests: asking someone to do something*
  for you chôo-ay + *verb* + nòy
▶ *verbs of saying and thinking with* wâh
▶ *how to seek advice and make suggestions*
▶ *miscellaneous spelling rules*

Dialogues

kǒr pôot gùp kOOn sǒmchai nòy

Peter telephones Somchai at home, but it is Somchai's daughter who takes the call:

QUICK VOCAB

hun-lǒh	*hello* (on the telephone)	ฮัลโหล
ror	*to wait*	รอ
sùk krôo	*a moment*	สักครู่
òrk	*to go out*	ออก
kûng nôrk	*outside, out*	ข้างนอก
ja	*future time marker*	จะ
glùp	*to return*	กลับ
mêu-rài?	*when?*	เมื่อไร
sâhp	*to know* (formal)	ทราบ
dtorn yen	*evening*	ตอนเย็น
toh	*to telephone, call*	โทร
mài	*again; new*	ใหม่

Peter	ฮัลโหล ขอพูดกับ	hun-lŏh. kŏr pôot gùp
	คุณสมชายหน่อย	kOOn Sŏmchai nòy
	ได้ไหมครับ	dâi mái krúp?
Daughter	รอสักครู่นะคะ	ror sùk krôo ná ká. ... ...
	คุณพ่อไม่อยู่ค่ะ	kOOn pôr mâi yòo kà.
	ออกไปข้างนอกแล้ว	òrk bpai kûng nôrk láir-o.
Peter	หรือครับ	lĕr krúp?
	จะกลับมาเมื่อไร	ja glùp mah mêu-rài?
Daughter	ไม่ทราบค่ะ	mâi sâhp kà.
	คิดว่าจะกลับมา	kít wâh ja glùp mah
	ตอนเย็นค่ะ	dtorn yen kà.
Peter	ไม่เป็นไรครับ	mâi bpen rai krúp.
	ตอนเย็นจะโทรมาใหม่	dtorn yen ja toh mah mài.
Daughter	ค่ะ สวัสดีค่ะ	kà. sa-wùt dee kà.
Peter	สวัสดีครับ	sa-wùt dee krúp.

● INSIGHT

Somchai's daughter uses the formal word **sâhp** (*to know*) when speaking to her father's friend; with her own friends she would use the informal **róo**.

1 Where is Somchai?

2 When will Somchai return home?

3 What does Peter decide to do?

chôo-ay pôot dung dung nòy dâi mái?

Peter calls back that same evening:

QUICK VOCAB

chôo-ay … nòy	*please…*	ช่วย...หน่อย
dung	*loud*	ดัง
săi	*(telephone) line*	สาย
dee	*good*	ดี

dâi yin	to hear	ได้ยิน
fàhk	to leave, entrust, deposit	ฝาก
kôr kwahm	message	ขอความ
bòrk wâh	to say that; tell someone that	บอกว่า
prÔOng née	tomorrow	พรุ่งนี้

🔊 12.02

Peter	ฮัลโหล ขอพูดกับ	hun-lŏh. kŏr pôot gùp
	คุณสมชายหน่อย	kOOn Sŏmchai nòy
	ได้ไหมครับ	dâi mái krúp?
Daughter	ใครพูดคะ	krai pôot ká?
Peter	ผมปีเตอร์ครับ	pŏm Peter krúp.
Daughter	ใครนะ	krai ná?
	ช่วยพูดดังๆหน่อย	chôo-ay pôot dung dung nòy
	ได้ไหมคะ	dâi mái ká?
	สายไม่ดี ไม่ได้ยิน	săi mâi dee. mâi dâi yin.
Peter	ครับ ผมปีเตอร์ครับ	krúp. pŏm Peter krúp.
Daughter	ออ คุณปีเตอร์หรือคะ	ôr kOOn Peter lĕr ká?
	คุณพอยังไม่กลับค่ะ	kOOn pôr yung mâi glùp kà.
	จะฝากขอความไหมคะ	ja fàhk kôr kwahm mái ká?
Peter	ช่วยบอกคุณพ่อว่า	chôo-ay bòrk kOOn pôr wâh
	ปีเตอร์โทรมาครับ	Peter toh mah krúp.
	แล้วพรุ่งนี้	láir-o prÔOng née
	จะโทรมาใหม่	ja toh mah mài.
Daughter	ค่ะ สวัสดีค่ะ	kà. sa-wùt dee kà.
Peter	สวัสดีครับ	sa-wùt dee krúp.

1 Why can't Somchai's daughter understand Peter at first?

2 What does she tell Peter?

3 What message does Peter leave?

póp gun têe-nǎi dee?

Malee calls Sue and they arrange to meet:

QUICK VOCAB

sa-bai dee	*to be well*	สบายดี
gin kâo	*to eat*	กินข้าว
dôo-ay gun	*together*	ด้วยกัน
see	(See Language notes)	ซี
póp	*to meet*	พบ
nâh	*in front of*	หน้า
děe-o	*in a minute, shortly*	เดี๋ยว
jer	*to meet (informal)*	เจอ

 12.03

Malee	ฮัลโหล	hun-lǒh.
	คุณซูใช่ไหมคะ	kOOn Sue châi mái ká?
Sue	ใช่ค่ะ	châi kà.
Malee	มาลีพูดนะคะ	Malee pôot ná ká.
	เป็นอย่างไรบ้างคะ	bpen yung-ngai bâhng ká?
	สบายดีไหม	sa-bai dee mái?
Sue	สบายดีค่ะ	sa-bai dee kà.
Malee	คุณซูกินข้าวหรือยัง	kOOn Sue gin kâo réu yung?
Sue	ยังค่ะ	yung kà.
Malee	ไปกินด้วยกันไหม	bpai gin dôo-ay gun mái?
Sue	ดีซีคะ	dee see ká.
	พบกันที่ไหนดี	póp gun têe-nǎi dee?
Malee	หน้าออฟฟิศฉัน ดีไหม	nâh órp-fìt chún dee mái?
Sue	ดีซีคะ	dee see ká.
Malee	โอเค เดี๋ยวเจอกันนะ	oh kay, děe-o jer gun ná.
	หวัดดีค่ะ	wùt dee kà.
Sue	ค่ะ หวัดดีค่ะ	kà. wùt dee ká.

1 Why does Malee call Sue?

2 Where do they arrange to meet?

โทรศัพท์	โทร	โท	ศูนย์
toh-ra-sùp	**toh**	**toh**	**sŏon**
telephone	*phone/tel.*	*two*	*zero*

Key phrases and expressions

🔊 12.04

1 Could I speak to … please?

kŏr pôot gùp … nòy dâi mái?   ขอพูดกับ...หน่อยได้ไหม

2 Who's speaking, please?

krai pôot krúp/ká?   ใครพูดครับ/คะ

3 Hold on a moment, please

ror sùk krôo   รอสักครู่

4 Could you speak up a bit, please?

chôo-ay pôot dung dung   ช่วยพูดดังๆหน่อยได้ไหม
    nòy dâi mái?

5 Khun X isn't in.

kOOn X mâi yòo

คุณ X ไม่อยู่

6 Do you want to leave a message?

ja fàhk kôr kwahm mái?

จะฝากข้อความไหม

7 The line is bad.

săi mâi dee

สายไม่ดี

8 I can't hear.

mâi dâi yin

ไม่ได้ยิน

9 This is … speaking.

… pôot

… พูด

10 How are you?

bpen yung-ngai bâhng?

เป็นอย่างไรบ้าง

sa-bai dee mái?

สบายดีไหม

11 I'll ring back.

ja toh mah mài

จะโทรมาใหม่

12 Could I have extension …, please?

kŏr dtòr ber …

ขอต่อเบอร์ …

13 Sorry, I've got the wrong number.

kŏr-tôht toh pìt ber

ขอโทษ โทรผิดเบอร์

Language notes

1 TALKING ABOUT THE FUTURE: *ja* + VERB

As we have already mentioned, Thai verbs do not change their endings to indicate tense in the same way as verbs in European languages. Often it is only from the context that you can tell whether a Thai is talking about something that will happen in the future or something that has already happened in the past. When you want to be quite specific about referring to the future, you add the word **ja** immediately before the verb; but **ja** is frequently omitted when an expression of time makes it clear that the speaker is referring to the future.

káo (ja) glùp mah dtorn bai

เขา(จะ)กลับมาตอนบ่าย

He'll be back in the afternoon.

prÔOng née (ja) toh mah mài

พรุ่งนี้(จะ)โทรมาใหม่

I'll ring back tomorrow.

ja fàhk kôr kwahm mái ká?

จะฝากข้อความไหม

Do you want to leave a message?

2 'WHEN?' QUESTIONS

The question word **mêu-rài?** (*when?*) normally occurs at the end of a sentence. A time expression alone is often sufficient answer, but this may be preceded by a verb:

káo ja glùp mah mêu-rài?

เขาจะกลับมาเมื่อไร

When will he be back?

- (káo ja glùp mah) dtorn bai

- (เขาจะกลับมา)ตอนบ่าย

(He'll be back) in the afternoon.

When **mêu-rài** occurs at the beginning of the question, it often conveys a sense of urgency or irritation on the part of the speaker:

mêu-rài káo ja glùp mah?

เมื่อไรเขาจะกลับมา

When will he be back?

mêu-rài kOOn ja bòrk káo?

เมื่อไรคุณจะบอกเขา

When will you tell him?

3 PARTS OF THE DAY

dtorn means *section* or *period of time*. It occurs commonly with the words for *morning*, *afternoon* and *evening*. When referring to the time of day when an action takes place, Thai does not need the word for *in*:

glùp mah dtorn yen

กลับมาตอนเย็น

He'll be back in the evening.

dtorn cháo	*morning, in the morning*	ตอนเช้า
dtorn bài	*afternoon, in the afternoon*	ตอนบ่าย
dtorn yen	*evening, in the evening*	ตอนเย็น

| dtorn glahng wun | daytime, in the daytime | ตอนกลางวัน |
| dtorn glahng keun | night time, in the night time | ตอนกลางคืน |

Time expressions can occur at the beginning or end of a sentence:

rao ja bpai dtorn yen

เราจะไปตอนเย็น

We'll go in the evening.

dtorn yen rao ja bpai

ตอนเย็นเราจะไป

In the evening we'll go.

4 POLITE REQUESTS: ASKING SOMEONE TO DO SOMETHING

When asking someone to do something, the pattern **chôo-ay** + VERB (**+ nòy**) is used.
nòy is optional but makes the request more polite; you can add … **dâi mái?** for additional politeness:

chôo-ay pôot dung dung nòy dâi mái

ช่วยพูดดังๆหน่อยได้ไหม

Could you speak louder please?

chôo-ay bòrk kOOn pôr wâh Peter toh mah

ช่วยบอกคุณพ่อว่าปีเตอร์โทรมา

Please tell your father that Peter rang.

Be careful not to confuse **chôo-ay** …, used when asking someone else to do something, and
kǒr … (Unit 7), used when asking to do something yourself:

chôo-ay pôot gùp kOOn Sǒmchai nòy

ช่วยพูดกับคุณสมชายหน่อย

Please speak to Khun Somchai.

kǒr pôot gùp kOOn Sǒmchai nòy?

ขอพูดกับคุณสมชายหน่อย

Could I speak to Khun Somchai, please?

chôo-ay jòrt rót têe nôhn dâi mái?

ช่วยจอดรถที่โน่นได้ไหม

Could you park the car over there, please?

kŏr jòrt rót têe nôhn dâi mái?

ขอจอดรถที่โน่นได้ไหม

Can I park the car over there, please?

5 VERBS OF THINKING/SAYING/KNOWING + *wâh*

wâh links verbs of speaking (e.g. **bòrk** *to say*), mental activity (e.g. **kít** *to think*) and perception (e.g. **sâhp** *to know*) to a following clause; it is like English 'that' in *you said that …, he thinks that …, I know that …*:

kít wâh pah-săh tai pôot yâhk

คิดว่าภาษาไทยพูดยาก

I think Thai is difficult to speak.

káo bòrk wâh ja glùp mah dtorn yen

เขาบอกว่าจะกลับมาตอนเย็น

He said that he'd be back in the evening.

káo mâi sâhp wâh rao ja mâi bpai

เขาไม่ทราบว่าเราจะไม่ไป

He doesn't know we're not going.

When **wâh** occurs with **bòrk**, it can introduce both indirect and direct speech; in indirect speech **wâh** is equivalent to *that* and in direct speech it serves the same function as inverted commas:

káo bòrk wâh (káo) ja mâi bpai

เขาบอกว่า(เขา)จะไม่ไป

He said that he wasn't going.

káo bòrk wâh (pŏm) ja mâi bpai

เขาบอกว่า(ผม)จะไม่ไป

He said, 'I'm not going.'

Notice that when the pronouns in the second clause are omitted, indirect and direct speech are indistinguishable.

6 SEEKING ADVICE AND MAKING SUGGESTIONS

The question words *how?, where?, when?, who?* and *how many?* are used in the pattern verb + question word + **dee** when seeking advice:

póp gun têe-năi dee?

พบกันที่ไหนดี

Where shall we meet?

glùp mêu-rài dee?

กลับเมื่อไรดี

When shall we return?

bpai yung-ngai dee?

ไปอย่างไรดี

How shall I go?

A simple way of making a suggestion is to add ... **dee mái?** (*is it good?*) to the end of a statement:

póp gun nâh órp-fit chún dee mái?

พบกันหน้าออฟฟิศฉันดีไหม

Shall we meet in front of my office?

gin a-hâhn jeen dee mái?

กินอาหารจีนดีไหม

Shall we eat Chinese food?

glùp prÔOng née dee mái?

กลับพรุ่งนี้ดีไหม

Shall I go back tomorrow?

7 MOOD PARTICLE: *see* (II)

In Unit 10, you met the particle **see** used when contradicting a negative statement. Another use of **see**, illustrated in this unit, is to emphasize a *yes* answer to a question:

póp gun nâh órp-fit chún dee mái?

พบกันหน้าออฟฟิศฉันดีไหม

How about meeting in front of my office?

- dee see!

- ดีซี

- Ooh, yes!

ao ber toh-ra-sùp meu těu mái?

เอาเบอร์โทรศัพท์มือถือไหม

Do you want her mobile phone number?

- ao see

- เอาซี

- Ooh, yes, please!

Exercises

1 How would you:
  a *ask to speak to Malee?*
  b *ask someone to speak a little louder?*
  c *ask someone to hang on for a moment?*
  d *ask who is speaking?*
  e *ask when Malee will return?*

2 You are thinking of doing a number of things today. Use **pǒm/chún kít wâh ja ...** to state your intention to:
  a *go out in the morning.*
  b *go to the post office in the morning.*
  c *go to Somchai's house in the afternoon.*
  d *return in the evening.*

🔊 **12.05**

3 Khun Somchai has told you his plans for the day (in the following). Pass on the information to Malee, beginning **kOOn Sǒmchai bòrk wâh ja ...**:
  a *I'll go to the bank in the morning.*
  b *I'm going to Damrong's house in the afternoon.*
  c *I'll park my car in the Thammasat area.*
  d *I'll return home in the evening.*

🔊 **12.06**

4 Ask when Khun Somchai is going to do these things:
  a *return*
  b *be in/at home*
  c *know*
  d *ring*
  e *tell you*
  f *ring and tell you*

Reading and writing

You have now covered the principal features of the Thai writing system. This unit looks at some of the most common spelling irregularities and miscellaneous diacritics that you are likely to encounter when reading an ordinary passage of Thai.

1 THE LETTER ร

The letter ร is normally pronounced **n** at the end of a word:

อาหาร	**ah-hăhn**	*food*
ควร	**koo-un**	*should*
ผู้จัดการ	**pôo-jùt gahn**	*manager*

In a number of words, however, ร is pronounced **orn** at the end of a word:

พร	**porn**	*gift, blessing*
ละคร	**la-korn**	*theatre*
นคร	**na-korn**	*Nakhorn (in place names)*

In certain words, ร is not pronounced at all:

| จริง | **jing** | *true* |
| สระ | **sà** | *swimming pool* |

ทร at the beginning of a word is pronounced **s**:

ทราบ	**sâhp**	*to know*
ทรง	**song**	*breast*
ทราย	**sai**	*sand*

When -รร occurs at the end of a word or syllable it is pronounced **-un**; if it is followed by a final consonant it is pronounced **-u**:

รถบรรทุก	**rót bun-tÓOk**	*lorry*
พรรค	**púk**	*(political) party*
กรรม	**gum**	*fate, karma*

2 *r* IN *ung-grìt*

The Thai spelling of **ung-grìt** (*English*) uses the rare symbol ฤ to represent the **ri** sound:

| อังกฤษ | **ung-grìt** | *English* |

3 LETTERS THAT ARE NOT PRONOUNCED AT THE END OF A WORD

When the symbol ◌์ (**gah-run**) occurs above a consonant, that consonant is not pronounced. It occurs in words of foreign origin and reflects the spelling in the original language.

เบอร์	ber	number
จอห์น	jorn	John
เสาร์	săo	Saturday
อาทิตย์	ah-tít	Sunday, week

Sometimes it is not only the consonant below ◌์ that is not pronounced, but also the one immediately preceding it:

| จันทร์ | jun | Monday, moon |
| ศาสตร์ | sàht | science |

In some cases, even though there is no ◌์, the final consonant is still not pronounced:

| บัตร | bùt | card |
| สมัคร | sa-mùk | to join |

And in other cases, a short vowel at the end of a word is not pronounced:

| ชาติ | châht | nation |
| เหตุ | hàyt | reason |

4 LINKER SYLLABLES

There are a number of words that appear to have only two syllables but in fact are joined by a linker syllable so that they become three-syllable words. The final consonant of the first syllable also acts as the initial consonant of the linker syllable which has a short **a** vowel:

| ชนบท | chon-na-bòt | countryside |
| ผลไม้ | pôn-la-mái | fruit |

5 MISMATCH BETWEEN PRONUNCIATION AND SPELLING

There are a few common words that are pronounced with a high tone in normal conversation when the spelling suggests that the tone should be rising. When these words are spoken in isolation, however, they will be pronounced with a rising tone.

ไหม	mái	(question particle)
ฉัน	chún	I
เขา	káo	he, she, they

6 SYMBOLS ๆ AND ฯ

You are most likely to meet the symbol ฯ in the word **grOOng-tâyp**, the Thai name for Bangkok. It really means 'etc.' and is used to abbreviate the extremely long full name of the capital. The symbol ๆ indicates that the preceding word should be repeated:

| กรุงเทพฯ | **grOOng-tâyp** | *Bangkok* |
| ช้าๆ | **cháh cháh** | *slow(ly)* |

How are you progressing?

You have now covered the main features of the Thai writing system and you should find that if you cover up the romanized part of the dialogues and focus on just the Thai script you can read every word.

At this point, it is worth going back over the earlier units and working through all the dialogues again, reading just the Thai script. It will almost certainly be slow work at first. But if you keep re-reading the same dialogues, you will find that your reading speed steadily improves and that your eye begins to skim quickly over letters without having to pause to think carefully about each one.

The reading speed that you develop on familiar passages will gradually transfer itself to new, previously unseen passages.

Reading practice

1 A number of provinces include the word **na-korn** in their name. **na-korn** comes from a Sanskrit word meaning city. Match the Thai script spelling with the normal romanization of these place names:

i	นครปฐม	a	**Nakhorn Ratchasima**
ii	นครนายก	b	**Nakhorn Phanom**
iii	นครสวรรค์	c	**Sakol Nakhorn**
iv	นครราชสีมา	d	**Nakhorn Srithammarat**
v	นครพนม	e	**Nakhorn Sawan**
vi	สกลนคร	f	**Nakhorn Nayok**
vii	นครศรีธรรมราช	g	**Nakhorn Pathom**

2 Here are some words from earlier units with the 'killer' symbol over one of the letters. Some of these words are recognizably from English while others come from Sanskrit, the classical language of India:

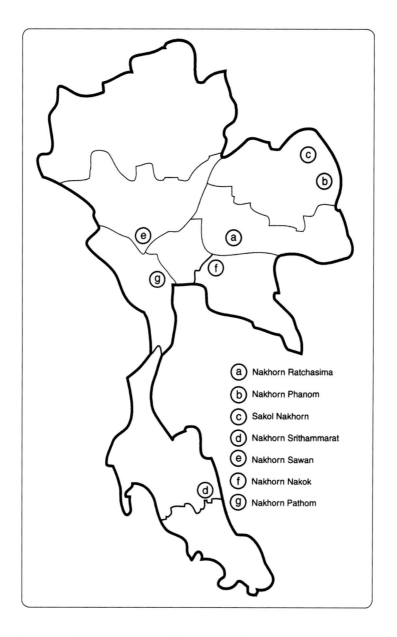

a. Nakhorn Ratchasima

b. Nakhorn Phanom

c. Sakol Nakhorn

d. Nakhorn Srithammarat

e. Nakhorn Sawan

f. Nakhorn Nakok

g. Nakhorn Pathom

ปีเตอร์ อาจารย์   ธรรมศาสตร์ อินเตอร์เนท
เบอร์ ไปรษณีย์ โทรศัพท์   สถานีรถเมล์

3 DIALOGUE

In the middle of a telephone conversation, Sue gets flustered but regains her poise when Damrong comes to her aid:

🔊 12.07

Sue	ฮัลโหล ขอพูดกับคุณน้อยได้ไหมคะ
Thai voice	ใครนะคะ
Sue	อะไรนะคะ
Thai voice	คุณอยากจะพูดกับใคร
Sue	ฮัลโหล คุณน้อยอยู่ไหมคะ
Thai voice	ไม่ได้ยิน พูดดังๆ หน่อยได้ไหม
Sue	ขอโทษ คุณพูดภาษาอังกฤษเป็นไหมคะ
Thai voice	ออ รอสักครู่นะคะ
Damrong	ฮัลโหล ออ ... คุณซูใช่ไหมครับ
Sue	ใช่ค่ะ อยากจะพูดกับคุณน้อยค่ะ
Damrong	คุณน้อยไม่อยู่ครับ เอาเบอร์โทรศัพท์มือถือไหม
Sue	เอาซีค่ะ ช้าๆนะคะ
Damrong	โอเค เบอร์ ๐๑ ๕๖๔ ๕๖๖๔
Sue	ขอบคุณมากค่ะ สวัสดีค่ะ
Damrong	หวัดดีครับ

1 Who does Sue want to talk to?

2 Why can't she?

3 What assistance does Damrong offer?

Key points

1 To talk about future events, use **ja** + VERB.

2 **... mêu-rài?** (*when?*) normally occurs at the end of a sentence.

3 When asking someone to do something for you, use **chôo-ay** + VERB + **nòy**.

4 **wâh** links verbs of speaking, thinking, knowing to a following clause.

5 The pattern VERB + *wh-* QUESTION WORD + **dee** is used when seeking advice.

6 **... dee mái?** can be added to the end of a statement to turn it into a suggestion.

13 *mâi kâo jai*
I don't understand
ไม่เข้าใจ

In this unit, you will learn:
▶ *coping strategies for when you don't understand*
▶ *to know:* sâhp, róo *and* róo-jùk
▶ *another use of* hâi
▶ *don't ...*
▶ *names of letters*
▶ *how to use a dictionary*

Dialogues

Sue has accompanied some Thai friends to a restaurant:

mâi kâo jai

QUICK VOCAB

bplah	fish	ปลา
kem	salty	เค็ม
èek tee	again	อีกที
kâo jai	to understand	เข้าใจ
cháh	slow	ช้า

 13.01

Chanida	ปลาเค็มมากไหมคะ	bplah kem mâhk mái ká?
Sue	อะไรนะคะ	a-rai ná ká?
	พูดอีกทีได้ไหม	pôot èek tee dâi mái?
Chanida	ปลาเค็มมากไหม	bplah kem mâhk mái?
Sue	ไม่เข้าใจ	mâi kâo jai
	พูดช้าๆหน่อย	pôot cháh cháh nòy
	ได้ไหม	dâi mái?

pah-săh ung-grìt bplair wâh a-rai?

Sue has asked Chanida to speak more slowly, but she's still struggling to understand:

QUICK VOCAB

róo-jùk	*to know*	รู้จัก
kum	*word*	คำ
bplair	*to translate*	แปล
… bplair wâh a-rai?	*what does … mean?*	…แปลว่าอะไร
sa-gòt	*to spell*	สะกด

🔊 13.02

Chanida	ปลาเค็มมากไหม	bplah - kem – mâhk - mái?
Sue	ไม่รู้จักคำว่า เค็ม	mâi róo-jùk kum wâh 'kem'.
	ภาษาอังกฤษ แปลว่า	pah-săh ung-grìt bplair wâh
	อะไร	a-rai?
Chanida	แปลว่า *salty*	bplair wâh 'salty'.
Sue	อ๋อ เข้าใจแล้ว เค็มค่ะ	ôr kâo jai láir-o kem
	เค็มมาก	kà. kem mâhk.
	เค็ม สะกดอย่างไร	'kem' sa-gòt yung-ngai?

● **INSIGHT**

Full marks to Sue for wanting to learn the spelling of a new word, but if she doesn't know the names of Thai letters (given later in this unit), she may be floored by the answer. Maybe Peter's strategy, in the next conversation, is better.

1 What was the Thai word that Sue didn't know?

2 How did she try to ensure that she would remember it in future?

3 How did she answer Chanida's original question?

fung róo rêu-ung mái?

Peter is also in a restaurant. His Thai companions are chattering away in Thai when Somchai suddenly turns to him:

QUICK VOCAB

fung	*to listen*	ฟัง
róo rêu-ung	*to understand*	รู้เรื่อง
fa-rùng	*'farang', Caucasian*	ฝรั่ง
ngong	*to be dazed, confused*	งง
ray-o	*quickly*	เร็ว
nin-tah	*to gossip*	นินทา
yàh	*don't*	อย่า
chêu-a	*to believe*	เชื่อ
pôot lên	*to joke*	พูดเล่น
sa-měr	*always*	เสมอ
hâi	*for*	ให้

🔊 13.03

Somchai	คุณ *Peter* ฟังรู้เรื่อง ไหม	kOOn Peter fung róo rêu-ung mái?
Peter	อะไรนะครับ	a-rai ná krúp?
Malee	ฝรั่งงง	fa-rùng ngong.
Somchai	ฟังรู้เรื่องไหม	fung róo rêu-ung mái?
Peter	ไม่รู้เรื่อง ถ้าพูดเร็ว ผมก็ไม่รู้เรื่องเลย	mâi róo rêu-ung. tâh pôot ray-o pǒm gôr mâi róo rêu-ung ler-ee.
Malee	ไม่เป็นไรหรอก เรานินทาคุณเท่านั้น	mâi bpen rai ròrk. rao nin-tah kOOn tâo-nún.
Peter	นินทาแปลว่าอะไร	'nin-tah' bplair wâh a-rai?
Somchai	แปลว่า *gossip* แต่อย่าไปเชื่อ มาลีนะ คุณมาลีชอบ พูดเล่นเสมอ	bplair wâh 'gossip'. dtàir yàh bpai chêu-a Malee ná. kOOn Malee chôrp pôot lên sa-měr.
Peter	ช่วยเขียน นินทา ให้หน่อย	chôo-ay kěe-un 'nin-tah' hâi nòy.

160

1 What joke does Malee make?

2 Why doesn't Peter get it?

3 What does Peter ask Somchai to do?

● **INSIGHT**

Although you will find Thais extremely complimentary about your attempts to learn Thai, you will almost certainly feel that your linguistic inadequacies are exposed with alarming frequency in the initial stages. One obvious problem is vocabulary. Thai words sound quite unlike any European language and so there is little scope for latching onto a familiar word and then guessing what people are talking about. Even when you stay within your linguistic limitations, you may find a Thai looking absolutely bewildered by your best attempts, only to repeat, with a sudden expression of enlightenment, *exactly* what you just said. Well, *almost* exactly. Maybe you got a tone wrong, a vowel not quite right or maybe your Thai friend was simply more accustomed to foreigners speaking Thai with a German accent. The important thing is not to get discouraged by these little setbacks. Relax. Recognize that on some days you are going to be on better form than on others. Don't worry if everything is going over your head. Be prepared to laugh at yourself. But, most important of all, have some positive strategy for dealing with communication breakdowns and try to analyse where your individual weaknesses lie. Learn different ways of asking someone to repeat something – for even the most patient of Thais may tire of the *farang* whose every other utterance is **a-rai ná?** A knowledge of Thai script is invaluable here, because you can always ask how something is written in Thai (**pah-săh tai kĕe-un yung-ngai?**); and if you weren't sure what tone the word was when you heard it, you can check from the spelling.

Key phrases and expressions

 13.04

How to say

1 Pardon?

a-rai ná?　　　อะไรนะ

2 Could you say that again?

pôot èek tee dâi mái?　　　พูดอีกทีได้ไหม

3 I don't understand.

mâi kâo jai　　　ไม่เข้าใจ

mâi róo rêu-ung　　　ไม่รู้เรื่อง

4 Could you speak slowly, please?

pôot cháh cháh nòy dâi mái?   พูดช้าๆหน่อยได้ไหม

5 I don't know the word ...

mâi róo-jùk kum wâh ...   ไม่รู้จักคำว่า ...

6 What's that in English?

pah-săh ung-grìt bplair wâh a-rai?   ภาษาอังกฤษแปลว่าอะไร

7 What does ... mean?

... bplair wâh a-rai?   ... แปลว่าอะไร

... măi kwahm wâh a-rai?   ... หมายความว่าอะไร

8 How do you spell/write it?

sa-gòt/kĕe-un yung-ngai?   สะกด/เขียนอย่างไร

9 Please write it down for me.

chôo-ay kĕe-un hâi nòy   ช่วยเขียนให้หน่อย

Language notes

1 WHAT DOES THAT MEAN?

There are two ways of asking what something means: **bplair wâh a-rai?** is a request for a translation, while **măi kwahm wâh a-rai?** seeks clarification or an explanation:

pah-săh ung-grìt bplair wâh a-rai?

ภาษาอังกฤษแปลว่าอะไร

What's that in English?

kOOn măi kwahm wâh a-rai?

คุณหมายความว่าอะไร

What do you mean?

2 UNDERSTAND

kâo jai and **róo rêu-ung** both mean *to understand*.

kâo jai literally means 'enter-heart'. It is one of numerous verbs in Thai in which **jai** (*heart*) is the second element Some other common examples are:

dee jai	*to be happy (good + heart)*	ดีใจ
sa-bai jai	*to be happy (well + heart)*	สบายใจ
por jai	*to be satisfied (enough + heart)*	พอใจ

róo rêu-ung often occurs after the verbs **fung** (*to listen*) and **àhn** (*to read*) as a 'resultative verb', where it indicates the 'result' (i.e. understanding) that follows the action of the first verb (i.e. listening, reading):

róo rêu-ung mái?

รู้เรื่องไหม

Do you understand?

fung róo rêu-ung mái?

ฟังรู้เรื่องไหม

Do you understand? (by listening)

àhn róo rêu-ung mái?

อ่านรู้เรื่องไหม

Do you understand? (by reading)

It is the resultative verb that is used for *yes* answers and which is negated for *no* answers:

fung róo rêu-ung mái?

ฟังรู้เรื่องไหม

Do you understand? (by listening)

- róo rêu-ung/mâi róo rêu-ung

- รู้เรื่อง/ไม่รู้เรื่อง

- Yes/No.

Similarly, in negative statements, it is the resultative verb that is negated:

mâi róo rêu-ung

ไม่รู้เรื่อง

I don't understand.

fung mâi róo rêu-ung

ฟังไม่รู้เรื่อง

I don't understand (what I hear).

àhn mâi róo rêu-ung

อ่านไม่รู้เรื่อง

I don't understand (what I read).

3 TO KNOW

Earlier you met two words that mean *to know*: the formal **sâhp** and the informal **róo**. Both of these words are used when talking about knowing something or knowing facts. When you want to answer *I don't know*, you say **mâi róo** or **mâi sâhp**.

Be careful not to confuse **sâhp** and **róo** with **róo-jùk**; **róo-jùk** means *to know* in the sense of being familiar or acquainted with someone, somewhere or something.

mâi róo-jùk kum wâh 'kem'

ไม่รู้จักคำว่า เค็ม

I don't know the word 'kem'.

róo-jùk rohng rairm ree-noh mái?

รู้จักโรงแรมรีโนไหม

Do you know the Reno Hotel?

4 DON'T

Negative commands follow the pattern **yàh** (*don't*) + VERB. They can be made milder by adding the particle **ná** (*right, OK?*) after the verb:

yàh bpai chêu-a Malee ná

อย่าไปเชื่อมาลีนะ

Don't go believing Malee, OK?

yàh bòrk káo ná

อย่าบอกเขานะ

Don't tell him, OK?

yàh tum pèt mâhk ná

อย่าทำเผ็ดมากนะ

Don't make it very spicy, OK?

5 lên

As a main verb, **lên** means to play:

lên fÓOt-born	*to play football*	เล่นฟุตบอล
lên gee-dtah	*to play the guitar*	เล่นกีตาร์

When **lên** follows another verb, it indicates that the action of the first verb is being carried out for fun or in a not very serious manner:

pôot	*to speak*	**pôot lên**	*to joke*	พูดเล่น
chêu	*to be named*	**chêu lên**	*to be nicknamed*	ชื่อเล่น

dern	to walk	dern lên	to go for a walk	เดินเล่น
àhn	to read	àhn lên	to read for pleasure	อ่านเล่น
gin	to eat	gin lên	to eat for fun (e.g. mid-meal snacks)	กินเล่น

kOOn Malee chôrp pôot lên

คุณมาลีชอบพูดเล่น

Khun Malee likes joking.

6 hâi

In Unit 9, you met **hâi** as a causative verb meaning *to get someone to do something*.

Another important use of **hâi** is to indicate the beneficiary of an action, when it can be translated as *for*; this usage often confuses the learner, because in spoken Thai the beneficiary is normally understood from the context and therefore omitted. Thus, when Peter asked Somchai to write down a word for him, there was no need for him to use **pǒm**:

chôo-ay kěe-un 'nin-tah' hâi (pǒm) nòy

ช่วยเขียน นินทา ให้(ผม)หน่อย

Please write 'nin-tah' down for me.

Here are some more examples. Remember, that Thais will often omit the word in brackets. Learning to work out what the omitted word is when Thais use **hâi** will help you to understand and be able to use it more quickly.

krai séu hâi (kOOn)?

ใครซื้อให้(คุณ)

Who bought it for you?

lót hâi (rao) nòy dâi mái?

ลดให้(เรา)หน่อยได้ไหม

Can you give us a discount?

káo sùng a-hǎhn hâi (chún)

เขาสั่งอาหารให้(ฉัน)

He ordered food for me.

Exercises

1 How would you:

   a *tell someone you did not understand?*

   b *ask someone to repeat something?*

   c *ask someone what something means?*

   d *ask someone to speak slowly?*

   e *ask someone how to write something?*

 13.05

2 Use the pattern **chôo-ay** + VERB + **hâi** + **nòy** + **dâi mái?** to ask Khun Somchai to do the following things for you:

   a *park the car for you*

   b *buy some cigarettes for you*

   c *order a plate of chicken fried rice for you*

   d *tell Chanida for you*

 13.06

3 In the last exercise, there was no need to use the pronoun **pǒm/chún** after **hâi** because it was clear that you were asking Khun Somchai to do something for you.

Now ask Khun Somchai to do the same favours for Khun Malee:

EXAMPLE

   a *park the car for Khun Malee*

   chôo-ay jòrt rót hâi kOOn Malee nòy dâi mái?

   b *buy some cigarettes for Khun Malee*

   c *order a plate of chicken fried rice for Khun Malee*

   d *tell Chanida for Khun Malee*

4 Here's Peter, locked in conversation with Malee and stubbornly refusing to be limited by his lack of vocabulary. What do you think he said?

Malee	ker-ee bpai doo nǔng tai mái?
Peter	_____.
Malee	ker-ee bpai doo nǔng tai mái?
Peter	_____.
Malee	ker-ee - bpai - doo - nǔng - tai - mái?
Peter	_____.
Malee	nǔng bplair wâh 'movie' kâo jai mái?
Peter	_____.
Malee	ker-ee - bpai - doo - nǔng - tai - mái?
Peter	mâi ker-ee.

Reading and writing

1 NAMES AND DICTIONARY ORDER OF CONSONANTS

The following table (which should be read from left to right) shows the consonants in alphabetical order with the names of the letters. Most Thais will assume that if you can read and write Thai, you will have learned the consonants in this order and will know the names of all the letters. Some might be quite appalled to know that you have been learning consonants in an apparently random fashion without learning the names of the letters. By all means, learn the names if you wish to impress Thais. But if you feel your brain has limited storage capacity at this stage, and that that storage space should be reserved for practical information, leave this for a rainy day; rest assured that there are many foreigners who read Thai fluently without knowing the consonant names.

ก	ข	ค	ฆ	ง	
gor gài	**kŏr kài**	**kor kwai**	**kor ra-kung**	**ngor ngoo**	
(chicken)	*(egg)*	*(buffalo)*	*(bell)*	*(snake)*	

จ	ฉ	ช	ซ	ฌ	ญ
jor jahn	**chŏr chìng**	**chor cháhng**	**sor sôh**	**chor (ga)** **cher** *(tree)*	**yor yĭng**
(plate)	*(small cymbals)*	*(plate)*	*(chain)*		*(girl)*

ฎ	ฏ	ฐ	ฑ	ฒ	ณ
dor chá-dah	**dtor bpa-dtùk**	**tŏr tăhn**	**tor mon-toh**	**tor tâo** *(old person)*	**nor nayn**
(theatrical crown)	*(goad)*	*(base)*	*(Indra's Queen)*		*(novice)*

ด	ต	ถ	ท	ธ	น
dor dèk *(child)*	**dtor dtào**	**tŏr tŏOng**	**tor ta-hăhn**	**tor tong**	**nor nŏo**
	(turtle)	*(bag)*	*(soldier)*	*(flag)*	*(mouse)*

บ	ป	ผ	ฝ	พ	ฟ	ภ	ม
bor bai mái	**bpor bplah**	**pŏr pêung**	**fŏr făh**	**por pahn**	**for fun**	**por sŭm-pao**	**mor máh**
(leaf)	*(fish)*	*(bee)*	*(lid)*	*(tray)*	*(tooth)*	*(sailing ship)*	*(horse)*

ย	ร	ล	ว	ศ	ษ	ส
yor yúk	**ror reu-a**	**lor ling**	**wor wǎirn**	**sǒr sǎh-lah**	**sǒr reu-sěe**	**sǒr sěu-a**
(giant)	(boat)	(monkey)	(ring)	(pavilion)	(hermit)	(tiger)

ห	ฬ	อ	ฮ
hǒr hèep	**lor jOO-lah**	**or àhng**	**hor nók hôok**
(box)	(kite)	(bowl)	(owl)

2 DICTIONARY ORDER OF VOWELS

The Thai word for vowel is **sa-rà** (สระ). When Thais say the name of a vowel symbol, the vowel sound is preceded by the word **sa-rà**. Thus a Thai would read –า as **sa-rà ah**.

-อ	-ะ	-ึ	-ัว	-า	-ำ	-ิ	-ี
– or	**– a**	**– u**	**– oo-a**	**– ah**	**– um**	**– i**	**– ee**
-ึ	-ื	-ุ	-ู	เ-	เ-ี	เ-ย	เ-อ
– eu	**– eu**	**– OO**	**– oo**	**– ay**	**– e**	**– er-ee**	**– er**
เ-อะ	เ-ะ	เ-า	เ-าะ	เ-	เ-ย	เ-ยะ	เ-ือ
– er	**– e**	**– ao**	**– or**	**– er**	**– ee-a**	**– ee-a**	**– eu-a**
แ-	แ-ื	แ-ะ	โ-	ใ-	ไ-		
– air	**– air**	**– air**	**– oh**	**– ai**	**– ai**		

3 HOW TO USE A DICTIONARY

Words are arranged in alphabetical order of consonants. Thus words beginning with **dor dèk** appear before those that begin with **bor bai mái**. Words that begin with a vowel *sound* (e.g. **àhn**, **òrk**) are written with an initial 'zero' consonant and therefore appear near the end of the dictionary under **or àhng**. Words written with a silent **hǒr hèep** also appear near the end of the dictionary under that letter.

Words beginning with the same consonant are then further arranged in order of, first, consonants and then vowels. Thus words with no written vowel, like บก (**bòk**), บท (**bòt**) and บน (**bon**), appear before words that do have a vowel symbol, such as บาท (**bàht**), บีบ (**hèep**) and ใบ (**bai**).

When the spelling of two word is differentiated only by tone mark, the dictionary order of entry is: *no tone mark*, ่, ้, ๊, ๋.

Although the symbols ร and ว are sometimes read as vowels, their position in the normal order of consonants remains unchanged. Thus กรรม (**gum**) appears before กัน (**gun**).

It will take a little while to find your way around a dictionary and at first it may take several minutes to locate a word. Start by looking up familiar words to build up your confidence. Some dictionaries are listed in the Appendices.

Reading practice

1 DIALOGUE

A foreign businessman is being interviewed about his experience of learning Thai:

QUICK VOCAB

เวลา	*when*	ตำรา	*textbook*
บางครั้ง	*sometimes*	ใช้	*to use*
เหมือนกัน	*similarly, likewise*	ซีดี	*CD*
โรงเรียน	*school*	คง	*sure to, bound to*

 13.07

Interviewer	คุณอยู่เมืองไทยนานไหมครับ
Businessman	ไม่นานครับ ประมาณ ๖ เดือนเท่านั้น
Interviewer	คุณพูดไทยเก่งมากครับ
Businessman	ไม่หรอกครับ เวลาคนไทยพูด บางครั้งผมฟังไม่รู้เรื่องเลย แล้ว เวลาผมพูดภาษาไทย บางครั้งคนไทยก็ฟังไม่รู้เรื่องเหมือนกัน
Interviewer	คุณเรียนภาษาไทยที่ไหนครับ
Businessman	เรียนที่โรงเรียนสอนภาษาอยู่แถวถนนสุขุมวิท แล้วใช้ตำรากับซีดี เรียนที่บ้าน
Interviewer	ภาษาไทยยากไหมครับ
Businessman	ยากครับ แต่ถ้าไม่มีซีดีฟัง ก็คงยากกว่า
Interviewer	แล้วคุณอ่านและเขียนภาษาไทยเป็นไหมครับ
Businessman	อ่านเป็นนิดหน่อยครับ ถ้าเป็นคำง่ายๆ แต่เขียนไม่ค่อยได้

1 How long has the businessman been in Thailand?
2 What communication problems does he sometimes encounter?
3 How did he learn Thai?
4 Can he read and write Thai?

Key points

1 To ask for a translation of a word/sentence, use **bplair wâh a-rai**?

2 Expect to be asked **fung róo rêu-ung mái?** and to hear Thais mutter to each other – in reference to you – **fung mâi róo rêu-ung**; if you do catch this, console yourself with that fact that you are understanding something!

3 **róo-jùk** means *to be acquainted with someone, somewhere or something*.

4 **sâhp** and **róo** mean *to know something/facts*.

5 Negative commands follow the pattern, **yàh** + VERB + (**ná**).

6 VERB + **lên** means that the activity of the verb is done for fun.

7 When **hâi** is used to indicate the beneficiary of an action, it can be translated as *for*.

8 If you ask Thais how to spell a word, you need to know the names of the consonants. You can conceal the fact that you don't know the names by asking someone to write the word down for you.

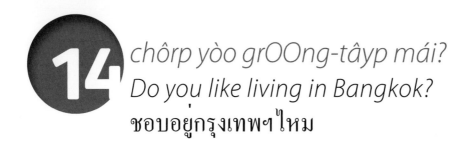

14 chôrp yòo grOOng-tâyp mái?
Do you like living in Bangkok?
ชอบอยู่กรุงเทพฯไหม

In this unit, you will learn:
▶ *how to talk about living and working in Bangkok*
▶ *how to talk about things that happened in the past*
▶ *ker-ee + verb*
▶ *some ways of intensifying adjectives and adverbs*
▶ *some more uses of gôr*

Dialogues

chôrp yòo grOOng-tâyp mái?

Chanida is asking Sue how she likes Bangkok:

QUICK VOCAB

nâh sǒn jai	*interesting*	น่าสนใจ
wâh	*to think, say*	ว่า
nâh yòo	*nice to live (in/at)*	น่าอยู่
nâirn	*crowded*	แน่น
ah-gàht	*air; weather*	อากาศ
sa-àht	*clean*	สะอาด
dtàhng jung-wùt	*upcountry, outside Bangkok*	ต่างจังหวัด

Chanida	คุณซูชอบอยู่	kOOn Sue chôrp yòo
	กรุงเทพฯไหม	grOOng-tâyp mái?
Sue	ชอบค่ะ	chôrp kà.
	คิดว่าน่าสนใจมาก	kít wâh nâh sŏn jai mâhk.
Chanida	จริงหรือคะ	jing lěr ká?
	ฉันว่ากรุงเทพฯ	chún wâh grOOng-tâyp
	ไม่น่าอยู่เลย	mâi nâh yòo ler-ee.
	รถมันติด คนก็แน่น	rót mun dtìt, kon gôr nâirn,
	อากาศก็ไม่สะอาด	ah-gàht gôr mâi sa-àht.
	อยากอยู่ต่างจังหวัด	yàhk yòo dtàhng jung-wùt
	มากกว่า	mâhk gwàh.

1 Why does Sue say she likes living in Bangkok?

2 Why doesn't Chanida like Bangkok?

yái mah yòo têe nêe mêu-a chún yung dèk

Chanida tells Sue a little about her background:

QUICK VOCAB

yái	to move house	ย้าย
mêu-a	when	เมื่อ
yung	still	ยัง
dèk	child	เด็ก
dtorn nún	at that time; then	ตอนนั้น
dtèuk	concrete building	ตึก
sŏong	tall	สูง
mêu-a gòrn	formerly, before	เมื่อก่อน
bòy	often	บ่อย
yêe-um	to visit	เยี่ยม
yai	(maternal) grandmother	ยาย
krúng	time	ครั้ง

Sue	คุณชนิดาเป็น	kOOn cha-ni-dah bpen
	คนกรุงเทพฯ	kon grOOng-tâyp
	ใช่ไหมคะ	châi mái ká?
Chanida	ไม่ใช่ค่ะ พ่อแม่เขา	mâi châi kà. pôr mâir káo
	ย้ายมาอยู่ที่นี่	yái mah yòo têe nêe
	เมื่อฉันยังเด็ก	mêu-a chún yung dèk.
	ตอนนั้นรถไม่ค่อยมี	dtorn nún rót mâi kôy mee
	ตึกสูงก็ไม่ค่อยมี	dtèuk sŏong gôr mâi kôy mee.
Sue	เมื่อก่อนอยู่จังหวัด	mêu-a gòrn yòo jung-wùt
	อะไร	a-rai?
Chanida	เมื่อก่อนเราอยู่ภาคใต้	mêu-a gòrn rao yòo pâhk dtâi.
	ฉันเกิดที่จังหวัด	chún gèrt têe jung-wùt
	ภูเก็ต	poo-gèt.
Sue	กลับภาคใต้บ่อยไหมคะ	glùp pâhk dtâi bòy mái ká?
Chanida	กลับไปเยี่ยมคุณยาย	glùp bpai yêe-um kOOn yai
	ปีละสองสามครั้งค่ะ	bpee la sŏrng săhm krúng kà.

1 What province was Chanida born in?

2 When did she move to Bangkok?

3 What was Bangkok like then?

4 How often does she go back to the south?

dtôrng ton yòo

Peter asks Somchai about his job:

QUICK VOCAB

ngahn	*work*	งาน
mun	*it*	มัน
ngern deu-un	*salary*	เงินเดือน
chái dâi	*acceptable*	ใช้ได้
bèu-a	*to be bored, fed up*	เบื่อ

ker-ee	used to; to have ever done something	เคย
bpen bpai mâi dâi	it's impossible	เป็นไปไม่ได้
kong	sure to; probably	คง
hăh ngahn	to look for work	หางาน
yâir	to be a nuisance, a hassle	แย่
chôo-ay a-rai mâi dâi	it can't be helped	ช่วยอะไรไม่ได้
dtôrng	have to, must	ต้อง
ton	to put up with	ทน

🔊 14.03

Peter	งานเป็นอย่างไร	ngahn bpen yung-ngai?
Somchai	ก็ … ดีเหมือนกัน	gôr …dee mĕu-un gun.
	งานมันน่าสนใจ	ngahn mun nâh sŏn jai
	เงินเดือนก็ใช้ได้	ngern deu-un gôr chái dâi.
	แต่ …	dtàir …
Peter	แต่ อะไรครับ	dtàir a-rai krúp?
Somchai	ผมเบื่อกรุงเทพฯครับ	pŏm bèu-a grOOng-tâyp krúp.
Peter	เคยคิดจะไปอยู่	ker-ee kít ja bpai yòo
	ต่างจังหวัดไหม	dtàhng jung-wùt mai?
Somchai	เคย	ker-ee.
	แต่รู้ว่าเป็นไปไม่ได้	dtàir róo wâh bpen bpai mâi dâi.
	คงหางานทำไม่ได้	kong hăh ngahn tum mâi dâi.
Peter	แย่นะ	yâir ná.
Somchai	ใช่ แย่จริงๆ	châi yâir jing jing.
	แต่ช่วยอะไรไม่ได้	dtàir chôo-ay a-rai mâi dâi.
	ต้องทนอยู่	dtôrng ton yòo.

1 What does Somchai like about his job?

2 What doesn't he like about working in Bangkok?

3 Why doesn't he look for a job outside Bangkok?

mêu-a gòrn chôrp

Chanida is talking to one of the receptionists at work:

QUICK VOCAB

dtorn née	*now*	ตอนนี้
róo-sèuk	*to feel*	รู้สึก
sa-nÒOk	*fun; to be fun*	สนุก
dĕe-o née	*now*	เดี๋ยวนี้
tum-mai lâ?	*why?*	ทำไมล่ะ
jung ler-ee	*really, very*	จังเลย

🔊 14.04

Chanida	งานตอนนี้	ngahn dtorn née
	เป็นอย่างไรคะ	bpen yung-ngai ká?
Receptionist	เมื่อก่อนชอบค่ะ	mêu-a gòrn chôrp kà.
	รู้สึกว่าสนุกดี	róo-sèuk wâh sa-nÒOk dee
	แต่เดี๋ยวนี้ไม่สนุกเลย	dtàir dĕe-o née mâi sa-nÒOk ler-ee.
Chanida	ทำไมล่ะคะ	tum-mai lâ ká?
Receptionist	งานมันน่าเบื่อและ	ngahn mun nâh bèu-a láir
	ผู้จัดการแย่มาก	pôo-jùt gahn yâir mâhk
	จังเลย	jung ler-ee.
Chanida	แย่อย่างไรคะ	yâir yung-ngai ká?
Receptionist	เขาไม่รู้เรื่องอะไร	káo mâi róo rêu-ung a-rai
	เลยค่ะ แล้วเขาไม่	ler-ee kà. láir-o káo mâi
	ชอบหนูด้วย	chôrp nŏo dôo-ay.

1 How has the receptionist's attitude to her job changed?

2 What does she think about her manager?

3 Why?

4 How does she refer to herself when speaking to Chanida?

Bangkok has the reputation of being one of the world's most congested cities. The massive building boom of the late 1980s and early 1990s saw multi-storey office blocks, shopping centres, hotels and condominiums spring up overnight, adding to the environmental nightmare. Special bus lanes, elaborate one-way systems, elevated bypasses and expressways, overhead and underground railway lines have improved the traffic situation enormously in recent years, but the traffic situation continues to affect the quality of life of most Bangkok residents, many leaving home early and returning late in order to avoid the worst of the traffic.

Language notes

1 mêu-a

mêu-a (*when*) is used when talking about things that happened in the past. *Previously/before* can be expressed by **mêu-a gòrn**, while **mêu-a** + TIME EXPRESSION + **gòrn** is one way of expressing ... *ago*:

rao yái mah yòo têe nêe mêu-a chún yung dèk

เราย้ายมาอยู่ที่นี่เมื่อฉันยังเด็ก

We moved here when I was still a child.

mêu-a gòrn rao yòo pâhk dtâi

เมื่อก่อนเราอยู่ภาคใต้

Before we lived in the south.

mêu-a gòrn chôrp

เมื่อก่อนชอบ

I used to like it.

mêu-a kOOn Chanida ah-yÓO hâh kòo-up

เมื่อคุณชนิดาอายุห้าขวบ

when Khun Chanida was five years old

mêu-a sâhm bpee gòrn

เมื่อสามปีก่อน

three years ago

2 *ker-ee* + VERB

The pattern **ker-ee** + VERB is used to indicate that the action of the verb has (1) occurred at least once in the past or (2) occurred habitually in the past:

rao ker-ee bpai têe-o poo-gèt

เราเคยไปเที่ยวภูเก็ต

We have been to Phuket.

pǒm ker-ee ree-un pah-sǎh tai

ผมเคยเรียนภาษาไทย

I used to study Thai.

The negative, **mâi ker-ee** + VERB, means *have never . . .*:

káo mâi ker-ee bpai

เขาไม่เคยไป

He's never been.

chún mâi ker-ee tum

ฉันไม่เคยทำ

I've never done it.

Questions that take the form **ker-ee** + VERB + **mái?** (*Have you ever . . . ?*) are answered either **ker-ee** (*yes*) or **mâi ker-ee** (*no*):

ker-ee bpai mái?

เคยไปไหม

Have you ever been there?

- ker-ee/ mâi ker-ee

- เคย/ไม่เคย

- Yes/No.

ker-ee gin mái?

เคยกินไหม

Have you ever eaten it?

- ker-ee/ mâi ker-ee

- เคย/ไม่เคย

- Yes/No.

ker-ee kít ja bpai yòo dtàhng jung-wùt mái?

เคยคิดจะไปอยู่ต่างจังหวัดไหม

Have you ever thought of going to live upcountry?

3 tum-mai lâ?

When Thais ask *why?* in response to a statement, they frequently add the particle **lâ** after **tum-mai**, as a way of pressing for an explanation; in informal speech **lâ** is often reduced to **â**:

děe-o née mâi sa-nÒOk ler-ee

เดี๋ยวนี้ไม่สนุกเลย

Now it's not fun at all.

- tum-mai lâ?

- ทำไมล่ะ

- Why?

4 gôr

gôr has occurred several times, as a hesitation device (Unit 5), in idiomatic expressions such as … **gôr láir-o gun** (Unit 6) and … **gôr dâi** (Unit 7) and in conditional sentences (**tâh** … **gôr** …, Unit 9). Two further uses are illustrated in this unit. First, **gôr** can mean *too, also*:

rót mâi kôy mee, dtèuk soˇong gôr mâi kôy mee

รถไม่ค่อยมีตึกสูงก็ไม่ค่อยมี

There were hardly any cars and hardly any tall buildings either/too.

rót mun dtìt, kon gôr nâirn

รถมันติด คนก็แน่น

The traffic is bad and it's crowded, too.

kon tai yér, fa-rùng gôr yér

คนไทยเยอะ ฝรั่งก็เยอะ

There were lots of Thais and lots of farangs, too.

Second, when the topic of the sentence occurs at the beginning of the sentence, **gôr** often occurs in the pattern **sòo-un** (*as for*) + TOPIC + **gôr** + VERB; it is rather as if **gôr** is saying 'statement on the topic now coming up':

sòo-un ah-hǎhn tai pǒm gôr chôrp

ส่วนอาหารไทยผมก็ชอบ

As for Thai food, I like it.

sòo-un pah-săh jeen gôr yâhk bpai

ส่วนภาษาจีนก็ยากไป

As for Chinese, it's too difficult.

In spoken Thai, **sòo-un** is often dropped:

ngern deu-un gôr chái dâi

เงินเดือนก็ใช้ได้

As for the salary, it's alright.

ah-hǎhn tai gôr a-ròy

อาหารไทยก็อร่อย

As for Thai food, it's tasty.

5 NOUN + PRONOUN + VERB

The pattern NOUN + PRONOUN + VERB, where the pronoun refers to the noun, occurs commonly in spoken Thai. You may hear some Thais carry the construction across to English, with statements like *My teacher, he is not nice:*

rót mun dtìt

รถมันติด

The traffic is bad.

pôr mâir káo yái mah yòo têe nêe ...

พ่อแม่เขาย้ายมาอยู่ที่นี่ ...

My parents moved here ...

In the second example, there is less stress on the word **káo** when it refers to the preceding noun rather than meaning *his/her/their*. It may take a while for you to hear this difference, but being aware of this pattern and listening out for it (and perhaps noting down examples) at this stage will certainly help to improve your aural comprehension. Thais have similar problems with English and sentences like *Park next to the green house and Park next to the greenhouse.*

6 INTENSIFICATION

The easiest way to intensify an adjective or adverb is to add **mâhk** (*very, much*) after it. In this unit, two additional ways of intensification are introduced: adding **jing jing** or **jung ler-ee** after the adjective, both of which can be translated as *really. . .* or *ever so. . . .* You can also use **mâhk** in front of **jing jing** and **jung ler-ee**; in the latter case it is very often abbreviated in speech to . . . **mâhk ler-ee**. You now have quite a selection of ways for intensifying adjectives, in both positive and negative ways:

dee (mâhk) jing jing	It's really (very) good	ดี(มาก)จริงๆ
dee (mâhk) jung ler-ee	It's really (very) good	ดี(มาก)จังเลย
dee mâhk ler-ee	It's really very good	ดีมากเลย
dee mâhk	It's very good	ดีมาก
dee	It's good	ดี
gôr … dee měu-un gun	Well … it's good (some reservations)	ก็ … ดีเหมือนกัน
mâi kôy dee (tâo-rài)	It's not very good	ไม่ค่อยดี(เท่าไหร่)
mâi dee	It's not good/it's bad	ไม่ดี
mâi dee ler-ee	It's not good at all/ it's very bad	ไม่ดีเลย

7 'BORED' AND 'BORING'

Thais use the word **bèu-a** (*bored, fed up*) and **nâh bèu-a** (*boring*) frequently when complaining:

pǒm bèu-a grOOng-tâyp

ผมเบื่อกรุงเทพฯ

I'm fed up with Bangkok.

ngahn mun nâh bèu-a

งานมันน่าเบื่อ

The work is boring.

Thai students often have difficulty in distinguishing between *bored* and *boring* in English; and when they tell their English teacher *I am very boring in your class,* they misinterpret his nod and smile as a sign that he will try to right matters.

Exercises

 14.05

1 Answer these questions with an emphatic *yes*, using the pattern … **mâhk jing jing** or … **mâhk jung ler-ee**:

   a chôrp mái?
   b dee mái?
   c nâh bèu-a mái?
   d gairng gài pèt mái?
   e a-hǎhn tai a-ròy mái?

2 Complete the following sentences:

    a pǒm/ chún gèrt têe …

    b mêu-a pǒm/ chún yung dèk bâhn pôr mâir yòo têe…

    c mêu-a pǒm/ chún ah-yÓO hâh kòo-up bpai ree-un têe …

    d mêu-a pǒm/ chún ah-yÓO … bpee yái bpai yòo …

3 You are weighing up the advantages and disadvantages of living in Bangkok with living outside the capital. Which statements would you list under each heading?

    a yòo grOOng-tâyp …

    b yòo dtàhng jung-wùt …

    i ah-gàht sa-àht gwàh.

    ii ngern deu-un gôr chái dâi.

    iii kon nâirn.

    iv rót mâi dtìt.

    v ah-gàht mâi dee.

    vi kon mâi kôy nâirn.

    vii rót dtìt jung ler-ee.

    viii ngern deu-un mâi kôy dee.

4 How would you ask someone if they had ever:

    a *been to America?*

    b *studied English?*

    c *eaten Japanese food?*

    d *visited Nakhorn Phanom Province?*

    e *worked outside Bangkok?*

Reading practice

1 Here is some more information about Chanida's family:

QUICK VOCAB

ตำรวจ*	*policeman*
แม่บ้าน	*housewife*
มหาวิทยาลัยมหิดล	*Mahidol University*

*The second syllable is pronounced with a low tone, not a falling tone as you might expect from the rules you have learned.

คุณชนิดาเป็นคนภาคใต้ เกิดที่จังหวัดภูเก็ต
พ่อเป็นตำรวจ แม่เป็นแม่บ้าน
พ่อแม่กับพี่น้องคุณชนิดาย้ายมาอยู่ที่กรุงเทพฯ
เมื่อคุณชนิดาอายุห้าขวบ ตอนนี้น้องชายคุณชนิดา
เรียนอยู่ที่มหาวิทยาลัยมหิดล เขาอยากจะเป็นหมอ
คุณพ่อชนิดาอยากจะให้น้องชายไปเรียนต่อที่
ประเทศอเมริกา

1 How old was Chanida when the family moved to Bangkok?
2 What is Chanida's younger brother doing at the moment?
3 What plans does Chanida's father have for his son's future?
2 Peter is asking Somchai about his place of birth:

Peter	คุณสมชายเป็นคนภาคเหนือใช่ไหม
Somchai	ใช่ ผมเกิดที่เชียงใหม่
	พ่อแม่ย้ายมาอยู่ที่นี่เมื่อสามสิบปีก่อนเมื่อผมยังเด็ก
	พ่ออยากให้ผมเรียนที่นี่เพราะว่าพ่อคิดว่าโรงเรียนที่นี่ดีกว่า
Peter	ชอบอยู่ที่นี่ไหม
Somchai	ไม่ค่อยชอบเท่าไหร่
	ที่นี่รถติดมากจังเลย
	อยู่เชียงใหม่อากาศสะอาดกว่า
	และรถไม่ติดเหมือนที่นี่

1 What province was Somchai born in?
2 How long ago did his parents move to Bangkok?
3 Why did the family move to Bangkok?
4 In what ways does Somchai feel that his place of birth is better than Bangkok?

3 In this passage, a young girl called Tui talks about leaving home and going to work in a noodle shop in Bangkok. Instead of using **chún** (*l*) she refers to herself by her nickname, Tui. This is very common in girls' speech. Here are the new words that you will meet:

QUICK VOCAB

หมู่บ้าน	*village*
ทำนา	*rice farming*
หนัก	*heavy, hard*
ร้านก๋วยเตี๋ยว	*noodle shop*
ล้าง	*to wash*
ชาม	*bowl*
ทั้งวัน	*all day*
บางวัน	*some days*

 14.08

ตุยเป็นคนอีสานค่ะ อยู่หมู่บ้านเล็กๆ ที่จังหวัดหนองคาย
เมื่อก่อนตุยทำนา แต่ไม่ชอบ เพราะว่าเป็นงานหนักมาก
ตุยก็คิดว่าย้ายมาทำงานที่นี่ดีกว่า ตอนนี้ทำงานอยู่ที่
ร้านก๋วยเตี๋ยวอยู่แถวสุขุมวิท ล้างจานล้างชามทั้งวัน
บางวันคิดว่าน่าเบื่อ แต่ไม่อยากกลับบ้านเพราะว่า
ไม่อยากทำนาและเงินเดือนที่นี่ก็ใช้ได้ ดีกว่าต่างจังหวัด

1 What work did Tui do in her village?

2 Why didn't she like it?

3 What does she do all day long in the noodle shop?

4 Is she happy in her work?

5 Why doesn't she want to go home?

Key points

1 **mêu-a** (*when*) is used when talking about things that happened in the past.

2 Use **ker-ee** + VERB to talk about something that occurred at least once in the past or occurred habitually in the past.

3 When you want to ask *why?* in response to a statement, use **tum-mai lâ?**

4 **gôr** can mean *too, also;* another usage is to signal that a statement is about to be made about the topic just mentioned.

5 NOUN + PRONOUN + VERB, where the pronoun refers to the noun, is a common structure in spoken Thai.

6 **jing jing** (*really, very*) and **jung ler-ee** (*really, very*) are used after adjectives or adverbs to intensify the meaning.

7 Be careful to distinguish between **bèu-a** (*bored, fed up*) and **nâh bèu-a** (*boring*).

15 rót fai òrk gèe mohng?
What time does the train leave?
รถไฟออกกี่โมง

In this unit, you will learn:
▶ *how to make travel arrangements*
▶ *to visit: têe-o and yêe-um*
▶ *how to express distance between two places*
▶ *how to tell the time*

Dialogues

dtôrng jorng dtǒo-a lôo-ung nâh

Sue is planning a trip to the northeast. What travel advice does Chanida offer?

QUICK VOCAB

nûng	*to sit; travel by*	นั่ง
rót fai	*train*	รถไฟ
têe-o	*to visit, go out*	เที่ยว
na-korn pa-nom	*Nakhorn Phanom*	นครพนม
ah-tít	*week*	อาทิตย์
nâh	*next*	หน้า
dtòr	*to continue*	ต่อ
rót too-a	*tour bus*	รถทัวร์
kǒrn-gàirn	*Khonkaen*	ขอนแก่น
hàhng jàhk	*to be at a distance from*	ห่างจาก
gi-loh	*kilometre*	กิโล
lǎi	*many; several*	หลาย
chôo-mohng	*hour*	ชั่วโมง
jorng	*to book*	จอง
dtǒo-a	*ticket*	ตั๋ว
lôo-ung nâh	*in advance*	ล่วงหน้า

186

Sue	เราคิดจะนั่งรถไฟ	rao kít ja nûng rót fai
	ไปเที่ยวนครพนม	bpai têe-o na-korn pa-nom
	อาทิตย์หน้า	ah-tít nâh.
Chanida	นั่งรถไฟไป	nûng rót fai bpai
	นครพนมไม่ได้	na-korn pa-nom mâi dâi.
	ถ้าอยากไปรถไฟ	tâh yàhk bpai rót fai
	ก็ต้องต่อรถทัวร์	gôr dtôrng dtòr rót too-a
	ที่ขอนแก่น	têe kŏrn-gàirn.
Sue	หรือคะ ขอนแก่นอยู่	lĕr ká? kŏrn-gàirn yòo
	ห่างจากนครพนม	hàhng jàhk na-korn pa-nom
	กี่กิโลคะ	gèe gi-loh ká?
Chanida	ไม่ทราบค่ะ	mâi sâhp kà.
	คงหลายชั่วโมง	kong lăi chôo-mohng.
	ฉันว่า นั่งรถทัวร์	chún wâh nûng rót too-a
	จากกรุงเทพฯดีกว่า	jàhk grOOng-tâyp dee gwàh.
	แต่ต้องจองตั๋ว	dtàir dtôrng jorng dtŏo-a
	ล่วงหน้า	lôo-ung nâh.

rót òrk gèe mohng?

Peter is booking tickets to Nakhorn Phanom:

QUICK VOCAB

têe	*place*	ที่
gèe mohng?	*what time?*	กี่โมง
sèe tÔOm krêung	*10.30 pm*	สี่ทุ่มครึ่ง
tĕung	*to reach*	ถึง
dtee hâh	*5.00 am*	ตีห้า
kêun	*to get on*	ขึ้น

Peter	ขอโทษครับ	kǒr -tôht krúp.
	ไปนครพนม	bpai na-korn pa-nom
	จองตั๋วที่ไหน	jorng dtǒo-a têe-nǎi?
Clerk	ที่นี่ค่ะ	têe-nêe kâ.
	จะไปเมื่อไร	ja bpai mêu-rài?
Peter	พรุ่งนี้ครับ	prÔOng née krúp.
Clerk	พรุ่งนี้เย็นนะคะ	prÔOng née yen ná ká.
	เอากี่ที่คะ	ao gèe têe ká?
Peter	สองครับ	sǒrng krúp.
Clerk	เการ้อยแปดสิบบาทค่ะ	gâo róy bpàirt sìp bàht kà.
Peter	รถออกกี่โมงครับ	rót òrk gèe mohng krúp?
Clerk	สี่ทุ่มครึ่งค่ะ	sèe tÔOm krêung kà.
	ถึงนครพนม	těung na-korn pa-nom
	ประมาณตีห้า	pra-mahn dtee hâh.
Peter	แล้วขึ้นรถที่ไหน	láir-o kêun rót têe-nǎi?

1 When does Peter want to go to Nakhorn Phanom?

2 What time does his bus leave?

3 What time does it arrive?

4 How much does he pay for tickets?

● **INSIGHT**

Travel outside Bangkok is cheap and convenient. Tour buses, operated by the state-owned Mass Transport Organization (MTO) provide a frequent and efficient service to every province in the country. Refreshments are served en route and, on longer journeys, a simple meal is provided at a highway café on showing your ticket. When travelling upcountry, it is normally necessary to book in advance at the Bangkok terminus.

Key phrases and expressions

🔊 **15.03**

How to

1 ask where to book a ticket

jorng dtŏo-a têe-năi?   จองตั๋วที่ไหน

2 ask to book a ticket to …

kŏr jorng dtŏo-a bpai …   ขอจองตั๋วไป …

3 ask what time the bus/train leaves

rót/rót fai òrk gèe mohng?   รถ/รถไฟออกกี่โมง

4 ask what time the bus/train arrives

rót/rót fai tĕung gèe mohng?   รถ/รถไฟถึงกี่โมง

5 ask where to get on/off a bus or train

kêun /long rót têe-năi?   ขึ้น/ลงรถที่ไหน

6 ask how long a journey takes

chái way-lah dern tahng gèe chôo-a-mohng?   ใช้เวลาเดินทางกี่ชั่วโมง

Language notes

1 VISIT

The verb to visit is **têe-o** when referring to places and **yêe-um** when referring to people:

rao kít ja bpai têe-o na-korn pa-nom

เราคิดจะไปเที่ยวนครพนม

We're thinking of going to (visit) Nakhorn Phanom.

glùp bpai yêe-um kOOn yai

กลับไปเยี่ยมคุณยาย

I go back to visit my granny.

The expression **bpai têe-o** can sometimes mean a rather vague *I'm going out* and is often used in response to the greeting **bpai năi?** (*Where are you going?*). The expression **têe-o pôo-yǐng** is a euphemism for 'visiting' prostitutes. **têe-o** can also be used as a noun, when it means *trip*:

wun la sŏrng têe-o

วันละสองเที่ยว

two trips a day

2 BY TRAIN

No preposition is needed in Thai to translate *by* in expressions like *by bus, by train, by car* and so on. It is sufficient to use the pattern **bpai** + VEHICLE:

rao ja bpai rót fai

เราจะไปรถไฟ

We are going by train.

Alternatively, the pattern **nûng** (*to sit*)/**kùp** (*to drive*) +VEHICLE + **bpai/mah** can be used to specify whether someone is a passenger or driver and whether they are coming or going:

nûng rót fai bpai mâi dâi

นั่งรถไฟไปไม่ได้

You can't go by train.

pǒm kùp rót mah

ผมขับรถมา

I drove here (by car).

3 DISTANCES

The distance in kilometres between two places is expressed by the pattern A **yòo hàhng jàhk** B + NUMBER + **gi-loh**:

nǒrng-kai yòo hàhng jàhk grOOng-tâyp 614 gi-loh

Nongkhai is 614 kilometres from Bangkok.

หนองคายอยู่ห่างจากกรุงเทพฯ ๖๑๔ กิโล

kǒrn-gàirn yòo hàhng jàhk na-korn pa-nom gèe gi-loh?

How many kilometres from Nakhorn Phanom is Khonkaen?

ขอนแก่นอยู่ห่างจากนครพนมกี่กิโล

4 QUESTIONS ABOUT TIME

There are two ways of asking *What time is it?*:

gèe mohng láir-o?   กี่โมงแล้ว

way-lah tâo-rài láir-o?   เวลาเท่าไหร่แล้ว

Likewise, there are two ways of asking what time something happens:

rót fai òrk gèe mohng?

รถไฟออกกี่โมง

What time does the train leave?

rót fai òrk way-lah tâo-rài?

รถไฟออกเวลาเท่าไหร่

What time does the train leave?

When asking how many hours something takes, the word **chôo-a mohng** (*hour*) is used:

gèe chôo-a mohng?

กี่ชั่วโมง

How many hours?

káo bpai gèe chôo-a mohng?

เขาไปกี่ชั่วโมง

How many hours was he gone?

chái way-lah gèe chôo-a mohng?

ใช้เวลากี่ชั่วโมง

How many hours does it take?

5 TELLING THE TIME
Hours

midnight	**têe-ung keun**	เที่ยงคืน
1 a.m.	**dtee nèung**	ตีหนึ่ง
2 a.m.	**dtee sŏrng**	ตีสอง
3 a.m.	**dtee săhm**	ตีสาม
4 a.m.	**dtee sèe**	ตีสี่
5 a.m.	**dtee hâh**	ตีห้า
6 a.m.	**hòk mohng cháo**	หกโมงเช้า
7 a.m.	**jèt mohng cháo**	เจ็ดโมงเช้า
8 a.m.	**bpàirt mohng cháo**	แปดโมงเช้า
or	**sŏrng mohng cháo**	สองโมงเช้า
9 a.m.	**gâo mohng cháo**	เก้าโมงเช้า
or	**săhm mohng cháo**	สามโมงเช้า
10 a.m.	**sìp mohng cháo**	สิบโมงเช้า
or	**sèe mohng cháo**	สี่โมงเช้า

11 a.m.	**sìp-èt mohng cháo**	สิบเอ็ดโมงเช้า
or	**hâh mohng cháo**	ห้าโมงเช้า
midday	**têe-ung wun**	เที่ยงวัน
1 p.m.	**bài mohng**	บ่ายโมง
2 p.m.	**bài sǒrng mohng**	บ่ายสองโมง
3 p.m.	**bài sǎhm mohng**	บ่ายสามโมง
4 p.m.	**bài sèe mohng**	บ่ายสี่โมง
5 p.m.	**hâh mohng yen**	ห้าโมงเย็น
6 p.m.	**hòk mohng yen**	หกโมงเย็น
7 p.m.	**tÔOm nèung**	ทุ่มหนึ่ง
8 p.m.	**sǒrng tÔOm**	สองทุ่ม
9 p.m.	**sǎhm tÔOm**	สามทุ่ม
10 p.m.	**sèe tÔOm**	สี่ทุ่ม
11 p.m.	**hâh tÔOm**	ห้าทุ่ม

Half hours

Half past the hour is expressed as HOUR TIME + **krêung** (*half*); the words **cháo** (6 am to 11 a.m.) and **yen** (4–5 p.m.) are normally omitted:

2.30 a.m.	**dtee sǒrng krêung**	ตีสองครึ่ง
8.30 a.m.	**bpàirt mohng krêung**	แปดโมงครึ่ง
3.30 p.m.	**bài sǎhm mohng krêung**	บ่ายสามโมงครึ่ง
5.30 p.m.	**hâh mohng krêung**	ห้าโมงครึ่ง
11.30 p.m.	**hâh tÔOm krêung**	ห้าทุ่มครึ่ง

MINUTES PAST, MINUTES TO THE HOUR

There is no special word for *quarter past* or *quarter to* the hour. Minutes past the hour are expressed as HOUR TIME + NUMBER + **nah-tee** (*minute*):

11.15 a.m.	**sìp-èt mohng sìp-hâh nah-tee**	สิบเอ็ดโมงสิบห้านาที
3.10 p.m.	**bài sǎhm mohng sìp nah-tee**	บ่ายสามโมงสิบนาที
8.15 p.m.	**sǒrng tÔOm sìp-hâh nah-tee**	สองทุ่มสิบห้านาที

Minutes to the hour are expressed as **èek** (*further, more*) + NUMBER + **nah-tee** + HOUR TIME:

9.45 a.m.	**èek sìp-hâh nah-tee sìp mohng cháo**	อีกสิบห้านาทีสิบโมงเช้า
4.40 p.m.	**èek yêe-sìp nah-tee hâh mohng yen**	อีกยี่สิบนาทีห้าโมงเย็น
11.50 p.m.	**èek sìp nah-tee têe-ung keun**	อีกสิบนาทีเที่ยงคืน

24-HOUR CLOCK

In the 24-hour clock system, the word **nah-li-gah** is used for *hours* and half hours are expressed as *30 minutes past*:

20:00	**yêe-sìp nah-li-gah**	ยี่สิบนาฬิกา
22:30	**yêe-sìp sǒrng nah-li-gah**	ยี่สิบสองนาฬิกา
	sǎhm-sìp nah-tee	สามสิบนาที

Exercises

1 Match up the following times:

a **èek sìp nah-tee têe-ung wun**	**i**	05:30
b **hâh tÔOm yêe-sìp hâh nah-tee**	**ii**	16:10
c **bài sèe mohng sìp nah-tee**	**iii**	11:45
d **dtee hâh krêung**	**iv**	23:25

2 What time is it?
- **a** 09:30
- **b** 14:20
- **c** 17:00
- **d** 21:45

3 How would you ask:
- **a** *where to book a ticket for Chiangmai?*
- **b** *what time the Chiangmai bus leaves?*
- **c** *how many kilometres Chiangmai is from Bangkok?*
- **d** *where to get on the bus?*

Reading practice

1 Mineko seeks advice about a trip she plans to make:

QUICK VOCAB

friend   เพื่อน

Mineko	ฉันคิดจะไปเที่ยวจังหวัดตรังค่ะ
Damrong	หรือครับ ไปทำอะไรที่ตรัง
Mineko	ไปเยี่ยมเพื่อนค่ะ
	ไม่ทราบว่าจะไปอย่างไรดี
Damrong	ไปรถไฟก็ได้ รถทัวร์ก็ได้
	ผมว่าไปรถไฟสบายกว่า
	แต่ต้องจองตั๋วล่วงหน้า

1 Where is Mineko going?

2 Why?

3 How does Damrong suggest she get there?

4 What further advice does he give her?

2 Here is some information from a tour company's brochure about trips to Nongkhai. When you have fully understood the passage, write full sentence answers in Thai to the questions:

QUICK VOCAB

จำกัด	*Ltd*
ปรับอากาศ	*air conditioned*
ชั้นหนึ่ง	*first class*
เที่ยว	*trip*
เดินทาง	*to travel*

หนองคายอยู่ห่างจากกรุงเทพฯ ๖๑๔ กิโลเมตร
บริษัท วี ไอ พี จำกัด มีรถปรับอากาศชั้นหนึ่งออก
จากกรุงเทพฯวันละ ๒ เที่ยว เวลา ๐๘.๐๐ และ ๒๑.๐๐
นาฬิกา ใช้เวลาเดินทางประมาณ ๑๐ ชั่วโมง

QUESTIONS

1 หนองคายอยู่ห่างจากกรุงเทพฯ กี่กิโลเมตร

2 บริษัท วี ไอ พี จำกัดมีรถไปหนองคายวันละกี่เที่ยว

3 รถไปหนองคายออกกี่โมง

4 ใช้เวลาเดินทางกี่ชั่วโมง

Key points

1 **têe-o** is used for visiting places and **yêe-um** for visiting people.

2 Use the pattern **nûng rót fai/rót bpai …** to talk about travelling somewhere by train or coach.

3 Distance between two places is expressed as A **yòo hàhng jàhk** B + NUMBER + **gi-loh**.

4 To ask the time, use **gèe mohng láir-o?** or **way-lah tâo-rài láir-o?**

5 To ask what time X happens/happened, use X **gèe mohng?** or X **way-lah tâo-rài?**

6 To ask how many hours something takes, use … **gèe chôo-a mohng**?

7 In the 24-hour clock system, **nah-li-gah** is used for hours.

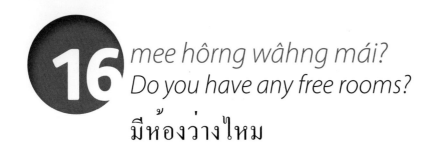

16 mee hôrng wâhng mái?
Do you have any free rooms?
มีห้องว่างไหม

In this unit, you will learn:
- ▶ *how to book a hotel room*
- ▶ *days of the week*
- ▶ *... réu bplào? questions*
- ▶ *verb + wái*
- ▶ *noun + classifier + adjective*

Dialogues

mee hôrng wâhng mái?

Peter and Sue have arrived at a small hotel in the provincial capital of Nakhorn Phanom:

QUICK VOCAB

hôrng	room	ห้อง
wâhng	to be free, vacant	ว่าง
púk	to stay	พัก
keun	night	คืน
nâir	to be sure	แน่
àht ja	may, might	อาจจะ
jon tĕung	until	จนถึง
wun săo	Saturday	วันเสาร์
wun ah-tít	Sunday	วันอาทิตย์
air	air conditioning	แอร์
... réu bplào?	... or not?	... หรือเปล่า
bper sen	per cent	เปอร์เซ็นต์

Peter	มีห้องว่างไหมครับ	mee hôrng wâhng mái krúp?
Clerk	มีครับ	mee krúp.
	จะพักกี่คืนครับ	ja púk gèe keun krúp?
Peter	ยังไม่แน่ครับ	yung mâi nâir krúp.
	อาจจะอยู่จนถึง	àht ja yòo jon tĕung
	วันเสาร์หรือวันอาทิตย์	wun săo réu wun ah-tít.
	ห้องมีแอร์หรือเปล่า	hôrng mee air réu bplào?
Clerk	มีครับ	mee krúp.
Peter	ค่าห้องคืนละเท่าไหร่ครับ	kâh hôrng keun la tâo-rài krúp?
Clerk	คืนละแปดร้อยบาทครับ	keun la bpàirt róy bàht krúp.
	ถ้าอยู่อาทิตย์หนึ่ง	tâh yòo ah-tít nèung
	ก็จะลดให้สิบเปอร์เซ็นต์	gôr ja lót hâi sìp bper sen.

1 How many nights do Sue and Peter plan to stay?

2 How much does the room cost per night?

3 How does the clerk try to persuade Peter to stay longer?

kŏr doo hôrng gòrn dâi mái?

Peter asks to see the room:

QUICK VOCAB

chern tahng née	*please come this way*	เชิญทางนี้
mÓOng lôo-ut	*mosquito screen*	มุงลวด
sĕe-a	*broken*	เสีย
sôrm	*to repair*	ซ่อม
chèet	*to spray*	ฉีด
yah gun yOOng	*mosquito repellant*	ยากันยุง

Peter	ขอดูห้องก่อนได้ไหม	kŏr doo hôrng gòrn dâi mái?
Clerk	ได้ครับ	dâi krúp.
	เชิญทางนี้ครับ	chern tahng née krúp.
Peter	มุ้งลวดเสียครับ	mÓOng lôo-ut sĕe-a krúp.
Clerk	ครับ เดี๋ยวจะซ่อมให้	krúp. dĕe-o ja sôrm hâi.
Peter	ช่วยฉีดยากันยุง	chôo-ay chèet yah gun yOOng
	ให้ด้วยนะ	hâi dôo-ay ná.

● **INSIGHT**

Note the use of **hâi** to mean *for* in this conversation. The clerk could have added the word **kOOn** after **hâi**, while Peter could have added **pŏm** after his **hâi**.

---

1 What problem does Peter discover?
2 What does the clerk agree to do?
3 What else does Peter ask him to do?

fàhk kŏrng wái têe-nêe dâi mái?

Peter and Sue have agreed to take the room and are now going out:

QUICK VOCAB

... **wái**	*see* Language notes	...ไว้
kŏrng	*thing(s)*	ของ
glôrng tài rôop	*camera*	กล้องถ่ายรูป
gra-bpăo	*bag*	กระเป๋า
bai	*classifier for bags*	ใบ
bplòrt-pai	*safe (adj.)*	ปลอดภัย
gèp	*to keep*	เก็บ
dtôo sáyf	*safe (noun)*	ตู้เซฟ
gOOn-jair	*key*	กุญแจ

Clerk	ไปไหนครับ	bpai năi krúp?
Peter	ไปทานข้าวครับ	bpai tahn kâo krúp.
	ขอโทษครับ	kŏr-tôht krúp
	ฝากของไว้ที่นี่	fàhk kŏrng wái têe-nêe
	ได้ไหม	dâi mái?
Clerk	ของอะไรครับ	kŏrng a-rai krúp?
Peter	กล้องถ่ายรูปและ	glôrng tài rôop láir
	กระเป๋าใบเล็ก	gra-bpăo bai lék.
Clerk	ได้ครับ	dâi krúp.
	ฝากไว้ที่นี่ปลอดภัย	fàhk wái têe-nêe bplòrt-pai.
	ผมจะเก็บไว้ให้	pŏm ja gèp wái hâi
	ในตู้เซฟ	nai dtôo sáyf.
Peter	ขอบคุณมากครับ	kòrp-kOOn mâhk krúp.
	ฝากกุญแจห้อง	fàhk gOOn-jair hôrng
	ด้วยนะ	dôo-ay ná.

1 Where are Peter and Sue going?

2 What valuables do they want to leave in the safe?

Key phrases and expressions

 16.04

How to

1 ask if there are any free rooms

mee hôrng wâhng mái?　　มีห้องว่างไหม

2 say you will stay until Saturday

ja yòo jon tĕung wun săo　　จะอยู่จนถึงวันเสาร์

3 ask whether the room is air conditioned

hôrng mee air réu bplào?　　ห้องมีแอร์หรือเปล่า

4 ask how much a room costs per night

kâh hôrng keun la tâo-rài?　　ค่าห้องคืนละเท่าไหร่

5 ask to see the room

kŏr doo hôrng gòrn dâi mái?　　ขอดูห้องก่อนได้ไหม

6 say X is broken and ask for it to be fixed

X sĕe-a　　X เสีย

chôo-ay sôrm hâi dôo-ay ná　　ช่วยซ่อมให้ด้วยนะ

7 ask to leave something

fàhk kŏrng wái têe-nêe dâi mái?　　ฝากของไว้ที่นี่ได้ไหม

Language notes

1 DAYS OF THE WEEK

 16.05

wun jun	*Monday*	วันจันทร์
wun ung-kahn	*Tuesday*	วันอังคาร
wun pÓOt	*Wednesday*	วันพุธ
wun pa-réu-hùt	*Thursday*	วันพฤหัส
wun sÒOk	*Friday*	วันศุกร์
wun săo	*Saturday*	วันเสาร์
wun ah-tít	*Sunday*	วันอาทิตย์

The word **wun** (*day*) usually prefaces the name of the day. When talking about the day on which something happens, Thai does not use a preposition corresponding to English *on*:

wun jun bpai tum ngahn

วันจันทร์ไปทำงาน

On Monday I'm going to work.

káo ja glùp mah wun săo

เขาจะกลับมาวันเสาร์

He's coming back on Saturday.

2 AIR CONDITIONED

The English word **air** is frequently used to mean *air conditioned*, in expressions like **mee/dtìt air** (*air conditioned*), **hôrng air** (*air-conditioned room*), **rót air** (*air-conditioned bus*). The more formal Thai word for *air conditioned* is **bprùp ah-gàht** (lit., *adjust air*), while an air conditioner is **krêu-ung** (*machine*) **bprùp ah-gàht.**

3 … *réu bplào?* QUESTIONS

… réu bplào? literally means … *or not?* although the English translation makes this question form sound rather more abrupt than it is in Thai. There is nothing brusque about **… réu bplào?** questions; they simply require a clear *yes* or *no* answer:

bpai réu bplào?

ไปหรือเปล่า

Are you going (or not)?

hôrng mee air réu bplào?

ห้องมีแอร์หรือเปล่า

Does the room have air conditioning (or not)?

Yes/No answers are formed as follows:

a if the question refers to the present or future:

Yes: VERB

No: **(bplào) mâi** + VERB

bpai réu bplào?

ไปหรือเปล่า

Are you going (or not)?

- **bpai/(bplào) mâi bpai**

- ไป/(เปล่า)ไม่ไป

- *Yes/No.*

a-ròy réu bplào?

อร่อยหรือเปล่า

Is it tasty (or not)?

- **a-ròy/(bplào) mâi a-ròy**

- อร่อย/(เปล่า)ไม่อร่อย

- *Yes/No.*

b if the question refers to the past, action verbs (e.g. *to go, to eat, to study,* etc.) behave differently from stative verbs (e.g. *to be expensive, to be bored, to be tasty*) and so on:

Action verbs

Yes: VERB + **láir-o**

No: (**bplào**) **mâi dâi** + VERB

káo toh mah réu bplào?

เขาโทรมาหรือเปล่า

Did he phone (or not)?

- **toh mah láir-o/(bplào) mâi dâi toh mah**

- โทรมาแล้ว/(เปล่า)ไม่ได้โทรมา

- *Yes/No.*

Stative verbs

Yes: VERB

No: (**bplào**) **mâi** + VERB

pairng réu bplào?

แพงหรือเปล่า

Was it expensive (or not)?

- **pairng/(bplào) mâi pairng**

แพง/(เปล่า)ไม่แพง

- *Yes/No.*

4 POLITE REQUESTS: ASKING SOMEONE TO DO SOMETHING (II)

chôo-ay occurs with the particle **dôo-ay** in polite requests/commands, in the basic pattern **chôo-ay** + VERB + **dôo-ay**; this can optionally be expanded by the addition of **nòy** and/or **dâi mái?**:

chôo-ay chèet yah gun yOOng hâi dôo-ay ná

ช่วยฉีดยากันยุงให้ด้วยนะ

Please spray mosquito repellant (for me), OK?

chôo-ay bòrk káo dôo-ay

ช่วยบอกเขาด้วย

Please tell him.

chôo-ay bòrk káo nòy dôo-ay

ช่วยบอกเขาหน่อยด้วย

Could you tell him, please?

chôo-ay bòrk káo nòy dôo-ay dâi mái?

ช่วยบอกเขาหน่อยด้วยได้ไหม

Could you tell him, please?

Note that **chôo-ay** is sometimes omitted, for example in the expression **gèp dtung dôo-ay** (see Unit 8).

5 VERB + *wái*

The word **wái** occurs after verbs of action to indicate that the action is being done for future use or reference; it occurs commonly with the verbs **gèp** (*to keep*) and **fàhk** (*to deposit*):

fàhk kǒrng wái têe-nêe dâi mái?

ฝากของไว้ที่นี่ได้ไหม

Can I leave some things here?

fàhk wái têe-nêe bplòrt-pai

ฝากไว้ที่นี่ปลอดภัย

It's safe to leave them here.

pǒm ja gèp wái hâi nai dtôo sáyf

ผมจะเก็บไว้ให้ในตู้เซฟ

I'll keep them for you in the safe.

6 NOUN + CLASSIFIER + ADJECTIVE

While a noun can be followed immediately by an adjective, nouns and adjectives are also commonly linked by a classifier in the pattern, NOUN + CLASSIFIER + ADJECTIVE:

gra-bpǎo bai lék

กระเป๋าใบเล็ก

a small bag

kâo pùt jahn yài

ข้าวผัดจานใหญ่

a large plate of fried rice

rót kun* mài

รถคันใหม่

a new car

Exercises

 16.06

1 Use the pattern **bplào krúp (kâ), mâi dâi** + VERB, to signal a firm *no* to the following questions asking whether you did something:

  a bpai bâhn kOOn sǒm-chai réu bplào?

  b sùng kâo pùt réu bplào?

  c jorng dtǒo-a réu bplào?

  d bòrk kOOn mah-lee réu bplào?

 16.07

2 Use the pattern **bplào krúp (kâ), mâi** + VERB, to signal a firm *no* to the following questions:

  a pairng réu bplào?

  b bèu-a réu bplào?

  c pèt réu bplào?

  d glai réu bplào?

3 How would you ask to leave the following articles in the hotel safe?

  a *keys*

  b *camera*

  c *mobile phone*

  d *train ticket*

  e *a small bag*

*Classifier for cars

Reading practice

1 Sue and Peter are thinking about visiting the province's famous temple, Wat That Phanom. Here are the new words you will meet:

QUICK VOCAB

วัดธาตุพนม	*Wat That Phanom*
คิดดู	*to think about, consider*

🔊 **16.08**

Clerk	ไปเที่ยววัดธาตุพนมหรือยังครับ
Sue	ที่ไหนนะคะ
Clerk	วัดธาตุพนมครับ
Sue	ยังค่ะ อยากไปแต่ไม่ทราบว่าจะไปอย่างไรดี
Clerk	ไปกับทัวร์ได้ครับ มีรถแอร์ไปทุกเช้ากลับเย็น
Sue	หรือคะ ค่าทัวร์เท่าไหร่คะ
Clerk	พันสองร้อยห้าสิบบาทครับ
Sue	รถออกกี่โมงคะ
Clerk	แปดโมงเช้าครับ
	ออกจากหน้าโรงแรม
	แล้วกลับมาที่นี่เวลาห้าโมงเย็น
Sue	แล้วถ้าไป จองตั๋วได้ที่ไหน
Clerk	ผมจองให้ได้ครับไปพรุ่งนี้ใช่ไหมครับ
Sue	เดี๋ยว ๆ ฉันคิดดูก่อนนะคะ

a How does the clerk suggest Sue gets to Wat That Phanom?

b How much will it cost?

c What time will they leave and return?

d What does the clerk offer to do for Sue?

e Does Sue accept his offer?

2 Once at Wat That Phanom Sue asks a student if taking photographs is allowed:

QUICK VOCAB

ห้าม	*to forbid*
ถ่ายรูป	*to take a photograph*
ถาม	*to ask*
เจ้าหน้าที่	*official*
คนต่างชาติ	*foreigner*
ถอด	*to take off*
เข้า	*to enter*

 16.09

Sue	ขอโทษค่ะ ที่นี่ห้ามถ่ายรูปหรือเปล่า
Student	คิดว่าไม่ห้ามครับ เดี๋ยวจะไปถามเจ้าหน้าที่ให้ ... ขอโทษครับ มีคนต่างชาติถามว่า ที่นี่ห้ามถ่ายรูปหรือเปล่า
Official	ที่นี่ไม่ห้าม แต่ข้างในห้ามครับ ช่วยบอกเขาด้วยว่า ต้องถอด รองเท้าก่อนเข้าไปข้างใน
Student	ครับ ขอบคุณครับ

a What does the student offer to do for Sue?

b What message does the official ask the student to convey to Sue?

3 Match the prohibition notices with the correct translation:

a ห้ามถ่ายรูป		**i**	No parking
b ห้ามจอดรถ		**ii**	Sale prohibited
c ห้ามสูบบุหรี่		**iii**	No entry
d ห้ามเข้า		**iv**	No smoking
e ห้ามขาย		**v**	Photography forbidden

⁇ Key points

1 **wun** (*day*) occurs at the beginning of names of days. There is no preposition in Thai corresponding to English *on Monday*.

2 An air conditioner is **krêu-ung bprùp ah-gàht** or **krêu-ung air**.

3 *Yes/No* answers to **... réu bplào?** (*... or not?*) questions depend on whether the question refers to the past or present, and whether the verb is an action verb or a stative verb.

4 The pattern **chôo-ay** + VERB + **dôo-ay** is used in polite requests/commands.

5 **wái** occurs after verbs such as **gèp** (*to keep*) and **fàhk** (*to deposit*): to indicate that the action is being done for future use or reference.

6 A noun is commonly linked to an adjective by its classifier, in the pattern NOUN + CLASSIFIER + ADJECTIVE.

17 mee a-páht-mén hâi châo mái?
Do you have any apartments for rent?

มือพาร์ทเมนท์ให้เช่าไหม

In this unit, you will learn:
▶ *gum-lung ja + verb*
▶ *negative questions*
▶ *relative pronouns*
▶ *months and seasons*
▶ *dates and ordinal numbers*
▶ *hâi: to give*
▶ *mâi dâi + verb*

Dialogues

mee a-páht-mén hâi châo mái?

Somchai has gone to an estate agent in search of a new apartment:

QUICK VOCAB

a-páht-mén	*apartment*	อพาร์ทเมนท์
châo	*to rent*	เช่า
hâi châo	*for rent*	ให้เช่า
têe	*relative pronoun*	ที่
BTS	(Bangkok Mass Transit System)	บีทีเอส
lŭng	classifier for apartments	หลัง
a-sòhk	*Asoke* (name of station)	อโศก
prórm pong	*Phrom Phong* (name of station)	พร้อมพงษ์
léuk	*deep*	ลึก
soy	*soi, lane*	ซอย
bpàhk	*mouth, entrance*	ปาก
bpáirp dee-o	*just a second/moment*	แป๊บเดียว

Somchai	มีอพาร์ทเมนท์	mee a-páht-mén
	ให้เช่าไหมครับ	hâi châo mái krúp?
Agent	มีค่ะ คุณต้องการ	mee kà. kOOn dtôrng-gahn
	กี่ห้องนอนคะ	gèe hôrng norn ká?
Somchai	สองครับ	sŏrng krúp.
	แถวสุขุมวิท	tǎir-o sÒO-kǒOm-wít.
	ต้องการอพาร์ทเมนท์	dtôrng-gahn a-páht-mén
	ที่อยู่ใกล้ๆ สถานี บีทีเอส	têe yòo glâi glâi sa-tǎh-nee BTS.
Agent	มีหลังหนึ่งค่ะ	mee lǔng nèung kà.
	ที่สุขุมวิทซอย ๓๑	têe sÒO-kǒOm-wít soy sǎhm-sìp èt.
	อยู่ใกล้ๆสถานีอ่โศก	yòo glâi glâi sa-tǎh-nee a-sòhk
	และพร้อมพงษ์ค่ะ	láir prórm pong kà.
	อยู่ชั้นหกค่ะ	yòo chún hòk kà.
Somchai	อยู่ลึกในซอยไหม	yòo léuk nai soy mái?
Agent	ไม่ลึกค่ะ	mâi léuk kà.
	จากปากซอย	jàhk bpàhk soy
	เดินไปแป๊บเดียว	dern bpai bpáirp dee-o.
Somchai	ค่าเช่าเดือนละ	kâh châo deu-un la
	เท่าไหร่ครับ	tâo-rài krúp?

1 How many bedrooms does Somchai want?

2 In what location?

3 Where is the property the agent mentions?

4 Is it deep in the soi?

rao gum-lung ja yái bâhn

Sue tells Chanida of her plan to move home:

QUICK VOCAB

| **gum-lung ja …** | *to be about to …* | กำลังจะ … |
| **sǒo-un** | *garden* | สวน |

gloo-a	*to be afraid*	กลัว
ka-moy-ee	*burglar*	ขโมย
wun têe sìp-hâh	*the 15th*	วันที่ ๑๕

🔊 **17.02**

Sue	เรากำลังจะย้ายบ้านค่ะ	rao gum-lung ja yái bâhn kà.
Chanida	หรือคะ	lěr ká?
	อพาร์ทเมนท์ที่อยู่ตอนนี้	a-páht-mén têe yòo dtorn née
	ไม่ชอบหรือ	mâi chôrp lěr?
Sue	ชอบซีคะ	chôrp see ka.
	แต่เราอยากจะอยู่บ้าน	dtàir rao yàhk ja yòo bâhn
	ที่มีสวน	têe mee sǒo-un.
Chanida	แล้วไม่กลัวขโมยหรือ	láir-o mâi gloo-a ka-moy-ee lěr?
Sue	ก็ ... กลัวเหมือนกัน	gôr ... gloo-a měu-un gun.
Chanida	จะย้ายเมื่อไรคะ	ja yái mêu-rài ká?
Sue	วันที่ ๑๕ เดือนหน้า	wun têe sìp-hâh deu-un nâh.

1 Why does Sue want to move?

2 Where is she living at present?

3 When is she going to move?

bâhn bpen yung-ngai?

Chanida asks Sue what her new house is like:

QUICK VOCAB

hâi	*to give*	ให้
kâh mút-jum	*deposit* (noun)	ค่ามัดจำ
nâh fǒn	*rainy season*	หน้าฝน
tôo-um	*to flood*	ท่วม

Chanida	บ้านเป็นอย่างไรคะ	bâhn bpen yung-ngai ká?
Sue	ดีมากเลยค่ะ	dee mâhk ler-ee kà.
	สวนเล็กแต่น่ารัก	sŏo-un lék dtàir nâh rúk.
Chanida	เป็นบ้านสองชั้น ใช่ไหม	bpen bâhn sŏrng chún châi mái?
Sue	ใช่ค่ะ	châi kà.
Chanida	อยู่แถวไหน	yòo tăir-o năi?
Sue	สุขุมวิทซอย ๔๘	sÒO-kŎOm-wít soy sèe-sìp gâo
Chanida	ค่าเช่าแพงไหม	kâh châo pairng mái?
Sue	เดือนละสามหมื่น	deu-un la săhm mèun.
	แต่ต้องให้ค่ามัดจำเขา	dtàir dtôrng hâi kâh mút-jum káo
	หกหมื่นด้วย	hòk mèun dôo-ay.
Chanida	หน้าฝนน้ำท่วมไหม	nâh fŏn náhm tôo-um mái?
Sue	ไม่รู้ เราไม่ได้ถาม	mâi róo. rao mâi dâi tăhm.

1 Where is Sue's house situated?

2 What is the monthly rent?

3 How much deposit did she pay?

4 What did she forget to ask before deciding to rent the house?

> ● **INSIGHT**
>
> The BTS (Bangkok Mass Transit System) SkyTrain service provides a safe, efficient and comfortable way of getting around Bangkok, while bypassing the traffic jams below. Officially introduced on December 5, 1999, there are currently two lines, the Sukhumvit Line and the Silom Line, which cover much of central Bangkok. The service operates between 6.00 am and 12.00 midnight and trains are frequent.

Key phrases and expressions

 17.04

How to

1 ask if there are any apartments for rent

mee a-páht-mén hâi châo mái?   มีพาร์ทเมนท์ให้เช่าไหม

2 say you want an apartment ...

dtôrng-gahn a-páht-mén

ต้องการอพาร์ทเมนท์

... which is near a sky train station

... têe yòo glâi glâi sa-tăh-nee BTS...

ที่อยู่ใกล้ๆ สถานี บีทีเอส

... which is in the Sukhumwit area

... têe yòo tăir-o sŎO-kŎOm-wít

... ที่อยู่แถวสุขุมวิท

... which has two bedrooms

... têe mee sŏrng hôrng norn

... ที่มีสองห้องนอน

3 ask what the monthly rent is

kâh châo deu-un la tâo-rài?

ค่าเช่าเดือนละเท่าไหร่

4 ask if it floods in the rainy season

nâh fŏn náhm tôo-um mái?

หน้าฝนน้ำท่วมไหม

Language notes

1 soi

Major roads often have small roads or lanes called **soy** (spelt *soi* in English) leading off them. They may vary considerably in length from a few hundred metres to a kilometre or more, and while some are quiet residential areas, others have developed into major roads.

Longer sois often have a motorcycle taxi service running from the entrance to the soi (**bpàhk soy**) to the end of the soi (**sÒOt soy**). If you have asked a taxi to take you to, say Sukhumwit Soi 49, he will typically ask **kâo soy mái?** (*Do you want to go into the soi?*).

2 *gum-lung ja* + VERB

The pattern **gum-lung ja** + VERB is used to describe actions that are, or were, about to happen:

rao gum-lung ja yái bâhn

เรากำลังจะย้ายบ้าน

We are/were about to move house.

chún gum-lung ja gin kâo

ฉันกำลังจะกินข้าว

I am/was about to eat.

Be careful not to confuse this pattern with **gum-lung** + VERB (+ **yòo**) (Unit 7) used to describe continuous actions.

3 ROOMS

Names of rooms are preceded by **hôrng** (*room*):

hôrng norn   *bedroom*   ห้องนอน

hôrng sôo-um	*toilet*	ห้องส้วม
hôrng náhm	*bathroom*	ห้องน้ำ
hôrng kroo-a	*kitchen*	ห้องครัว
hôrng rúp kàirk	*living room*	ห้องรับแขก

The classifier for rooms is **hôrng**. But rather than the slightly long-winded phrase **mee hôrng norn sŏrng hôrng** (*there are two bedrooms*), which follows the grammatical rule NOUN + NUMBER + CLASSIFIER, Thais will often prefer the more economical **mee sŏrng hôrng norn**.

4 NEGATIVE QUESTIONS

Negative questions can be formed by the pattern, **mâi** + VERB + **lěr?**:

ah-hăhn mâi a-ròy lěr?

อาหารไม่อร่อยหรือ

Isn't the food tasty, then?

têe-o pút-ta-yah mâi sa-nÒOk lěr?

เที่ยวพัทยาไม่สนุกหรือ

Wasn't it fun visiting Pattaya, then?

a-páht-mén têe yòo mâi chôrp lěr?

อพาร์ทเมนท์ที่อยู่ไม่ชอบหรือ

You don't like the apartment where you're living, then?

(Note that these questions are all drawing a negative inference; they are quite different from English negative questions like *Didn't he do well?* and *Wasn't it awful?* which seek agreement.)

Yes/No answers to negative questions are confusing to English speakers, because Thais use **krúp/ kà** (*yes*) where English speakers say *no*:

| **kOOn mâi chôrp lěr?** | คุณไม่ชอบหรือ |
| **- krúp/kà (mâi chôrp)** | - ครับ/ค่ะ (ไม่ชอบ) |

You don't like it, then?

- No (I don't).

A *yes* answer is VERB + **see**, where the particle **see** is used to contradict the negative question (see also Unit 10):

| **kOOn mâi chôrp lěr?** | คุณไม่ชอบหรือ |
| **- chôrp see** | - ชอบซี |

You don't like it, then?

- Yes, I do.

ah-hăhn mâi a-ròy lěr? อาหารไม่อร่อยหรือ

- a-ròy see - อร่อยซี

Isn't the food tasty, then?

- Yes, it is.

5 RELATIVE PRONOUNS

A single relative pronoun, **têe**, can mean *where, which, who, when*:

bâhn têe rao yòo mee sŏo-un lék

บ้านที่เราอยู่มีสวนเล็ก

The house where we live has a small garden.

a-páht-mén têe châo yòo dee mâhk

อพาร์ทเมนท์ที่เช่าอยู่ดีมาก

The apartment which I'm renting is very good.

kon têe bòrk Malee mâi châi pŏm

คนที่บอกมาลีไม่ใช่ผม

The person who told Malee wasn't me.

deu-un têe bpai têe-o dtrung bpen nâh fŏn

เดือนที่ไปเที่ยวตรังเป็นหน้าฝน

The month when we went to Trang was the rainy season.

6 MONTHS

 17.05

mók-ga-rah-kom	*January*	มกราคม
gOOm-pah-pun	*February*	กุมภาพันธ์
mee-nah-kom	*March*	มีนาคม
may-săh-yon	*April*	เมษายน
préut-sa-pah-kom	*May*	พฤษภาคม
mí-tOO-nah-yon	*June*	มิถุนายน
ga-rúk-ga-dah-kom	*July*	กรกฎาคม
sĭng-hăh-kom	*August*	สิงหาคม

gun-yah-yon	*September*	กันยายน
dtOO-lah-kom	*October*	ตุลาคม
préut-sa-jìk-gah-yon	*November*	พฤศจิกายน
tun-wah-kom	*December*	ธันวาคม

The final syllable is **-kom** for months with 31 days, **-yon** for months with 30 days and **-pun** for the shortest month, February. In normal speech, the word **deu-un** (*month*) often occurs before the name of the month, while the final syllable is often omitted. Note that there is no preposition in Thai corresponding to English *in*:

bpai deu-un sĭng-hăh

ไปเดือนสิงหา

I'm going in August.

glùp deu-un tun-wah

กลับเดือนธันวา

He's coming back in December.

7 DATES, ORDINAL NUMBERS AND YEARS

Ordinal numbers (*first, second, third,* etc.) are formed by adding **têe** in front of the number:

têe nèung	*first*	ที่หนึ่ง
têe sŏrng	*second*	ที่สอง
têe săhm	*third*	ที่สาม

Dates are expressed using the pattern **wun** (*day*) + ORDINAL NUMBER + MONTH:

wun têe sìp-sèe dtOO-lah

วันที่ ๑๔ ตุลาฯ

14th October

wun têe sìp-hâh deu-un nâh

วันที่ ๑๕ เดือนหน้า

the 15th of next month

Years are counted according to Buddhist Era (BE), which dates from the birth of the Buddha, 543 years before the birth of Christ. To convert Thai years to AD, subtract 543. Thus, 2500 BE is 1957 AD, while 2000 AD is 2543 BE. BE and AD are abbreviated as follows:

por sŏr	*BE*	พศ
kor sŏr	*AD*	คศ

8 *hâi*: TO GIVE

You have already met **hâi** meaning (1) *to get someone to do something* (Unit 9) and (2) *for* (Unit 13). A third meaning of **hâi**, illustrated in this unit, is *to give*. Indirect and direct objects occur with **hâi** in the pattern (SUBJECT) + **hâi** + DIRECT OBJECT + INDIRECT OBJECT:

dtôrng hâi kâh mút-jum káo hòk mèun

ต้องให้ค่ามัดจำเขาหกหมื่น

I had to give them a deposit of 60,000.

fairn hâi ngern pǒm

แฟนให้เงินผม

My wife gave me the money.

rao hâi rót káo

เราให้รถเขา

We gave him a car.

9 SEASONS

There are three seasons in Thailand, the cool season (November to February), the hot season (March to June) and the rainy season (July to October). The formal word for season is **reu-doo**, but **nâh** is more commonly used in everyday conversation:

reu-doo/nâh nǎo	*cool season*	ฤดู/หน้าหนาว
reu-doo/nâh rórn	*hot season*	ฤดู/หน้าร้อน
reu-doo/nâh fǒn	*rainy season*	ฤดู/หน้าฝน

10 *mâi dâi* + VERB

You have previously met the pattern verb + **mâi dâi** meaning *can't ...* (see Unit 5). It is important not to confuse this with **mâi dâi** + VERB, which is used to state that an action did not take place in the past:

rao mâi dâi tǎhm

เราไม่ได้ถาม

We didn't ask.

chún mâi dâi bpai

ฉันไม่ได้ไป

I didn't go.

káo mâi dâi séu

เขาไม่ได้ซื้อ

He didn't buy it.

Exercises

🔊 **17.06**

1 How would you say you are about to do the following:
   a *move house?*
   b *order food?*
   c *go home?*
   d *buy a car?*
   e *go shopping?*

2 How would you say the following dates:
   a *9th January*
   b *19th June*
   c *31st August*
   d *5th November*
   e *3rd April*

3 Translate the following sentences into Thai, using the relative pronoun **têe**:
   a *The house where I'm staying is not very big.*
   b *The food which we eat is very spicy.*
   c *The Thais I know speak English very well.*
   d *The school where I teach is far away.*
   e *The teacher who teaches Thai comes from Chiangmai.*

4 Translate the following sentences into Thai:
   a *His mother gave him some money.*
   b *A friend gave me the CD.*
   c *We gave him a mobile phone.*
   d *He gave my younger sister a camera.*

Reading practice

In the following passages, you will meet the word **kwahm** for the first time. **kwahm** is used in front of verbs to form abstract nouns:

jing	*to be true*	**kwahm jing**	*truth*	ความจริง
dee	*to be good*	**kwahm dee**	*goodness*	ความดี
kít	*to think*	**kwahm kít**	*idea*	ความคิด
rúk	*to love*	**kwahm rúk**	*love*	ความรัก

1 Noi, a hotel worker, is talking about her work:

QUICK VOCAB

เกือบ	*almost*
ความสะอาด	*cleanliness, cleaning*
ซัก	*to wash (clothes)*
รีด	*to iron*
เสื้อผ้า	*clothes*
แขก	*guest*
ส่วนมาก	*mostly*
ฝรั่ง	*'farang', Caucasian*
เยอะ	*lots*
ใจดี	*kind (hearted)*
ทิป	*tip*
คุย	*to chat*
ทั้งวัน	*all day*

 17.07

น้อยทำงานอยู่ที่นี่เกือบ ๒๐ ปีแล้วค่ะ ทำความสะอาดห้อง
และซักรีดเสื้อผ้า มาทำงานเวลา ๒ โมงเช้าแล้วกลับบ้าน
บ่าย ๔ โมง แขกที่นี่ส่วนมากเป็นคนต่างชาติ ฝรั่งก็เยอะ
บางคนใจดีมาก ให้ทิปร้อยกว่าบาท สบาย
แต่ตอนนี้เป็นหน้าฝน แขกก็ไม่ค่อยมี งานก็ไม่ค่อยมาก
น้อยก็นั่งคุยกับเพื่อน กินเล่นทั้งวัน สบายอีกแบบหนึ่ง

2 Malee and Sue are discussing a visit Sue made to the seaside:

QUICK VOCAB

ชายทะเล	*seaside*
พัทยา	*Pattaya*
เงียบ	*quiet*
ทะเล	*sea*
นักท่องเที่ยว	*tourist*
น้อยกว่า	*fewer*

Malee	คุณซูเคยไปเที่ยวชายทะเลไหม
Sue	เคยค่ะ ไปพัทยาเมื่อ ๒-๓ เดือนก่อน
Malee	เป็นอย่างไร สนุกไหม
Sue	ก็ ... สนุกเหมือนกัน
	แต่มีคนเยอะ ชอบเงียบๆ มากกว่า
Malee	ถ้าไปชายทะเล ฉันว่าไปภาคใต้ดีกว่า
	ทะเลมันสวยกว่า นักท่องเที่ยวก็น้อยกว่า

3 John is having a problem with his hotel room:

QUICK VOCAB

เปลี่ยน	*to change*
เครื่องปรับอากาศ	*air conditioner*
ขึ้น	*to go up*

🔊 17.09

John	ขอเปลี่ยนห้องได้ไหมครับ
Clerk	ทำไมล่ะครับ
John	เครื่องปรับอากาศมันเสีย
Clerk	เดี๋ยวจะขึ้นไปดู
John	ไม่ต้องครับ
	ห้องน้ำใช้ไม่ได้ด้วย ไม่มีน้ำ
	อยากเปลี่ยนห้องดีกว่า
Clerk	เปลี่ยนไม่ได้ครับ
John	ทำไมล่ะครับ
Clerk	ห้องอื่นไม่มี

4 Lek, a Thai woman, talks about her language problems when she first came to England:

QUICK VOCAB

สามี	*husband*
แห่ง	*(classifier for companies)*

ความจริง	truth
นักเรียน	student
เยอรมัน	German
อาฟริกา	Africa(n)
อาหรับ	Arab
คือ	namely, that is
ดีขึ้น	to improve

🔊 **17.10**

เล็กแต่งงานที่กรุงเทพฯ ค่ะ สามีเป็นคนอังกฤษ
เคยทำงานที่บริษัทใหญ่แห่งหนึ่งแถวถนนสุขุมวิท
เรากลับมาอยู่ที่อังกฤษเมื่อสามปีก่อน
ความจริงเล็กไม่อยากมาอยู่อังกฤษเลย
เพราะว่าพูดภาษาอังกฤษไม่ค่อยเป็น
เล็กเคยเรียนที่โรงเรียนหลายปี แต่เรียนไม่เก่ง
คนอังกฤษพูด เล็กก็ฟังไม่ค่อยรู้เรื่อง
สามีก็ให้เล็กไปเรียนภาษาที่โรงเรียนแถวๆ บ้าน
ที่โรงเรียนมีนักเรียนทุกชาติ ญี่ปุ่นก็มี จีนก็มี
เยอรมันก็มี อาฟริกาก็มี แล้วก็มีอาหรับด้วย
เล็กต้องไปเรียนอาทิตย์ละ ๔ วัน คือวันจันทร์
วันอังคาร วันพุธ แล้ววันศุกร์ เรียนวันละ ๒-๓
ชั่วโมงตั้งแต่เก้าโมงเช้าจนถึงเที่ยง เรียนประมาณ
๖ เดือนแล้ว เล็กก็รู้สึกว่า ภาษาอังกฤษดีขึ้นมากเลย

? Key points

1 Be careful not to confuse **gum-lung ja** + VERB (*about to ...*) with **gum-lung** + VERB (+ **yòo**) (*in the process of ...ing*).

2 Negative questions take the form, **mâi** + VERB + **lěr**? In Thai, you say yes – to confirm the negative statement – where in English you say *no*.

3 The relative pronoun **têe** means *where, which, who, when*; in Thai this is spelt exactly the same as the location word **têe** (*at*).

4 Ordinal numbers are formed by adding **têe** in front of the cardinal number.

5 To convert BE years to AD, subtract 543.

6 The order of objects after **hâi** (*to give*) is **hâi** + DIRECT OBJECT + INDIRECT OBJECT.

7 Be careful not to confuse VERB + **mâi dâi** (*can't ...*) with **mâi dâi** + VERB (*didn't ...*).

8 Abstract nouns are formed by the pattern, **kwahm** + VERB.

Key to the exercises

Unit 1

Exercise 1

   a sa-wùt dee krúp/kà kOOn Mah-lee

   b sa-wùt dee krúp/kà kOOn mŏr

   c sa-wùt dee krúp/kà ah-jahn

Exercise 2

   a sa-wùt dee krúp/kà

   b wùt dee krúp/kà

   c bpai tÓO-rá krúp/kà; bpai têe-o krúp/kà

   d krúp/kà

READING PRACTICE

Exercise 2

nah	mah	ngah	rah	lah	yah	wah
num	mum	ngum	rum	lum	yum	wum
nor	mor	ngor	ror	lor	yor	wor

Exercise 3

ngahm	nahn	yahm	nahng	ngahn
norn	rorng	lorng	morng	yorm
mun	yung	rung	lung	wun
rai	lao	nai	rao	yahng

Exercise 4

nai	nai morng	nai morng nahng
yahm	yahm mah	yahm mah ror
nahng	nahng ngahm	nahng ngahm rum

Unit 2

Exercise 1

   a pŏm/chún chêu ...

   b pŏm/chún nahm sa-gOOn ...

c pǒm/chún bpen kon …

d châi/mâi châi

e pǒm/chún bpen kon jung-wùt …

Exercise 2

2 káo chêu John. nahm sa-gOOn Stevens. bpen kon a-may-ri-gun. mah jàhk niw yórk.

3 káo chêu Makoto. nahm sa-gOOn Ito. bpen kon yêe-bpÒOn. mah jàhk dtoh-gee-o.

4 káo chêu Paula. nahm sa-gOOn Besson. bpen kon fa-rung-sàyt. mah jàhk bpah-rít.

Exercise 3

2 Nicole mâi châi kon sa-bpayn. bpen kon fa-rung-sàyt.

3 Damrong mâi châi kon jeen. bpen kon tai.

4 Soonyoung mâi châi kon yêe-bpÒOn. bpen kon gâo-lĕe.

Exercise 4

a kOOn chêu a-rai?

b káo chêu Damrong châi mái?

c káo nahm sa-gOOn a-rai?

d káo bpen kon châht a-rai?

e káo bpen kon grOOng-tâyp châi mái?

f káo bpen kon jung-wùt a-rai?

g káo bpen kon pâhk nĕu-a châi mái?

READING PRACTICE

2 Words

gin	gun	goo	jai	jung	jum
doo	dee	dung	dtah	dtee	dtai
bin	bai	bpai	bpee	bpoo	yOOng
un	ai	ai	mee	mohng	rohng

3 Sentences

bin mah	bin bpai bin mah	yOOng bin bpai bin mah
mah doo	yin dee mah doo	lOOng yin dee mah doo
bpoo dum	mee bpoo dum	nai nah mee bpoo dum
ngoo dtai	dtee ngoo dtai	yahm lao dtee ngoo dtai
nahng ngahm dung	doo nahng ngahm dung	ror doo nahng ngahm dung

4 Match the dates

i c   **ii** d   **iii** a   **iv** b

Unit 3

Exercise 1

a iv   **b** iii   **c** ii   **d** i

Exercise 2

    a káo tum ngahn a-rai?

    b kOOn tum ngahn têe nǎi?

    c ah-jahn Araya sǒrn têe nǎi?

    d Khun Sunit ree-un têe nǎi?

    e têe tum ngahn kǒrng kOOn Chartchai yòo têe nǎi?

Exercise 3

kOOn Chartchai bpen núk tÓO-rá-kìt. bâhn yòo tǎir-o (ta-nǒn)

sÒO-kǑOm-wít. tum ngahn têe órp-fìt yòo têe ta-nǒn sÒO-kǑOm-wít.

ah-jahn Araya bpen ah-jahn. bâhn yòo têe grOOng-tâyp. sǒrn têe ma-hǎh-wít-ta-yah-lai yòo tǎir-o (ta-nǒn) sÒO-kǑOm-wít.

kOOn Sunit bpen núk sèuk-sǎh. bâhn yòo tǎir-o tâh prá jun. ree-un têe ma-hǎh wít-ta-yah-lai tum-ma-sàht yòo têe tâh prá jun.

Exercise 4

    a kOOn Chartchai bpen núk tÓO-rá-kìt.

    b bâhn Dr Saowanee yòo têe grOOng-tâyp.

    c kOOn Sunit ree-un têe ma-hǎh wít-ta-yah-lai tum-ma-sàht.

    d ma-hǎh wít-ta-yah-lai ah-jahn Araya yòo tǎir-o (ta-nǒn) sÒO-kǑOm-wít.

READING PRACTICE

1 Dead or live?

live	dead	dead	live	live	dead

2 What tone?

low	mid	low	low	high
mid	low	mid	low	mid
falling	mid	falling	falling	low

3 Words

yâhk	mee	nút	gùp	ngahn
yOOng	gùt	mâhk	jàhk	rêep
ai	norn	yorm	lôok	jòrt

Unit 4

Exercise 1

a tǎir-o née mee bprai-sa-nee mái?

b tǎir-o née mee ta-na-kahn mái?

c tǎir-o née mee bor-ri-gahn in-dter-net mái?

d tǎir-o née mee klí-nìk mái?

Exercise 2

a kǒr-tôht

b kòrp-kOOn

c mâi bpen rai

d yòo chún sǎhm

e yòo têe nôhn

f yòo glâi glâi ta-na-kahn

g yòo mâi glai

h yòo tǎir-o née

Exercise 3

a kǒr-tôht

b ta-na-kahn

c têe nôhn

d mái?

e glai

f bpai

g nah-tee

h kòrp-kOOn

READING PRACTICE

1 Words

chai	chahm	soi	bàht	kum	chôrp
tahng	pah	púk	tum	tÓOk	keun
deung	dtèuk	keu	ker-ee	ler-ee	pairng
dairng	bpàirt	yen	lék	bpen	jèt
gèp	bpèt	gôr	kon	long	mót

2 Some short sentences

bpàirt	bpàirt bàht	bpàirt bàht pairng	bpàirt bàht pairng bpai
jeen	kon jeen	bpen kon jeen	lOOng bpen kon jeen
bpai	mâhk bpai	jèt jahn mâhk bpai	gin jèt jahn mâhk bpai

Unit 5

Exercise 1

a bpai sa-tăh-nee rót fai mái?

b bpai sa-năhm bin mái?

c bpai ma-hăh wít-ta-yah-lai tum-ma-sàht mái?

d bpai ta-nŏn sÒO-kŎOm-wít mái?

Exercise 2

a jòrt têe-nêe

b jòrt têe-nôhn

c jòrt glâi glâi bprai-sa-nee

d jòrt glâi glâi ta-na-kahn

READING PRACTICE

1 Words

kăi	kŏr	kùp	chèet	tăhm
tòok	pìt	fàhk	sĕe	sÒOt
sŏrn	săo	sùk	sìp	hùk
hăh	lŭng	wùt	nŏo	lăi

2 Match the numbers

i f **ii** d **iii** b **iv** e **v** a **vi** c

3 Sentences

tai	kon tai	bpen kon tai	lOOng bpen kon tai
dtàhk	jung-wùt dtàhk	jàhk jung-wùt dtàhk	mah jàhk jung-wùt dtàhk
mâhk	lăhn mâhk	mee lăhn mâhk	yai mee lăhn mâhk
kon	sìp kon	lôok sìp kon	mee lôok sìp kon
kon	săhm kon	săo săhm kon	lôok săo săhm kon

Unit 6

Exercise 1

a sôm loh la tâo-rài?

b mǒo yâhng mái la tâo-rài?

c kâo něe-o hòr la tâo-rài?

d sôm dtum tǑOng la tâo-rài?

Exercise 2

b mái la sìp lěr krúp/ká? ao sǒrng mái krúp/kà.

c hòr la sìp lěr krúp/ká? ao sǒrng hòr krúp/kà.

d tǑOng la sǎhm sìp lěr krúp/ká? ao sǒrng tǑOng krúp/kà.

Exercise 3

a něe rêe-uk wâh a-rai krúp?

b a-rai ná krúp?

c ma-la-gor châi mái?

d lôok la tâo-rài ?

e lót nòy dâi mái?

READING PASSAGE

Winai is Thai. He comes from Lampang. Ling is Chinese. She is Winai's girlfriend. Winai and Ling work in an office in the Sukhumwit area.

Unit 7

Exercise 1

a rah-kah tâo-rài?

b kǒr doo nòy dâi mái?

c kǒr lorng sài doo nòy dâi mái?

d lót nòy dâi mái?

Exercise 2

a pairng bpai nòy. mâi ao.

b kúp bpai nòy. sài mâi dâi.

c glai bpai nòy. dern mâi dâi.

d glâi bpai nòy. mâi chôrp.

Exercise 3

a hòr

b dtoo-a

c mái

d lôok

e kon

f loh

g kôo

READING PRACTICE

1 Words

mâi	nêe	pôr	mâir	nèung	kôo
yòo	gài	dtàir	sùng	nòy	dtòr
chêu	châi	pêe	têe	àhn	wâh

2 Phrases

châi mái?	mâi châi	nêe tâo-rài	yêe sìp bàht
pairng bpai nòy	jòrt têe-nêe	mâi pairng ròrk	yòo têe-nôhn
mâi bpen rai	yòo têe-nǎi	àhn mâi yâhk	kít wâh mâi mah

3 Dialogue

Yupa is Thai. She comes from Loei. Somchohk is Yupa's husband. He comes from Tak. Yupa and Somchohk have five children. They have two sons and three daughters.

Unit 8

Exercise 1

a kǒr/ao kâo pùt gÔOng sǎhm jahn

b kǒr/ao náhm sǒrng kòo-ut

c kǒr/ao núm sôm kún gâir-o nèung

d gèp dtung dôo-ay

Exercise 2

a sùng réu yung?

b séu meu těu réu yung?

c lorng doo réu yung?

d bpai têe-o chee-ung mài réu yung?

READING PRACTICE

1 Words

dtôrng	tíng	bâhn	hâi	róo
sôm	née	tâh	bpâi	náhm
láir-o	gÔOng	rórn	hôrng	séu
kâo	nóhn	gâir-o	nâh	dâi

2 Phrases

dâi mái	mâi dâi	săhm sìp hâh
róo-jùk mái	gôr láir-o gun	kâo pùt gÔOng
gâir-o nèung	tăir-o née	sŏrng róy bàht

3 Dialogue

Damrong	Have you bought a mobile phone yet?
Sue	Yes.
Damrong	Can I see it please?
Sue	Yes.
Damrong	Was it expensive?
Sue	No. Four thousand baht.
Damrong	Where did you buy it?
Sue	In the Sukhumwit area.

4 Dialogue

Somchai	Can I have two plates of duck rice, one plate of red pork rice and three glasses of fresh orange juice, please?
Waiter	We haven't got any fresh orange juice. Will Pepsi do?

Unit 9

- **a** bpen/mâi bpen
- **b** pèt/mâi pèt
- **c** bpen/mâi bpen
- **d** a-ròy/mâi a-ròy
- **e** sòop/mâi sòop

Exercise 2

- **a** gin ah-hăhn tai mâi bpen. pèt (gern) bpai.
- **b** ka-nŏm tai mâi a-ròy. wăhn (gern) bpai.
- **c** rao dern bpai mâi dâi. glai (gern) bpai.
- **d** káo mâi séu. pairng (gern) bpai.
- **e** sài mâi dâi. kúp (gern) bpai.

Exercise 3

- **a** (tâh) mâi sòop bÒO-rèe gôr krêe-ut. *If I don't smoke, I feel stressed.*
- **b** (tâh) pèt gern bpai gôr mâi a-ròy. *If it's too spicy, it's not tasty.*
- **c** (tâh) mâi pèt mâhk gôr gin dâi. *If it's not too spicy, I can eat it.*
- **d** (tâh) mâi glai bpai gôr dern dâi. *If it's not too far, I can walk.*
- **e** (tâh) pairng bpai gôr mâi séu. *If it's too expensive, I won't buy it?*

READING PRACTICE

1 Words

pâhk	pah-săh	yài	yĭng	kOOn	kâh
rao	káo	ao	kâo	tâo-rài	tâo-nún
ree-un	kĕe-un	lée-o	mêu-a	mĕu-un	pêu-un
dtoo-a	hŏo-a	woo-a	sŏo-ay	chôo-ay	dôo-ay
gern	gèrt	chern	dern	jer	ter
ja	ká	kà	ná	a-rai	ba-mèe

3 Dialogue

Chanida	Are you full?
Mineko	Yes.
Chanida	Is the food here tasty?
Mineko	Yes, very.
Chanida	Would you like coffee?
Mineko	No, thanks. I'm really full.

Unit 10

Exercise 1

  a bpen nít-nòy

  b mâi nahn

  c bpen nít-nòy

  d bpen nít-nòy

  e mâi kôy yâhk tâo-rài

Exercise 2

  a mâi kôy pairng tâo-rài

  b mâi kôy glai tâo-rài

  c mâi kôy a-ròy tâo-rài

  d mâi kôy dee tâo-rài

  e mâi kôy yâhk tâo-rài

Exercise 3

  a pairng gwàh

  b glai gwàh

  c a-ròy gwàh

  d dee gwàh

  e yâhk gwàh

Exercise 4

   a yâhk gwàh

   b ngâi gwàh

   c ngâi gwàh

   d yâhk gwàh

READING PRACTICE

1 Words

gwàh	kwǎh	grOOng	bpra-dtoo	bplah
bplào	dtrong	glai	glâi	glùp
krai	klái	krúp	kwahm	bpra-tâyt

2 More words

ta-nǒn	dta-lòk	ka-yǔn	sa-yǎhm	sa-pâhp
ka-nàht	sa-nÒOk	sa-tǎhn	sa-bai	bor-ri-sùt
cha-lǒrng	cha-làht	fa-rùng	ka-yà	bor-ri-gahn

3 Dialogue

Interviewer	You speak Thai well. Have you been in Thailand long?
Sarah	Not very long.
Interviewer	You speak Chinese, don't you?
Sarah	Yes. I lived in China for five years.
Interviewer	What were you doing over there?
Sarah	Teaching English.
Interviewer	Can you read and write Chinese?
Sarah	A little.

Unit 11

Exercise 1

   a mee pêe nórng gèe kon?

   b mee pêe sǎo gèe kon?

   c mee nórng chai gèe kon?

   d mee lôok gèe kon?

   e mee lôok chai gèe kon?

   f mee lôok sǎo gèe kon?

Exercise 2

   a séu rorng táo gèe kôo?

   b séu sêu-a gèe dtoo-a?

   c gin náhm gèe kòo-ut?

d gin núm sôm gèe gâir-o?

e ao sôm gèe loh?

f ao ma-môo-ung gèe lôok?

READING PRACTICE

1 Words

yé	lé té	dtè	gè gà
láir	gàir	páir	dtàir
dtó	lér tér	yér	yér yáir
prór	gòr	mòr	hǒo-a rór

2 Dialogue

Malee	How many children has your (older) brother got?
Somchai	Two. A boy and a girl.
Malee	How old are they?
Somchai	The son is 15. The daughter is 10.

3 Dialogue

a คุณชื่ออะไรคะ

b นามสกุลอะไรคะ

c อายุเท่าไหร่คะ

d แต่งงานหรือยังคะ

e มีลูกหรือยังคะ

Unit 12

Exercise 1

a kǒr pôot gùp kOOn Malee nòy dâi mái?

b chôo-ay pôot dung dung nòy dâi mái?

c ror sùk krôo

d krai pôot?

e kOOn Malee ja glùp mah mêu-rài?

Exercise 2

a pǒm/chún kít wâh ja òrk bpai kûng nôrk dtorn cháo.

b pǒm/chún kít wâh ja bpai bprai-sa-nee dtorn cháo.

c pǒm/chún kít wâh ja bpai bâhn kOOn Somchai dtorn bài.

d pǒm/chún kít wâh ja glùp mah dtorn yen.

Exercise 3

a kOOn Sŏmchai bòrk wâh (káo) ja bpai ta-na-kahn dtorn cháo.

b kOOn Sŏmchai bòrk wâh (káo) ja bpai bâhn kOOn Damrong dtorn bài.

c kOOn Sŏmchai bòrk wâh (káo) ja jòrt rót tăir-o tum-ma-sàht.

d kOOn Sŏmchai bòrk wâh (káo) ja glùp bâhn dtorn yen.

Exercise 4

a kOOn Somchai ja glùp mah mêu-rài?

b kOOn Somchai ja yòo mêu-rài?

c kOOn Somchai ja róo mêu-rài?

d kOOn Somchai ja toh mah mêu-rài?

e kOOn Somchai ja bòrk mêu-rài?

f kOOn Somchai ja toh mah bòrk mêu-rài?

READING PRACTICE

1

i g **ii** f **iii** e **iv** a **v** b **vi** c **vii** d

2

bpee-dter (Peter) ah-jahn tum-ma-sàht in-dter-net

ber bprai-sa-nee toh-ra-sùp sa-tăh-nee rót may

3 Dialogue

Sue	Hello, could I speak to Noi, please?
Thai voice	Who?
Sue	Pardon?
Thai voice	Who do you want to speak to?
Sue	Hello? Is Noi there?
Thai voice	I didn't hear. Could you speak up?
Sue	I'm sorry, do you speak English?
Thai voice	Ah, hang on a minute.
Damrong	Hello ... Ah, it's Sue, right?
Sue	Yes. I want to speak to Noi.
Damrong	Noi isn't in. Do you want her mobile number?
Sue	Yes, please. Slowly, OK?
Damrong	OK. The number is 01 564 5664
Sue	Thanks very much. Goodbye.
Damrong	'Bye.

Unit 13

Exercise 1

   a mâi kâo jai

   b pôot èek tee dâi mái?

   c bplair wâh a-rai?

   d pôot cháh cháh nòy dâi mái?

   e kěe-un yung-ngai?

Exercise 2

   a chôo-ay jòrt rót hâi nòy dâi mái?

   b chôo-ay séu bOO-rèe hâi nòy dâi mái?

   c chôo-ay sùng kâo pùt gài jahn nèung hâi nòy dâi mái?

   d chôo-ay bòrk kOOn Chanida hâi nòy dâi mái?

Exercise 3

   a chôo-ay jòrt rót hâi kOOn Malee nòy dâi mái?

   b chôo-ay séu bOO-rèe hâi kOOn Malee nòy dâi mái?

   c chôo-ay sùng kâo pùt gài jahn nèung hâi kOOn Malee nòy dâi mái?

   d chôo-ay bòrk kOOn Chanida hâi kOOn Malee nòy dâi mái?

Exercise 4

   a a-rai ná krúp?

   b pôot cháh cháh nòy dâi mái?

   c nǔng bplair wâh a-rai?

   d kâo jai

READING PRACTICE

1 Dialogue

Interviewer	Have you been in Thailand long?
Businessman	No. Only about six months.
Interviewer	You speak Thai very well.
Businessman	No, not at all. When Thais speak, sometimes I don't understand at all. And when I speak Thai, likewise, Thais sometimes don't understand me.
Interviewer	Where did you learn Thai?
Businessman	I studied at a language school in the Sukhumwit area. And I used a textbook and CDs at home.
Interviewer	Is Thai difficult?
Businessman	Yes. But if I didn't have CDs to listen to, it would be more difficult.
Interviewer	And can you read and write Thai?
Businessman	I can read a little, if they are easy words. But I can't really write.

Unit 14

Exercise 1

a chôrp mâhk jing jing/mâhk jung ler-ee.

b dee mâhk jing jing/mâhk jung ler-ee.

c nâh bèu-a mâhk jing jing/mâhk jung ler-ee.

d pèt mâhk jing jing/mâhk jung ler-ee.

e a-ròy mâhk jing jing/mâhk jung ler-ee.

Exercise 3

a ii, iii, v, vii

b i, iv, vi, viii

Exercise 4

a ker-ee bpai a-may-ri-gah mái?

b ker-ee ree-un pah-săh ung-grìt mái?

c ker-ee gin ah-hăhn yêe-bpÔOn mái?

d ker-ee bpai têe-o jung-wùt na-korn pa-nom mái?

e ker-ee tum ngahn dtàhng jung-wùt mái?

READING PRACTICE

1

Khun Chanida is from the South. She was born in Phuket. Her father is a policeman and her mother a housewife. Chanida's parents and brothers and sisters moved to Bangkok when Chanida was five years old. Now her younger brother is studying at Mahidol University. He wants to be a doctor. Chanida's father wants her younger brother to continue his studies in America.

2

Peter	You're from the north, aren't you?
Somchai	Yes. I was born in Chiangmai. My parents moved here 30 years ago when I was still a child. My father wanted me to study here because he thought the schools here were better.
Peter	Do you like living here?
Somchai	Not very much. The traffic here is really bad. The air in Chiangmai is better and the traffic isn't congested like it is here.

3

I'm from the northeast. I live in a small village in Nongkhai. Before, I used to work in the rice fields. But I didn't like it because it's very hard work. So I thought it would be better to come and work here. Now I'm working in a noodle shop in the Sukhumwit area. I wash up all day long. Some days I think it is boring. But I don't want to go back home because I don't want to work in the rice fields and the salary here is alright. It's better than upcountry.

Unit 15

Exercise 1

a iii   **b** iv   **c** ii   **d** i

Exercise 2

a gâo mohng krêung

b bài sŏrng mohng yêe-sìp nah-tee

c hâh mohng yen

d èek sìp-hâh nah-tee sèe tÔOm

Exercise 3

a jorng dtŏo-a bpai chee-ung mài têe-nǎi?

b rót bpai chee-ung mài òrk gèe mohng?

c chee-ung mài yòo hàhng jàhk grOOng-tâyp gèe gi-loh?

d kêun rót têe-nǎi?

READING PRACTICE

1

Mineko	I'm thinking of going to Trang.
Damrong	Really? What are you going to do in Trang?
Mineko	I'm going to visit a friend. I don't know what the best way to get there is.
Damrong	You can go by train or coach. I think it's more comfortable to go by train. But you have to book your ticket in advance.

2

Nongkhai is 614 kilometres from Bangkok. VIP Co. Ltd has first-class air-conditioned coaches leaving Bangkok twice a day, at 08.00 hrs and 21.00 hrs. The journey takes approximately 10 hours.

Unit 16

Exercise 1

a bplào, mâi dâi bpai.

b bplào, mâi dâi sùng.

c bplào, mâi dâi jorng.

d bplào, mâi dâi bòrk.

Exercise 2

a bplào krúp (kâ), mâi pairng.

b bplào krúp (kâ), mâi bèu-a.

c bplào krúp (kâ), mâi pèt.

d bplào krúp (kâ), mâi glai.

Exercise 3

   a fàhk gOOn-jair wái nai dtôo sáyf dâi mái?

   b fàhk glôrng tài rôop wái nai dtôo sáyf dâi mái?

   c fàhk meu tĕu wái nai dtôo sáyf dâi mái?

   d fàhk dtŏo-a rót fai wái nai dtôo sáyf dâi mái?

   e fàhk gra-bpăo bai lék wái nai dtôo sáyf dâi mái?

READING PRACTICE

1

Clerk	Have you been to Wat That Phanom yet?
Sue	Where?
Clerk	Wat That Phanom.
Sue	Not yet. We'd like to go, but we don't know how to get there.
Clerk	You can go with a tour. There's an air-conditioned coach that goes every morning and comes back in the evening.
Sue	Really? What does the trip cost?
Clerk	One thousand two hundred and fifty baht.
Sue	What time does the coach leave?
Clerk	Eight o'clock. It leaves from in front of the hotel and returns here at five o'clock.
Sue	And if we go, where can we book tickets?
Clerk	I can book for you. You're going tomorrow, right?
Sue	Hang on a minute. I'll think about it first.

2

Sue	Excuse me. Is it forbidden to take photographs here?
Student	I don't think so. Hang on a minute, I'll go and ask the official for you ... Excuse me, there's a foreigner asking whether photography is forbidden here or not.
Official	Not here, but it is inside. Please tell them that they have to take their shoes off before going inside.
Student	Yes. Thank you.

3

   a v   **b** i   **c** iv   **d** iii   **e** ii

Unit 17

Exercise 1

   a gum-lung ja yái bâhn.

   b gum-lung ja sùng ah-hăhn.

   c gum-lung ja glùp bâhn.

   d gum-lung ja séu rót.

   e gum-lung ja bpai séu kŏrng.

Exercise 2

a wun têe gâo mók-ga-rah

b wun têe sìp-gâo mí-tOO-nah

c wun têe săhm-sìp-èt sǐng-hăh

d wun têe hâh préut-sa-jìk-gah

e wun têe săhm may-săh

Exercise 3

a bâhn têe pǒm (chún) púk yòo mâi kôy yài tâo-rài.

b ah-hăhn têe rao gin pèt mâhk.

c kon tai têe pǒm (chún) róo-jùk pôot pah-săh ung-grìt gèng.

d rohng ree-un têe pǒm (chún) sŏrn yòo glai.

e ah-jahn têe sŏrn pah-săh tai mah jàhk chee-ung mài.

Exercise 4

a mâir hâi ngern káo.

b pêu-un hâi see dee pǒm (chún).

c rao hâi meu těu káo.

d káo hâi glôrng tài rôop nórng săo pǒm (chún).

READING PRACTICE

1

I've worked here nearly 20 years. I clean the rooms and do the laundry. I come to work at eight o'clock in the morning and go home at four o'clock in the afternoon. Most of the guests here are foreigners. There are lots of farangs. Some are very kind. They give me tips of more than 100 baht. Contentment! But it's the rainy season now. There aren't many guests and there isn't much work, either. So I sit chatting with my friends and snacking all day long. Another kind of contentment!

2

Malee	Have you ever been to the seaside?
Sue	Yes. I went to Pattaya two or three months ago.
Malee	How was it? Did you enjoy it?
Sue	Well ... I did, quite. But there were a lot of people. I prefer it quiet.
Malee	If you're going to the seaside, I think it's better to go to the south. The sea is more beautiful and there are fewer tourists, too.

3

John	Can I change my room, please?
Clerk	Why?
John	The air conditioner is broken.
Clerk	I'll be up in a minute to look at it.
John	There's no need. I can't use the toilet either. There's no water. I'd rather change room.
Clerk	You can't.
John	Why not?
Clerk	There aren't any other rooms.

4

I got married in Bangkok. My husband is British. He used to work in a big company in the Sukhumwit Road area. We came back to live in England three years ago.

Actually, I didn't want to come and live in England at all, because I could hardly speak the language. I'd studied it at school, but I was no good at it. When English people spoke, I could scarcely understand. So my husband had me study the language at a school near home. At the school there were students of all nationalities. There were Japanese, Chinese, Germans, Africans and Arabs, too. I had to go and study four days a week, that is Monday, Tuesday, Wednesday and Friday. I studied two to three hours a day from 9 am until midday. After studying for about six months I felt that my English had really improved a lot.

Appendices

Consonant classes

The following chart lists all the Thai consonants according to class and gives the pronunciation for each consonant both at the beginning of a word and at the end. Perhaps the easiest way to remember the class of a consonant is to memorize the shorter lists of mid class and high class consonants so that everything not on those lists can be assumed to be low class.

LOW CLASS

	น	ม	ง	ร	ล	ย	ว
Initial	n	m	ng	r	l	y	w
Final	n	m	ng	n	n	y	w

	ค	ช	ซ	ท	พ	ฟ
Initial	k	ch	s	t	p	f
Final	k	t	t	t	p	p

	ฆ	ฌ	ฑ	ญ	ณ
Initial	k	t	p	y	n
Final	k	t	p	n	n

	ฒ	ธ	ฎ	ฬ	ฮ
Initial	ch	t	t	l	h
Final	-	t	t	n	-

MID CLASS

	ก	จ	ด	ต	บ	ป	อ	ฎ	ฏ
Initial	g	j	d	dt	b	bp	zero	d	dt
Final	k	t	t	t	p	p	-	t	t

HIGH CLASS

	ข	ฉ	ถ	ผ	ฝ	ศ ษ ส	ห	ฐ
Initial	k	ch	t	p	f	s	h	t
Final	k	t	t	p	p	t	-	t

Vowels

LONG VOWELS

-า	-อ	โ-	้	ู	้	เ-	แ-	เ-ีย	เ-ือ	-ัว	เ-
-ah	-or	-oh	-ee	-oo	-eu	-ay	-air	-ee-a	-eu-a	-oo-a	-er

SHORT VOWELS

-ั	ไ-	ใ-	-ิ	-ุ	-็	เ-็	แ-็	เ-า	-ะ
-u	-ai	-ai	-i	-OO	-eu	-e	-air	-ao	-a

Summary of tone rules

WORDS WITHOUT TONE MARKS

Initial consonant class	Live syllable	Dead syllable	
		Short vowel	Long vowel
Low class	Mid tone	High tone	Falling tone
Mid class	Mid tone	Low tone	Low tone
High class	Rising tone	Low tone	Low tone

WORDS WITH TONE MARKS

Initial consonant class	mái àyk ่	mái toh ้	mái dtree ๊	mái jùt-dta-wah ๋
Low class	Falling tone	High tone	High tone	Rising tone
Mid class	Low tone	Falling tone	High tone	Rising tone
High class	Low tone	Falling tone	High tone	Rising tone

Taking it further

The following books will be useful if you wish to further your knowledge of Thai.

DICTIONARIES

Thai–English Dictionary by Domnern Garden and Sathienpong Wannapok, Bangkok: Amarin Printing and Publishing, 1994.

Thai English Student's Dictionary by Mary Haas, Stanford, CA: Stanford University Press, 1964. This is the best dictionary for the serious beginner, with a romanized pronunciation guide to each Thai script entry and numerous examples of usage.

A New Thai Dictionary with Bilingual Explanation by Thianchai Iamwaramet, Bangkok: Ruam San, 1993.

Robertson's Practical English–Thai Dictionary by Richard Robertson, Rutland, Vermont and Tokyo: Charles E. Tuttle, 1969. A small, but invaluable dictionary for the beginner, which provides Thai script and romanized Thai equivalents to approximately 2,500 English words.

New Age Thai–English Dictionary by Wong Wattanaphichet, Bangkok: Thaiways Publications, 2006.

GRAMMAR

Thai: An Essential Grammar (Second Edition) by David Smyth, London: Routledge, 2014.

PHRASEBOOK

The Bua Luang What You See Is What You Say Thai Phrase Handbook, Bangkok: Bua Luang Books, 2003. This book is packed with information on Thai language and culture and includes extensive, thematically arranged vocabulary lists in both romanized Thai and Thai script.

READER

Thai for Advanced Readers by Benjawan Poomsan Becker, Berkeley, CA: Paiboon Publishing, 2000.

GENERAL

Linguistic Diversity and National Unity: Language Ecology in Thailand by William A. Smalley, Chicago and London: University of Chicago Press, 1994. This volume offers an invaluable insight into the relationship between the national language, regional dialects and minority languages in Thailand.

Thai–English vocabulary

[**Key:** adj. = adjective; f. = female; m. = male; n. = noun; vb = verb]

a-páht-mén	*apartment*	อพาร์ทเมนท์
a-rai	*what?*	อะไร
a-rai ná?	*pardon?*	อะไรนะ
a-ròy	*to be tasty*	อร่อย
ah-gàht	*air; weather*	อากาศ
ah-hăhn	*food*	อาหาร
ah-jahn	*teacher, professor, coach*	อาจารย์
ah-tít	*week*	อาทิตย์
ah-yÓO	*age*	อายุ
àhn	*read*	อ่าน
àht ja	*may, might*	อาจจะ
air	*air conditioning*	แอร์
ao	*want*	เอา
bâhn	*house, home*	บ้าน
bahng	*some*	บาง
bahng krúng	*sometimes*	บางครั้ง
bàht	*baht*	บาท
bai	*classifier for bags*	ใบ
bài	*afternoon*	บ่าย
bàirp	*style, type, kind*	แบบ
bàirp năi?	*what kind?*	แบบไหน
bee-a	*beer*	เบียร์
ber	*number; size*	เบอร์
bèu-a	*bored, fed up*	เบื่อ

bor-ri-gahn	service	บริการ
bor-ri-sùt	company	บริษัท
bòrk	say, tell	บอก
bòy	often	บ่อย
bÒO-rèe	cigarette	บุหรี่
bpàhk	mouth, entrance	ปาก
bpai	go	ไป
bpáirp dee-o	just a second/moment	แป๊บเดียว
bpee	year	ปี
bpen	to be; to be able to	เป็น
bpen bpai mâi dâi	it's impossible	เป็นไปไม่ได้
bper sen	per cent	เปอร์เซ็นต์
bplah	fish	ปลา
bplair	translate	แปล
… bplair wâh a-rai?	what does … mean?	…แปลว่าอะไร
bplòrt-pai	safe (adj.)	ปลอดภัย
bpra-tâyt	country	ประเทศ
bprai-sa-nee	post office	ไปรษณีย์
bprùp ah-gàht	air conditioned	ปรับอากาศ
cháh	slow	ช้า
chahm	bowl	ชาม
châht	nation	ชาติ
chái	use (vb)	ใช้
chái dâi	acceptable	ใช้ได้
châi	yes	ใช่
…. châi mái?	…, is that right?	…ใช่ไหม
cháo	morning	เช้า
châo	rent (vb)	เช่า

chèet	*spray* (vb)	ฉีด
chék bin	*can I have the bill?*	เช็คบิล
chern tahng née	*please come this way*	เชิญทางนี้
chêu	*first name*	ชื่อ
chêu-a	*believe*	เชื่อ
chim	*taste* (vb)	ชิม
chôo-a mohng	*hour*	ชั่วโมง
chôo-ay … nòy	*please …*	ช่วย …หน่อย
chôrp	*like* (vb)	ชอบ
chún	*I* (f.)	ฉัน
chún	*floor, storey*	ชั้น
chún nèung	*first class*	ชั้นหนึ่ง
dâi	*can*	ได้
dâi yin	*hear*	ได้ยิน
dee	*good*	ดี
dee gwàh	*better*	ดีกว่า
dĕe-o	*in a minute, shortly*	เดี๋ยว
dĕe-o née	*now*	เดี๋ยวนี้
dèk	*child*	เด็ก
dern	*walk* (vb)	เดิน
dern tahng	*travel* (vb)	เดินทาง
deu-un	*month*	เดือน
dèuk	*after dark; late at night*	ดึก
di-chún	*I* (f.)	ดิฉัน
doo	*look at*	ดู
dôo-ay	*too*	ด้วย
dôo-ay gun	*together*	ด้วยกัน
dung	*loud*	ดัง

dtàhng jung-wùt	*upcountry*	ต่างจังหวัด
dtàir	*but*	แต่
dtàirng ngahn	*marry*	แต่งงาน
dtèuk	*concrete building*	ตึก
dtìt	*stick/ be stuck*	ติด
dtòk long	*agree*	ตกลง
dtôm yum	*'tom yam'*	ต้มยำ
dtôo sáyf	*safe* (n.)	ตู้เซฟ
dtoo-a	*classifier for shirts*	ตัว
dtŏo-a	*ticket*	ตั๋ว
dtòr	*continue*	ต่อ
dtorn née	*now*	ตอนนี้
dtorn nún	*at that time; then*	ตอนนั้น
dtorn yen	*evening*	ตอนเย็น
dtôrng	*have to, must*	ต้อง
dtôrng-gahn	*need, want*	ต้องการ
dtum-rah	*textbook*	ตำรา
dtum-ròo-ut	*policeman*	ตำรวจ
dtung	*money, satang*	สตางค์
èek	*another*	อีก
èek tee	*again*	อีกที
èun	*other*	อื่น
fa-rùng	*'farang', Caucasian*	ฝรั่ง
fàhk	*leave, entrust, deposit*	ฝาก
fairn	*boy/girlfriend; spouse*	แฟน
fung	*to listen*	ฟัง
gài	*chicken*	ไก่

gâir-o	*glass*	แก้ว
gairng	*curry*	แกง
gaym	*game*	เกม
gèe	*how many?*	กี่
gèe mohng?	*what time?*	กี่โมง
gèng	*good at*	เก่ง
gèp	*collect, keep*	เก็บ
gern bpai	*too ...*	เกินไป
gèrt	*to be born*	เกิด
gèu-up	*almost*	เกือบ
gi-loh	*kilometre*	กิโล
gin, gin kâo	*eat*	กิน,กินข้าว
glai	*far*	ไกล
glâi	*near*	ใกล้
gloo-a	*to be afraid*	กลัว
glôo-ay	*banana*	กล้วย
glôrng tài rôop	*camera*	กล้องถ่ายรูป
glùp	*return*	กลับ
gôr ...	*er ...*	ก็ ...
gOOn-jair	*key*	กุญแจ
gÔOng	*shrimp*	กุ้ง
gra-bpǎo	*bag*	กระเป๋า
grOOng-tâyp	*Bangkok*	กรุงเทพฯ
gum-lung ... yòo	*to be ...ing*	กำลัง ... อยู่
gum-lung ja ...	*to be about to ...*	กำลังจะ ...
gùp	*with*	กับ
gwàh	*more than*	กว่า
hǎh ngahn	*look for work*	หางาน

hâhm	forbid	ห้าม
hàhng jàhk	at a distance from	ห่างจาก
hâi	get someone to do something; for; give	ให้
hòr	packet	ห่อ
hôrng	room	ห้อง
hôrng náhm	toilet	ห้องน้ำ
hun-loh	hello (on the telephone)	ฮัลโล
ìm	to be full	อิ่ม
ja	future time marker	จะ
jàhk	from	จาก
jahn	plate	จาน
jâo nâh- têe	official	เจ้าหน้าที่
jeen	Chinese	จีน
jer	meet	เจอ
jing	true	จริง
jing lĕr?	really?	จริงหรือ
jon tĕung	until	จนถึง
jor	screen	จอ
jorng	book (vb)	จอง
jòrt	park, pull up	จอด
jum-gùt	Ltd	จำกัด
jung ler-ee	really, very	จังเลย
jung-wùt	province	จังหวัด
kà, kâh, ká	polite particles	ค่ะ คะ
ka-moy-ee	burglar	ขโมย
ka-nŏm	dessert; cake	ขนม
kâh	cost	ค่า

kâh mút-jum	deposit (n.)	ค่ามัดจำ
káo	he, she, they	เขา
kâo	enter	เข้า
kâo jai	understand	เข้าใจ
kâo	rice	ข้าว
kâo něe-o	sticky rice	ข้าวเหนียว
kâo pùt	fried rice	ข้าวผัด
kěe-un	write	เขียน
kem	salty	เค็ม
ker-ee	used to (do); once (did)	เคย
keun	night	คืน
kêun	get on; go up	ขึ้น
kít	think; charge (money)	คิด
kít doo	consider	คิดดู
kon	person	คน
kon dee-o	alone	คนเดียว
kon dtàhng châht	foreigner	คนต่างชาติ
kong	sure to; probably	คง
kôo	pair	คู่
koo-un	should	ควร
kòo-up	years old (under 13)	ขวบ
kòo-ut	bottle	ขวด
kôr kwahm	message	ข้อความ
kǒr	I'd like (to) ...	ขอ
kǒr-tôht	excuse me	ขอโทษ
kǒrng	of; thing	ของ
kòrp-kOOn	thank you	ขอบคุณ
kOOn	you	คุณ

krai	*who?*	ใคร
krêe-ut	*stressed*	เครียด
krúng	*time*	ครั้ง
krúp	*polite particle*	ครับ
kum	*word*	คำ
kûng lǔng	*behind; at the back*	ข้างหลัง
kûng nâh	*in front of*	ข้างหน้า
kûng nôrk	*outside, out*	ข้างนอก
kúp	*tight*	คับ
kwǎh	*right (side)*	ขวา
láhng	*wash (plates)*	ล้าง
lǎi	*many; several*	หลาย
láir	*and*	และ
láir-o	*and; already*	แล้ว
láir-o … lâ?	*and how about …?*	แล้ว ...ล่ะ
lék	*small*	เล็ก
lên	*play*	เล่น
lěr?	question particle	หรือ
lêrk	*give up*	เลิก
léuk	*deep*	ลึก
loh	*kilo*	โล
lôo-ung nâh	*in advance*	ล่วงหน้า
lôok	*child*	ลูก
lôok chai	*son*	ลูกชาย
lôok sǎo	*daughter*	ลูกสาว
lorng	*try out*	ลอง
lót	*reduce, lower*	ลด
lǔng	classifier for apartments	หลัง

ma-hăh wít-ta-yah-lai	*university*	มหาวิทยาลัย
mah	*come*	มา
mâhk	*much, many; very*	มาก
mái?	*question particle*	ไหม
mái	*stick; wood; skewer*	ไม้
mâi	*no; not*	ไม่
mâi bpen rai	*never mind*	ไม่เป็นไร
mâi châi	*no; is not*	ไม่ใช่
mâi dâi	*can't*	ไม่ได้
mâi kôy … (tâo-rài)	*not very*	ไม่ค่อย … …(เท่าไหร่)
mâi … ler-ee	*not … at all*	ไม่ … เลย
mâi …ròrk	*not … at all*	ไม่ … หรอก
mài	*again; new*	ใหม่
mâir	*mother*	แม่
mâir bâhn	*housewife*	แม่บ้าน
may-noo	*menu*	เมนู
mee	*there is/are; have*	มี
meu těu	*mobile phone*	มือถือ
mêu-a	*when*	เมื่อ
mêu-a gòrn	*formerly, before*	เมื่อก่อน
mêu-rài?	*when?*	เมื่อไร
měu-un	*like, similar*	เหมือน
měu-un gun	*fairly; likewise*	เหมือนกัน
meu-ung tai	*Thailand*	เมืองไทย
mŏo	*pork, pig*	หมู
mòo-bâhn	*village*	หมู่บ้าน

mÓOng lôo-ut	mosquito screen	มุ้งลวด
mŏr	doctor	หมอ
mun	it	มัน
ná	question particle	นะ
nâh	next; season	หน้า
nâh fŏn	rainy season	หน้าฝน
nâh sŏn jai	interesting	น่าสนใจ
nâh yòo	nice to live (in/at)	น่าอยู่
nah-tee	minute	นาที
nahm sa-gOOn	family name	นามสกุล
náhm	water; drink	น้ำ
nahn	a long time	นาน
nâir	sure	แน่
nâirn	crowded	แน่น
nêe	this	นี่
nin-tah	gossip (vb)	นินทา
nít-nòy	a little bit	นิดหน่อย
nórng chai	younger brother	น้องชาย
nórng săo	younger sister	น้องสาว
nòy	a little	หน่อย
nóy-nàh	custard apple	น้อยหน่า
núk sèuk-săh	student	นักศึกษา
núk tÓO-rá-gìt	businessman	นักธุรกิจ
nùk	heavy, hard	หนัก
núm mun	petrol	น้ำมัน
núm sôm kún	fresh orange juice	น้ำส้มคั้น
nún	that	นั้น
nûng	sit; travel by	นั่ง

ngahn	*work* (n.)	งาน
ngâi	*easy*	ง่าย
ngern deu-un	*salary*	เงินเดือน
ngong	*dazed, confused*	งง
ngún	*in that case*	งั้น
òrk	*to go out*	ออก
órp-fìt	*office*	ออฟฟิศ
pah-săh	*language*	ภาษา
pâhk	*region*	ภาค
pairng	*expensive*	แพง
pêe chai	*older brother*	พี่ชาย
pêe nórng	*brothers and sisters*	พี่น้อง
pêe săo	*older sister*	พี่สาว
pèt	*hot, spicy*	เผ็ด
pêu-un	*friend*	เพื่อน
pŏm	*I* (m.)	ผม
póp	*meet*	พบ
pôo-chai	*boy, male*	ผู้ชาย
pôo-jùt-gahn	*manager*	ผู้จัดการ
pôo-yĭng	*girl, female*	ผู้หญิง
pôot	*speak*	พูด
pôot lên	*joke* (vb)	พูดเล่น
pôr	*father*	พอ
prór	*because*	เพราะ
prÔOng née	*tomorrow*	พรุ่งนี้
púk	*stay*	พัก
pun	*thousand*	พัน

pùt pùk roo-um mít	*mixed fried vegetables*	ผัดผักรวม มิตร
pùt tai	*Thai-style fried noodles*	ผัดไทย
rah-kah	*price*	ราคา
ráhn ah-hǎhn	*restaurant*	ร้านอาหาร
ráhn gǒo-ay dtěe-o	*noodle shop*	ร้านก๋วยเตี๋ยว
rao	*we*	เรา
ray-o	*quickly*	เร็ว
rêe-uk wâh ...	*it's called ...*	เรียกว่า ...
ree-un	*study, learn*	เรียน
réu	*or*	หรือ
réu bplào?	*or not?*	หรือเปล่า
réu yung?	*yet?*	หรือยัง
rohng rairm	*hotel*	โรงแรม
rohng ree-un	*school*	โรงเรียน
róo	*know (facts)*	รู้
róo rêu-ung	*understand*	รู้เรื่อง
róo-jùk	*know (people, places)*	รู้จัก
róo-sèuk	*feel*	รู้สึก
ror	*wait*	รอ
rorng táo	*shoe*	รองเท้า
rót	*car*	รถ
rót dtìt	*traffic jam*	รถติด
rót fai	*train*	รถไฟ
rót may	*bus*	รถเมล์
rót too-a	*tour bus; coach*	รถทัวร์
rÔOn	*model, version*	รุ่น
rúp	*receive*	รับ

sa-àht	clean	สะอาด
sa-bai dee	well, comfortable	สบายดี
sa-gòt	spell (vb)	สะกด
sa-měr	always	เสมอ
sa-nǎhm bin	airport	สนามบิน
sa-nÒOk	fun	สนุก
sa-tǎh-nee rót fai	railway station	สถานีรถไฟ
sa-wùt dee	hello	สวัสดี
sâhp	know (things)	ทราบ
sài	wear, put on	ใส่
sái	left (side)	ซ้าย
sǎi	(telephone) line	สาย
see	mood particle	ซี
see dee	CD	ซีดี
sěe	colour	สี
sěe dairng	red	สีแดง
sěe-a	broken	เสีย
sěe-ung	sound	เสียง
sên lék	'thin strip' noodles	เส้นเล็ก
sên yài	'broad strip' noodles	เส้นใหญ่
séu	buy	ซื้อ
sêu-a	shirt	เสื้อ
sôm	orange	ส้ม
sôm dtum	papaya salad	ส้มตำ
sòng	send	ส่ง
sǒo-ay	beautiful	สวย
sǒo-un	garden	สวน
sǒong	tall	สูง

sòop	*smoke* (vb)	สูบ
sôrm	*repair, mend*	ซ่อม
sŏrn	*teach*	สอน
soy	*soi, lane*	ซอย
sùk krôo	*a moment*	สักครู่
sùng	*order* (vb)	สั่ง
ta-na-kahn	*bank*	ธนาคาร
ta-nŏn	*road*	ถนน
tâh	*if*	ถ้า
tăhm	*ask*	ถาม
tahn	*eat*	ทาน
tài rôop	*take a photograph*	ถ่ายรูป
tăir- o	*locality, vicinity*	แถว
tâo-nún	*only*	เท่านั้น
tâo-rài?	*how much?*	เท่าไหร่
têe	*at; relative pronoun*	ที่
têe năi	*where?*	ที่ไหน
têe nêe	*here*	ที่นี่
têe nôhn	*over there*	ที่โน่น
têe-o	*visit, go out; trip*	เที่ยว
tĕung	*reach, arrive*	ถึง
toh	*telephone* (vb)	โทร
ton	*put up with*	ทน
tòok	*cheap*	ถูก
tôo-um	*flood* (vb)	ท่วม
tòrt	*take off (clothes)*	ถอด
tóOk	*every*	ทุก

tŏOng	*bag*	ถุง
tum	*do, make*	ทำ
tum nah	*rice farming*	ทำนา
tum ngahn	*work* (vb)	ทำงาน
tum-mai?	*why?*	ทำไม
túng wun	*all day*	ทั้งวัน
ung-grìt	*English, British*	อังกฤษ
wâh	*think, say*	ว่า
wâhng	*free, vacant*	ว่าง
wăhn	*sweet*	หวาน
way-lah	*time; when*	เวลา
wun	*day*	วัน
wun săo	*Saturday*	วันเสาร์
yah gun yOOng	*mosquito repellant*	ยากันยุง
yàh	*don't*	อย่า
yâhk	*difficult*	ยาก
yàhk ja	*want to*	อยากจะ
yai	*(maternal) grandmother*	ยาย
yài	*big*	ใหญ่
yái	*move house*	ย้าย
yâir	*to be a nuisance, a hassle*	แย่
yêe-bpÒOn	*Japan*	ญี่ปุ่น
yêe-um	*visit* (people)	เยี่ยม
yòo	*located at; live*	อยู่
yung	*still*	ยัง
yung-ngai?	*how?*	อย่างไร

English–Thai vocabulary

[**Key:** adj. = adjective; f. = female; m. = male; n. = noun; vb = verb]

about, approximately	**bpra-mahn**	ประมาณ
about to ...	**gum-lung ja ...**	กำลังจะ ...
acceptable	**chái dâi**	ใช้ได้
actually	**kwahm jing**	ความจริง
advance: in advance	**lôo-ung nâh**	ล่วงหน้า
afraid	**gloo-a**	กลัว
again	**èek tee; mài**	อีกที; ใหม่
age	**ah-yÓO**	อายุ
agree	**dtòk long**	ตกลง
air	**ah-gàht**	อากาศ
air conditioning	**air/ bprùp ah-gàht**	แอร์/ปรับอากาศ
airport	**sa-năhm bin**	สนามบิน
all day	**túng wun**	ทั้งวัน
almost	**gèu-up**	เกือบ
alone	**kon dee-o**	คนเดียว
already	**láir-o**	แล้ว
always	**sa-měr**	เสมอ
and	**láir/láir-o**	และ/แล้ว
another	**èek**	อีก
apartment	**a-páht-mén**	อพาร์ทเมนท์
arrive	**mah těung**	มาถึง
ask	**tăhm**	ถาม
at	**têe**	ที่
bag	**gra-bpǎo; tŎOng**	กระเป๋า; ถุง

baht	**bàht**	บาท
banana	**glôo-ay**	กล้วย
Bangkok	**grOOng-tâyp**	กรุงเทพฯ
bank	**ta-na-kahn**	ธนาคาร
bathroom	**hôrng náhm**	ห้องน้ำ
be: is, am are, etc.	**bpen**	เป็น
beautiful	**sŏo-ay**	สวย
because	**prór**	เพราะ
beer	**bee-a**	เบียร์
before	**gòrn**	ก่อน
behind; at the back	**kûng lǔng**	ข้างหลัง
believe	**chêu-a**	เชื่อ
better	**dee gwàh**	ดีกว่า
big	**yài**	ใหญ่
book (vb)	**jorng**	จอง
bored	**bèu-a**	เบื่อ
born	**gèrt**	เกิด
bottle	**kòo-ut**	ขวด
bowl	**chahm**	ชาม
boy	**pôo-chai**	ผู้ชาย
boyfriend	**fairn**	แฟน
broken	**sěe-a**	เสีย
brother: older brother	**pêe chai**	พี่ชาย
younger brother	**nórng chai**	น้องชาย
brothers and sisters	**pêe nórng**	พี่น้อง
building (concrete)	**dtèuk**	ตึก
burglar	**ka-moy-ee**	ขโมย
bus	**rót may**	รถเมล์

businessman	núk tÓO-rá-kìt	นักธุรกิจ
but	dtàir	แต่
buy	séu	ซื้อ
call: it's called ...	rêe-uk wâh ...	เรียกว่า ...
CD	see dee	ซีดี
camera	glôrng tài rôop	กล้องถ่ายรูป
can	dâi; bpen	ได้; เป็น
car	rót	รถ
certain	nâir	แน่
change (vb)	bplèe-un	เปลี่ยน
chat (vb)	koo-ee	คุย
cheap	tòok	ถูก
chicken	gài	ไก่
child	dèk; lôok	เด็ก; ลูก
Chinese	jeen	จีน
cigarette	bÒO-rèe	บุหรี่
class	chún	ชั้น
clean	sa-àht	สะอาด
clothes	sêu-a pâh	เสื้อผ้า
coach, tour bus	rót too-a	รถทัวร์
colour	sĕe	สี
come	mah	มา
company	bor-ri-sùt	บริษัท
confused	ngong	งง
continue	dtòr	ต่อ
cost	kâh	ค่า
country	bpra-tâyt	ประเทศ
crowded	nâirn	แน่น

curry	**gairng**	แกง
custard apple	**nóy-nàh**	น้อยหน่า
daughter	**lôok săo**	ลูกสาว
day	**wun**	วัน
deep	**léuk**	ลึก
deposit (n)	**kâh mút-jum**	ค่ามัดจำ
deposit (vb)	**fàhk**	ฝาก
dessert; cake	**ka-nŏm**	ขนม
difficult	**yâhk**	ยาก
do	**tum**	ทำ
doctor	**mŏr**	หมอ
don't	**yàh**	อย่า
easy	**ngâi**	ง่าย
eat	**gin/ tahn (kâo)**	กิน/ทาน(ข้าว)
English	**ung-grìt**	อังกฤษ
enough	**por**	พอ
enter	**kâo**	เข้า
entrust	**fàhk**	ฝาก
evening	**dtorn yen**	ตอนเย็น
every	**tÓOk**	ทุก
excuse me	**kŏr-tôht**	ขอโทษ
expensive	**pairng**	แพง
far	**glai**	ไกล
'farang', Caucasian	**fa-rùng**	ฝรั่ง
father	**pôr**	พ่อ
feel	**róo-sèuk**	รู้สึก
fish	**bplah**	ปลา

flood (vb)	tôo-um	ท่วม
floor, storey	chún	ชั้น
food	ah-hăhn	อาหาร
forbid	hâhm	ห้าม
foreigner	kon dtàhng châht	คนต่างชาติ
forget	leum	ลืม
formerly	mêu-a gòrn	เมื่อก่อน
free, vacant	wâhng	ว่าง
friend	pêu-un	เพื่อน
from	jàhk	จาก
front: in front of	kûng nâh	ข้างหน้า
full (of food)	ìm	อิ่ม
fun	sa-nÒOk	สนุก
game	gaym	เกม
garden	sŏo-un	สวน
get on (a train, bus)	kêun	ขึ้น
girl	pôo-ying	ผู้หญิง
girlfriend	fairn	แฟน
give	hâi	ให้
give up, cease	lêrk	เลิก
glass	gâir-o	แก้ว
go	bpai	ไป
go out	òrk	ออก
good	dee	ดี
good at	gèng	เก่ง
gossip (vb)	nin-tah	นินทา
grandmother (maternal)	yai	ยาย

hard (of work)	**nùk**	หนัก
have	**mee**	มี
he	**káo**	เขา
hear	**dâi yin**	ได้ยิน
hello	**sa-wùt dee**	สวัสดี
here	**têe nêe**	ที่นี่
hotel	**rohng rairm**	โรงแรม
hour	**chôo-a mohng**	ชั่วโมง
house	**bâhn**	บ้าน
housewife	**mâir bâhn**	แม่บ้าน
how?	**yung-ngai?**	อย่างไร
how many?	**gèe**	กี่
how much?	**tâo-rài?**	เท่าไหร่
I (f.)	**chún/ di-chún**	ฉัน/ดิฉัน
I (m.)	**pǒm**	ผม
if	**tâh**	ถ้า
impossible	**bpen bpai mâi dâi**	เป็นไปไม่ได้
in	**nai**	ใน
interesting	**nâh sǒn jai**	น่าสนใจ
is: there is/are	**mee**	มี
it	**mun**	มัน
Japan	**yêe-bpÒOn**	ญี่ปุ่น
joke (vb)	**pôot lên**	พูดเล่น
keep	**gèp**	เก็บ
key	**gOOn-jair**	กุญแจ
kilo	**loh**	โล
... per kilo	**loh la ...**	โลละ ...

266

kilometre	**gi-loh**	กิโล
kind, type	**bàirp**	แบบ
know (people, places)	**róo-jùk**	รู้จัก
know (facts)	**róo; sâhp**	รู้ ; ทราบ
language	**pah-sǎh**	ภาษา
left (side)	**sái**	ซ้าย
like (vb)	**chôrp**	ชอบ
like, similar	**měu-un**	เหมือน
likewise	**měu-un gun**	เหมือนกัน
line	**sǎi**	สาย
listen	**fung**	ฟัง
little: a little bit	**nít-nòy**	นิดหน่อย
live	**yòo**	อยู่
long (time)	**nahn**	นาน
look at	**doo**	ดู
loud	**dung**	ดัง
Ltd	**jum-gùt**	จำกัด
man	**pôo-chai**	ผู้ชาย
manager	**pôo-jùt-gahn**	ผู้จัดการ
many	**lǎi**	หลาย
married	**dtàirng ngahn**	แต่งงาน
may, might	**àht ja**	อาจจะ
mean: what does ... mean	**... bplair wâh a-rai?**	...แปลว่าอะไร
meet	**póp; jer**	พบ ; เจอ
menu	**may-noo**	เมนู
message	**kôr kwahm**	ข้อความ
minute	**nah-tee**	นาที

mobile phone	meu tĕu	มือถือ
model, version	rÔOn	รุ่น
money	ngern; 'dtung	เงิน; สตางค์
month	deu-un	เดือน
more than	gwàh	กว่า
morning	cháo	เช้า
mosquito	yOOng	ยุง
mosquito repellant	yah gun yOOng	ยากันยุง
mosquito screen	mÓOng lôo-ut	มุงลวด
mother	mâir	แม่
mouth	bpàhk	ปาก
move (house)	yái	ย้าย
much, many	mâhk	มาก
must	dtôrng	ต้อง
name (first)	chêu	ชื่อ
name: family name	nahm sa-gOOn	นามสกุล
nation	châht	ชาติ
near	glâi	ใกล้
need, want	dtôrng-gahn	ต้องการ
never mind	mâi bpen rai	ไม่เป็นไร
new	mài	ใหม่
next	nâh	หน้า
night	keun	คืน
no; not	mâi	ไม่
noodle shop	ráhn gŏo-ay dtĕe-o	ร้านก๋วยเตี๋ยว
not … at all	mâi … ler-ee	ไม่ …เลย
not … at all	mâi …ròrk	ไม่ … หรอก

not very ...	mâi kôy ... (tâo-rài)	ไม่ค่อย ...(เท่าไหร่)
now	dĕe-o née; dtorn née	เดี๋ยวนี้; ตอนนี้
nuisance: to be a nuisance	yâir	แย่
number	ber	เบอร์
of	kŏrng	ของ
office	órp-fít	ออฟฟิศ
official	jâo nâh- têe	เจ้าหน้าที่
often	bòy	บ่อย
only	tâo-nún	เท่านั้น
or	réu	หรือ
... or not?	... réu bplào?	... หรือเปล่า
orange	sôm	ส้ม
orange juice (fresh)	núm sôm kún	น้ำส้มคั้น
order (vb)	sùng	สั่ง
other	èun	อื่น
outside	kûng nôrk	ข้างนอก
packet	hòr	ห่อ
pair	kôo	คู่
pardon?	a-rai ná?	อะไรนะ
park (vb)	jòrt	จอด
per cent	bper sen	เปอร์เซ็นต์
person	kon	คน
petrol	núm mun	น้ำมัน
photograph (vb)	tài rôop	ถ่ายรูป
plate	jahn	จาน
play (vb)	lên	เล่น
please ...	chôo-ay ... nòy	ช่วย ... หน่อย

policeman	dtum-ròo-ut	ตำรวจ
pork	mŏo	หมู
post office	bprai-sa-nee	ไปรษณีย์
price	rah-kah	ราคา
province	jung-wùt	จังหวัด
put up with	ton	ทน
quickly	ray-o	เร็ว
railway station	sa-tăh-nee rót fai	สถานีรถไฟ
rainy season	nâh fŏn	หน้าฝน
reach	tĕung	ถึง
read	àhn	อ่าน
really?	jing lĕr?	จริงหรือ
really, very	jung ler-ee	จังเลย
reduce, lower	lót	ลด
region	pâhk	ภาค
rent (vb)	châo	เช่า
repair	sôrm	ซ่อม
restaurant	ráhn ah-hăhn	ร้านอาหาร
return	glùp	กลับ
rice	kâo	ข้าว
fried rice	kâo pùt	ข้าวผัด
sticky rice	kâo nĕe-o	ข้าวเหนียว
rice farming	tum nah	ทำนา
right (side)	kwăh	ขวา
road	ta-nŏn	ถนน
room	hôrng	ห้อง
safe (adj.)	bplòrt-pai	ปลอดภัย

270

safe (n.)	dtôo sáyf	ตู้เซฟ
salary	ngern deu-un	เงินเดือน
salty	kem	เค็ม
say (that)	bòrk wâh	บอกว่า
school	rohng ree-un	โรงเรียน
screen	jor	จอ
season	nâh	หน้า
send	sòng	ส่ง
service	bor-ri-gahn	บริการ
she	káo	เขา
shirt	sêu-a	เสื้อ
shoe	rorng táo	รองเท้า
should	kong	คง
shrimp	gÔOng	กุ้ง
sister: older sister	pêe săo	พี่สาว
younger sister	nórng săo	น้องสาว
sit	nûng	นั่ง
situated, located (at/in/on)	yòo (têe)	อยู่(ที่)
skewer	mái	ไม้
slow	cháh	ช้า
small	lék	เล็ก
smoke (vb)	sòop	สูบ
some	bahng	บาง
sometimes	bahng krúng	บางครั้ง
soi, lane	soy	ซอย
son	lôok chai	ลูกชาย
sound	sĕe-ung	เสียง

speak	**pôot**	พูด
spell (vb)	**sa-gòt**	สะกด
spicy	**pèt**	เผ็ด
spray (vb)	**chèet**	ฉีด
stay	**púk**	พัก
stick, stuck	**dtìt**	ติด
still	**yung**	ยัง
stressed	**krêe-ut**	เครียด
student	**núk sèuk-săh**	นักศึกษา
study (vb)	**ree-un**	เรียน
style	**bàirp**	แบบ
sure	**nâir**	แน่
sweet (adj.)	**wăhn**	หวาน
take off (clothes)	**tòrt**	ถอด
tall	**sŏong**	สูง
taste (vb)	**chim**	ชิม
tasty	**a-ròy**	อร่อย
teach	**sŏrn**	สอน
teacher	**ah-jahn**	อาจารย์
telephone (vb)	**toh**	โทร
textbook	**dtum-rah**	ตำรา
Thai	**tai**	ไทย
Thailand	**meu-ung tai**	เมืองไทย
thank you	**kòrp-kOOn**	ขอบคุณ
that	**nún**	นั้น
then	**dtorn nún**	ตอนนั้น
there	**têe nôhn**	ที่โน่น

they	**káo**	เขา
thing	**kŏrng**	ของ
think	**kít**	คิด
this	**nêe**	นี่
thousand	**pun**	พัน
ticket	**dtŏo-a**	ตั๋ว
tight	**kúp**	คับ
time	**way-lah**	เวลา
time, occasion	**krúng**	ครั้ง
today	**wun née**	วันนี้
together	**dôo-ay gun**	ด้วยกัน
toilet	**hôrng náhm**	ห้องน้ำ
tomorrow	**prÔOng née**	พรุ่งนี้
too, also	**dôo-ay**	ด้วย
too ...	**gern bpai**	เกินไป
traffic jam	**rót dtìt**	รถติด
train	**rót fai**	รถไฟ
translate	**bplair**	แปล
travel (vb)	**dern tahng**	เดินทาง
true	**jing**	จริง
try out	**lorng**	ลอง
understand	**kâo jai; róo rêu-ung**	เข้าใจ; รู้เรื่อง
university	**ma-hăh wít-ta-yah-la**	มหาวิทยาลัย
until	**jon tĕung**	จนถึง
upcountry	**dtàhng jung-wùt**	ต่างจังหวัด
use (vb)	**chái**	ใช้
used to, formerly	**ker-ee**	เคย

very	**mâhk**	มาก
village	**mòo-bâhn**	หมู่บ้าน
visit (people)	**yêe-um**	เยี่ยม
visit (places)	**têe-o**	เที่ยว
wait	**ror**	รอ
walk	**dern**	เดิน
want (something)	**ao**	เอา
want (to do something)	**yàhk ja**	อยากจะ
wash (clothes)	**súk**	ซัก
wash (dishes)	**láhng**	ล้าง
water	**náhm**	น้ำ
we	**rao**	เรา
wear	**sài**	ใส่
week	**ah-tít**	อาทิตย์
well, in good health	**sa-bai dee**	สบายดี
what?	**a-rai?**	อะไร
what time?	**gèe mohng?**	กี่โมง
when?	**mêu-rài?**	เมื่อไร
when	**way-lah; mêu-a**	เวลา;เมื่อ
where?	**têe nǎi?**	ที่ไหน
who?	**krai?**	ใคร
why?	**tum-mai?**	ทำไม
with	**gùp**	กับ
woman	**pôo-yǐng**	ผู้หญิง
word	**kum**	คำ
work (n.)	**ngahn**	งาน
work (vb)	**tum ngahn**	ทำงาน

write	**kěe-un**	เขียน
year	**bpee**	ปี
... yet?	**... réu yung?**	... หรือยัง
you	**kOOn**	คุณ

Grammar index

Numbers in parentheses refer to the unit in which the topic is covered.

Notes

Notes

Notes